OXFORD REVISE

OCR GCSE

GEOGRAPHY B

COMPLETE REVISION AND PRACTICE

Series Editor: Tim Bayliss

Tim Bayliss

Rebecca Priest

OXFORD

UNIVERSITY PRESS

Contents

Shade in each level of the circle as you feel more confident and ready for your exam.

How to use this book

This book uses a three-step approach to revision: **Knowledge**, **Retrieval**, and **Practice**.
It is important that you do all three; they work together to make your revision effective.

 Knowledge

Knowledge comes first. Each chapter starts with a **Knowledge Organiser**. These are clear, easy-to-understand, concise summaries of the content that you need to know for your exam. The information is organised to show how one idea flows into the next so you can learn how everything is tied together, rather than lots of disconnected facts.

Case study

The **Case study** box highlights a popular case study that you may have studied in class.

SPECIFICATION TIP

Specification tips offer useful guidance and reminders about the specification.

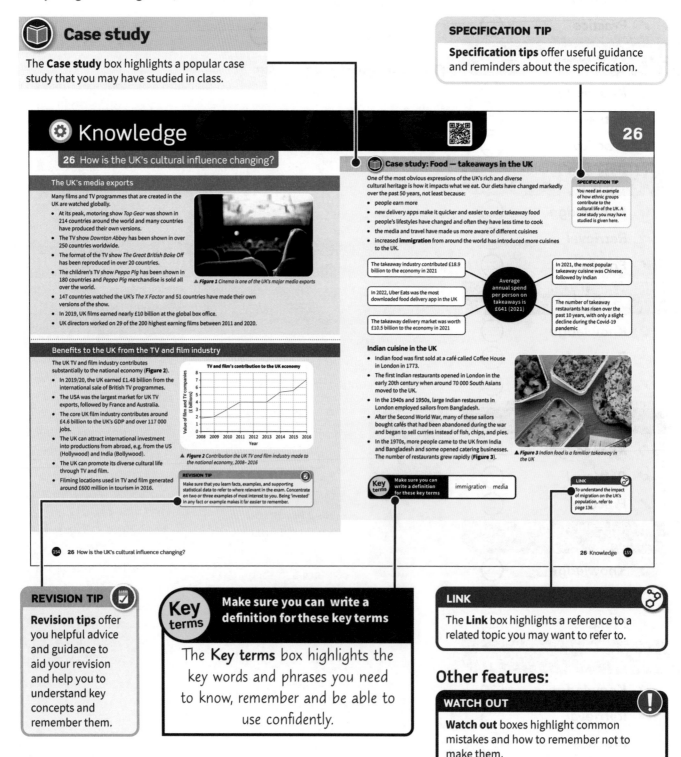

REVISION TIP

Revision tips offer you helpful advice and guidance to aid your revision and help you to understand key concepts and remember them.

Key terms
Make sure you can write a definition for these key terms

The **Key terms** box highlights the key words and phrases you need to know, remember and be able to use confidently.

LINK

The **Link** box highlights a reference to a related topic you may want to refer to.

Other features:

WATCH OUT

Watch out boxes highlight common mistakes and how to remember not to make them.

Retrieval

The **Retrieval questions** help you learn and quickly recall the information you've acquired. These are short questions and answers about the content in the Knowledge Organiser you have just reviewed. Cover up the answers with some paper and write down as many answers as you can from memory. Check back to the Knowledge Organiser for any you got wrong, then cover the answers and attempt all the questions again until you can answer *all* the questions correctly.

Make sure you revisit the retrieval questions on different days to help them stick in your memory. You need to write down the answers each time, or say them out loud, otherwise it won't work.

Previous questions

Each chapter also has some **Retrieval questions** from **previous chapters**. Answer these to see if you can remember the content from the earlier chapters. If you get the answers wrong, go back and do the Retrieval questions for the earlier chapters again.

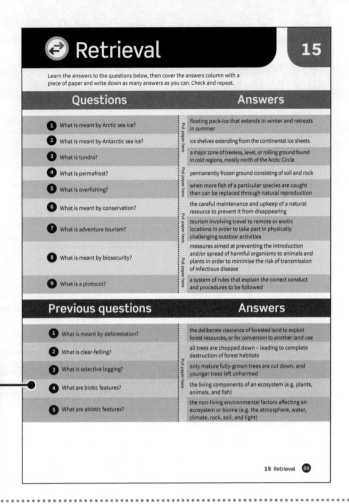

Practice

Once you think you know the Knowledge Organiser and Retrieval answers really well, you can move on to the final stage: **Practice**.

Each chapter has **exam-style questions**, including some questions from previous chapters, to help you apply all the knowledge you have learnt and can retrieve.

Answers and Glossary

You can scan the QR code at any time to access the sample answers and mark schemes for all the exam-style questions, glossary containing definitions of the key terms, as well as further revision support visit go.oup.com/OR/GCSE/OB/Geog

EXAM TIP

Exam tips show you how to interpret the questions, provide guidance on how to answer them, and advice on how to secure as many marks as possible. Guidance is also offered on how to approach different command words.

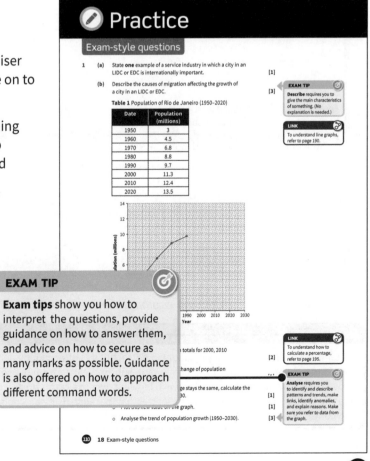

1 Global atmospheric circulation and weather

The global circulation system

- The **global circulation system**, involving interconnected cells of air, controls temperatures, rainfall distributions, prevailing winds, and creates distinctive climate zones (see **Figure 1**).

- Our **atmosphere**, winds, ocean currents and – principally – the Sun's energy (solar **insolation**), all work together to keep our planet habitable (see **Figure 2**).

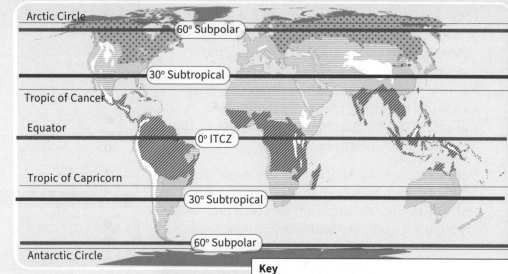

▲ **Figure 1** *How high and low pressure belts help to explain world climate zones*

Key
- ━ Low pressure: rising air and high precipitation
- ━ High pressure: sinking air and low precipitation
- ▨ Tropical climate: hot and wet
- ▤ Dry climate: hot and dry
- ▦ Mild climate: warm and wet
- ⣿ Continental climate: cold and wet
- ■ Polar climate: very cold and dry
- ▢ Mountain: altitude affects climate

- **Hadley cells** – the largest atmospheric circulation cells – cause heavy rain over the **Inter-Tropical Convergence Zone (ITCZ)** and **arid deserts** around 30° north and 30° south (see **Figure 3**).

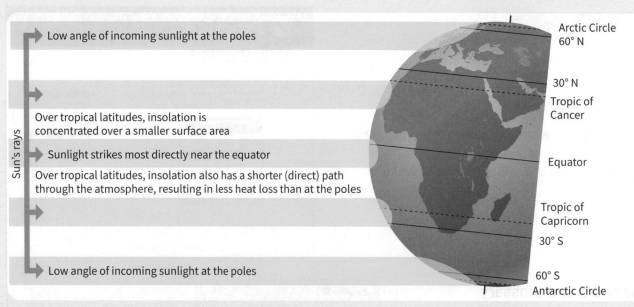

▲ **Figure 2** *How solar insolation varies around the Earth*

> **WATCH OUT** ①
>
> UK temperatures are unusually mild for 60° north, but it is often cloudy and wet. Cold polar air from the north meets warm sub-tropical air from the south above the UK. Winds from the south-west, blowing over the warm North Atlantic Drift, usually bring warm and wet weather, because rising air cools and condenses to form clouds.

How the global circulation system causes extremes in weather conditions

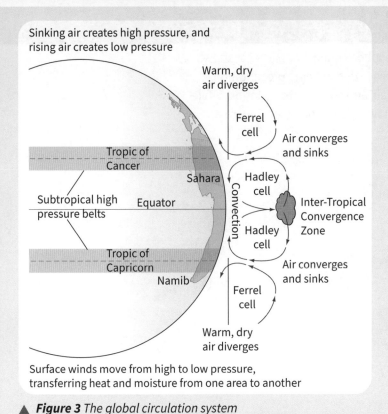

Sinking air creates high pressure, and rising air creates low pressure

- Warm, dry air diverges
- Ferrel cell
- Air converges and sinks
- Tropic of Cancer
- Sahara
- Hadley cell
- Inter-Tropical Convergence Zone
- Subtropical high pressure belts
- Equator
- Convection
- Hadley cell
- Tropic of Capricorn
- Namib
- Air converges and sinks
- Ferrel cell
- Warm, dry air diverges

Surface winds move from high to low pressure, transferring heat and moisture from one area to another

▲ **Figure 3** *The global circulation system*

Winds

Wind is the movement of air from high pressure to low pressure. The greater the difference in pressure, the stronger the wind. Wind types include:

- very strong **jet streams** high in the atmosphere
- **trade winds** blowing along the surface from high pressure belts to low pressure belts
- prevailing winds – wind from the most common direction in any given place
- katabatic winds – heavy air flowing downhill
- tropical storms and tornadoes – very strong rotating winds.

Temperature patterns

Solar insolation heats the Earth's surface (see **Figure 2**) – and is strongest where it is focused on low (tropical) **latitudes**. But other factors affect temperatures in different parts of the world.

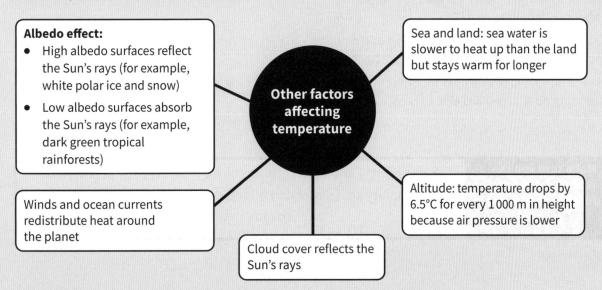

Albedo effect:
- High albedo surfaces reflect the Sun's rays (for example, white polar ice and snow)
- Low albedo surfaces absorb the Sun's rays (for example, dark green tropical rainforests)

Sea and land: sea water is slower to heat up than the land but stays warm for longer

Other factors affecting temperature

Winds and ocean currents redistribute heat around the planet

Altitude: temperature drops by 6.5°C for every 1000 m in height because air pressure is lower

Cloud cover reflects the Sun's rays

The hottest place on Earth is the Lut desert in Iran – there are no clouds, insolation is intense, and dark lava absorbs the Sun's rays. In contrast, the coldest place is Antarctica – insolation is spread, and ice and snow reflect the Sun's rays.

 # Knowledge

1 Global atmospheric circulation and weather

Precipitation

Precipitation is any moisture falling from the atmosphere – rain, hail, sleet, or snow. The global circulation system plays an important role in determining precipitation patterns because areas of low pressure have rising air, and so high precipitation, while areas of high pressure have descending air, and so low precipitation (see **Figure 4**).

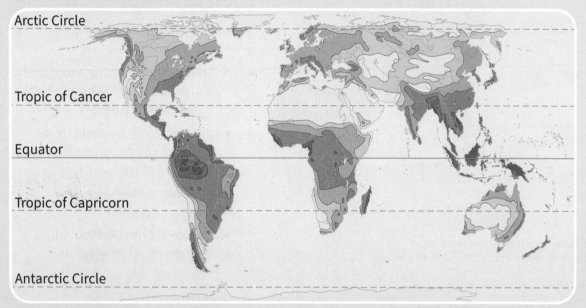

Key
mm
3 000
2 000
1 000
500
250
0

▲ **Figure 4** *Average annual precipitation*

At a global, regional, or local scale all precipitation is caused by warm air (containing water vapour) rising, cooling, and condensing into clouds. Precipitation may be:

- convectional – intense insolation heating the ground and air above it (for example, ITCZ)

- frontal – a warm air mass meeting cooler air and rising at the 'front' (for example, much of the UK's precipitation)

- relief – warm air forced to rise over mountains (causing heavy precipitation) but descending on the leeward side to create a dry **rain shadow**.

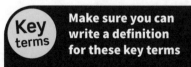 **Make sure you can write a definition for these key terms**

albedo effect   arid desert   atmosphere   global circulation system
Hadley cell   insolation   ITCZ   jet stream   latitude
rain shadow   trade wind

Retrieval

Learn the answers to the questions below, then cover the answers column with a piece of paper and write down as many answers as you can. Check and repeat.

Questions	Answers
1 What is meant by 'insolation'?	the amount of heat (radiation) from the Sun that reaches the Earth's surface
2 What is the prevailing wind?	wind from the most common direction in any given place
3 Why are Britain's temperatures unusually mild for 60° north?	surface prevailing winds from the south-west blow over the warm North Atlantic Drift, causing warmer temperatures than normal for this latitude
4 What is the albedo effect?	the amount a surface reflects the Sun's rays back into space
5 Why is solar insolation more intense at tropical latitudes?	the Sun's heat is concentrated most at lower latitudes and the rays also pass directly through the atmosphere, so less heat is lost
6 What is the Inter-Tropical Convergence Zone (ITCZ)?	a narrow zone of low air pressure, from 5° north to 5° south of the equator, where northern and southern air masses meet
7 What is the Hadley cell?	the largest atmospheric circulation cell which causes heavy rain over the ITCZ and deserts around 30° north and south
8 Why is it hot over the equator?	because the Sun's rays are strongest there
9 Why is it humid over the equator?	hot, humid air rises, cools, and condenses, causing heavy rain
10 Why is it hot and dry about 30° north and 30° south?	as cool air sinks, it creates a belt of high pressure with little rain and hot daytime temperatures
11 What is precipitation?	any moisture falling from the atmosphere, such as rain, hail, sleet, or snow
12 What causes precipitation?	warm air containing water vapour rises, cools, and condenses into clouds
13 What is a rain shadow?	the leeward side of mountains, where there is little rain
14 What is a jet stream?	a very strong wind high in the atmosphere
15 What are trade winds?	winds that blow along the surface from high pressure belts to low pressure belts
16 What is a katabatic wind?	a wind caused by heavy air flowing downhill

Put paper here

Practice

Exam-style questions

▲ **Fig. 1** – A satellite image of West Africa

1   **(a)**   Study **Fig. 1**, a satellite image of West Africa.

     (i)   Label the UK.   [1]

     (ii)   Label the Inter-Tropical Convergence Zone (ITCZ).   [1]

     (iii)   Outline the climatic conditions experienced in West
     Africa's ITCZ.   [3]

> **EXAM TIP**
>
> **Labels** simply identify or name features. **Annotations** give details such as explanations.

  (b)   Explain how the global circulation system affects rainfall distribution
  in West Africa.   [4]

  (c)   Draw an annotated sketch of atmospheric circulation to explain the
  global location of **either** the Inter-Tropical Convergence Zone (ITCZ)
  or arid deserts.   [4]

> **EXAM TIP**
>
> In the exam, you will be given answer lines to write on. Use the number of lines given as a guide to how much you are expected to write.

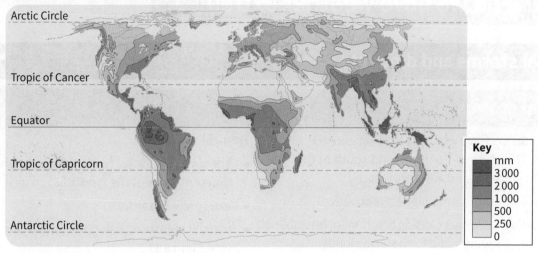

Arctic Circle

Tropic of Cancer

Equator

Tropic of Capricorn

Antarctic Circle

Key
mm
3 000
2 000
1 000
500
250
0

▲ *Fig. 2* – *Global annual precipitation*

2   **(a)**   Study **Fig. 2**, a map of average annual precipitation across the world. Select which statement is **true**.

A   The driest continent is South America.

B   Annual precipitation over the equator is less than 500 mm.

C   UK average precipitation is 500–1 000 mm per year.

D   Central Australia's average precipitation is less than 250 mm per year.

Write the correct letter in the box. ☐   [1]

(b)   Describe the distribution of average annual precipitation exceeding 3 000 mm.   [2]

> **EXAM TIP**
>
> **Describe** requires you to give the main characteristics of something. (No explanation is needed.)

(c)   Explain why arid areas are often found 30° north and 30° south of the equator.   [2]

(d)   Explain why Antarctica is so cold.   [4]

> **EXAM TIP**
>
> **Explain** requires you to give reasons why something happens.

2 Why do we have weather extremes?

Tropical storms and droughts

Tropical storms

Tropical storms have wind speeds that exceed 118 km/h. They form 5–15° north and south of the equator, in summer and autumn, where:

- ocean temperatures are highest (above 26.5°C)
- two Hadley cells meet causing hot, humid, unstable air to rise, condense and form storm clouds
- the **Coriolis effect** of the Earth's rotation is very strong – which starts the storm spinning.

Tropical storms are:

- known as cyclones, hurricanes, or typhoons in different parts of the world
- extremely hazardous
- usually measured using the **Saffir–Simpson scale** (see **Figure 1**).

Trade winds are responsible for the mainly east–west tropical storm paths.

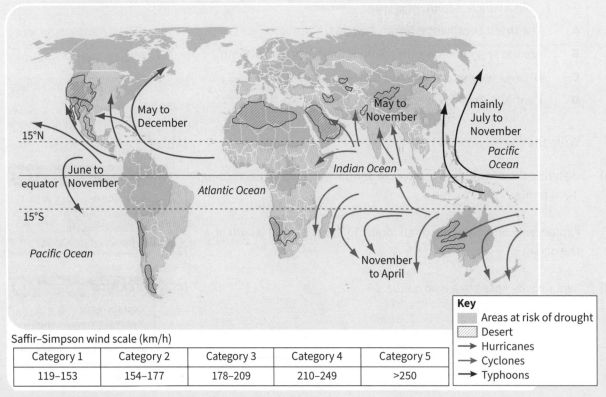

Saffir–Simpson wind scale (km/h)

Category 1	Category 2	Category 3	Category 4	Category 5
119–153	154–177	178–209	210–249	>250

Key
- Areas at risk of drought
- Desert
- → Hurricanes
- → Cyclones
- → Typhoons

▲ **Figure 1** *Global distribution of tropical storms and droughts*

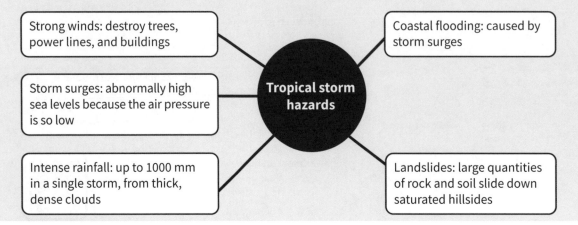

Strong winds: destroy trees, power lines, and buildings

Coastal flooding: caused by storm surges

Storm surges: abnormally high sea levels because the air pressure is so low

Tropical storm hazards

Intense rainfall: up to 1000 mm in a single storm, from thick, dense clouds

Landslides: large quantities of rock and soil slide down saturated hillsides

How do tropical storms form?

Rising air draws huge quantities of evaporated water vapour up from the ocean surface. This then cools and condenses to form towering thunderstorm clouds.	As the water vapour condenses, it releases heat which powers the storm and draws up more water vapour.	Multiple thunderstorms join to form a giant rotating storm.

LINK

To understand how tropical storm formation and movement is affected by the global circulation system, refer to pages 2–4.

The Coriolis effect spins the storm at over 118 km/h, creating a vast cloud spiral.	Prevailing winds move the storm over the ocean surface like a spinning top. The storm gathers strength as it picks up more and more energy from the evaporated water.	On reaching land, the energy supply (evaporated water) is cut off and the storm weakens.

What are the structure and features of a tropical storm?

Figure 2 shows a cross-section through the centre of a tropical storm:

- The centre is the **eye** – a column of rapidly sinking, cool air where conditions are fairly calm and there are no clouds.
- At the outer edge of the eye is the **eye wall** – the most severe conditions with very strong winds (including tornadoes) and torrential rainfall.
- Cumulonimbus clouds swirling around beyond the eye wall bring more rain.

REVISION TIP

Remember, tropical storms rotate anticlockwise in the northern hemisphere and clockwise in the southern hemisphere.

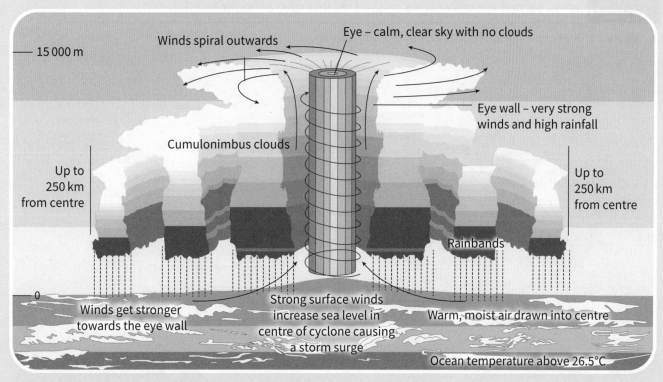

▲ *Figure 2* The structure and features of a tropical storm

Tropical storms are associated with extremely strong winds – often gusting more than 300 km/h – but they move over the ocean slowly.

Knowledge

2 Why do we have weather extremes?

Droughts

Droughts are long periods when there is much less precipitation than usual leading to water shortages. They are:

- linked to long periods of high pressure
- increasing in frequency – possibly due to long-term climate change
- less violent than tropical storms, but their impact can be deadly.

LINK

To understand more about climate change and its impacts, refer to pages 31–34.

El Niño and La Niña

El Niño and **La Niña** events are caused by changes in the sea surface temperature in a band across the Pacific Ocean (**Figures 3** and **4**).

Event	Causes	Consequences
El Niño	Weaker trade winds increase the sea temperature in the tropical eastern Pacific causing an El Niño effect every three to seven years	• Changes to world precipitation patterns (see **Figure 4**) • More tropical storms in the Pacific • Fewer tropical storms in the Atlantic • More droughts in Asia
La Niña	Stronger trade winds decrease the sea temperature in the tropical eastern Pacific causing a La Niña effect every three to five years	• Changes to world precipitation patterns • Weaker tropical storms in the Pacific • Stronger tropical storms in the Atlantic • Droughts in South America

▲ **Figure 3** Causes and consequences of El Niño and La Niña events

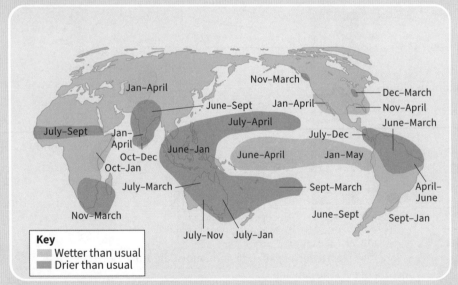

▲ **Figure 4** The impact of El Niño on world precipitation patterns

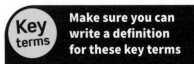 **Make sure you can write a definition for these key terms**

Coriolis effect   drought   El Niño   eye   eye wall
La Niña   Saffir–Simpson scale   storm surge   tropical storm

Learn the answers to the questions below, then cover the answers column with a piece of paper and write down as many answers as you can. Check and repeat.

Questions

Answers

	Questions	Answers
1	What is a tropical storm?	a powerful, rapidly spinning storm that forms 5–15° north and south of the equator
2	What hazards are associated with tropical storms?	strong winds, storm surges, intense rainfall, landslides, and coastal flooding
3	What is a storm surge?	abnormally high sea levels caused by very low air pressure during a tropical storm
4	What effect can a storm surge cause?	coastal flooding
5	What is the Saffir–Simpson scale?	a scale used to measure the wind strength of a tropical storm from category 1 to 5
6	What is the Coriolis effect?	the way the Earth's rotation causes rotating weather systems and tropical storms
7	What is the eye of a tropical storm?	a column of rapidly sinking cool air where conditions are fairly calm and there are no clouds at the centre of a storm
8	What is the eye wall of a tropical storm?	the outer edge of the eye with the most severe conditions of very strong winds and torrential rainfall
9	What is a drought?	a long period when there is much less precipitation than is usual, leading to water shortages
10	What is El Niño?	a Pacific Ocean event occurring when weak trade winds, blowing east to west, increase surface temperatures in the eastern Pacific
11	What is La Niña?	a Pacific Ocean event occurring when strong trade winds, blowing east to west, reduce surface temperatures in the eastern Pacific

Put paper here

Previous questions

Now go back and use the questions below to check your knowledge of previous topics.

Previous questions

Answers

	Previous questions	Answers
1	What is meant by 'insolation'?	the amount of heat (radiation) from the Sun that reaches the Earth's surface
2	Why is solar insolation more intense at tropical latitudes?	the Sun's heat is concentrated most at lower latitudes and the rays also pass directly through the atmosphere, so less heat is lost
3	What is the Hadley cell?	the largest atmospheric circulation cell which causes heavy rain over the ITCZ and deserts around 30° north and south

Put paper here

Exam-style questions

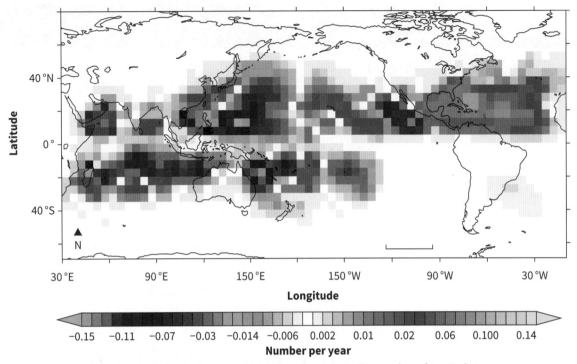

$$\begin{array}{cccccccccccc} -0.15 & -0.11 & -0.07 & -0.03 & -0.014 & -0.006 & 0.002 & 0.01 & 0.02 & 0.06 & 0.100 & 0.14 \end{array}$$

Number per year

The colour variation indicates an increase or decrease in the number of tropical storms per year

▲ *Fig. 1 — Distribution of tropical storms, 1980–2018*

1   (a)   Study **Fig. 1**, a map of the distribution (frequency) of tropical storms, 1980–2018.

Select the statement that best describes how climate change has changed the global frequency of tropical cyclones between 1980 and 2018.

   A   During the period 1980–2018, the number of tropical storms originating in the North Atlantic and central Pacific decreased.

   B   During the period 1980–2018, more tropical storms occurred in the southern Indian Ocean and western North Pacific.

   C   The colours on the map suggest many changes, but most annual changes are between -0.1 and +0.1 per year.

   D   The colours on the map suggest frequent annual changes of more than 0.1 increase or decrease.

Write the correct letter in the box. ☐   [1]

   (b)   State what tropical storms are called in different parts of the world.   [2]

   (c)   Describe the eye of a tropical storm.   [2]

   (d)   Identify **two** hazards associated with tropical storms.   [2]

   (e)   Define the term 'drought'.   [2]

   (f)   Outline the causes of El Niño and La Niña events.   [3]

> **EXAM TIP**
>
> **Define** requires you to give the meaning of a word, phrase, or idea.

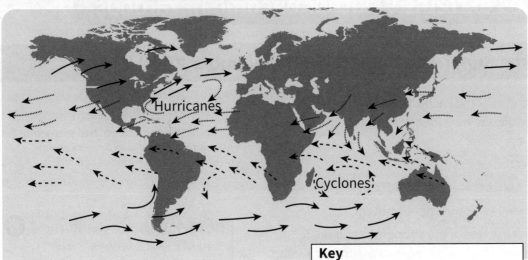

▲ **Fig. 2** – Effect of trade winds and westerlies on the paths of tropical storms

Key
— Westerlies
········· Trade winds (north-easterly)
--- Trade winds (south-easterly)

2   (a)   **Fig. 2** shows the effect of trade winds and westerlies on the paths of tropical storms. Using **Fig. 2** and your own understanding, explain the global distribution and movement of tropical storms.   **[4]**

Tropical storm	Location (and date)	Economic cost (US$ billions)	Number of deaths
Hurricane Sandy	USA (October 2012)	75	233
Typhoon Haiyan	Philippines (November 2013)	3	6300

▲ **Table 1**

(b)   Study the data in **Table 1**.

(i)   Calculate the ratio of the economic cost between the two tropical storms.   **[1]**

(ii)   Calculate the ratio of the number of deaths between the two tropical storms.   **[1]**

(iii)   Suggest reasons for these contrasts.   **[4]**

(c)   Explain the hazards associated with tropical storms.   **[4]**

(d)   Examine the causes **and** consequences of El Niño and La Niña events.   **[8]**

Questions referring to previous content

3   (a)   Explain how the albedo effect affects temperatures in different parts of the world.   **[2]**

(b)   Explain why air temperatures in the Inter-Tropical Convergence Zone (ITCZ) are so high.   **[4]**

EXAM TIP

Examine requires you to investigate in detail. Make sure you differentiate clearly between the events. Given the high number of marks allocated, it is essential you include detail.

 Case study: Super Typhoon Haiyan, November 2013

Typhoon Haiyan formed over the Pacific Ocean in November 2013 at 7 °N where conditions were ideal for tropical storm development, including:

- strong Coriolis effect
- deep ocean surface temperature over 26.5°C
- passing over little land to slow its development.

Figure 1 shows the track of one of the strongest Category 5 storms ever recorded – which is why it's called a 'super' typhoon. Very low air pressure caused a 5 m storm surge which was swept on shore by winds up to 275 km/h. Coastal devastation in the Philippines included 90% of Tacloban City destroyed by the storm surge (**Figure 2**).

> **SPECIFICATION TIP**
>
> You need case studies of **two** contrasting natural weather hazard events arising from extreme weather conditions.

> **REVISION TIP**
>
> The Philippines is an example of an **emerging and developing country (EDC)** – a country in transition from low-income and developing to advanced. EDCs have a medium to high Human Development Index (HDI).

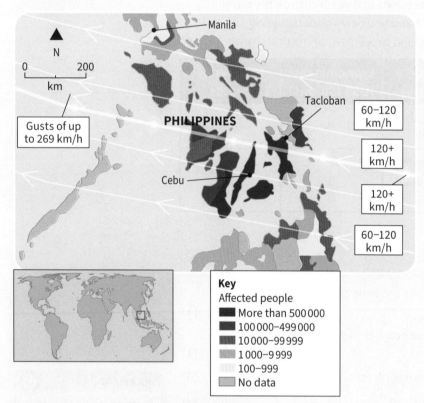

▲ *Figure 1 The track of super Typhoon Haiyan*

▲ *Figure 2 Destruction in Tacloban*

Consequences of and responses to Typhoon Haiyan

The consequences of natural disasters such as this are usually categorised as primary or secondary:

- Primary consequences are those experienced immediately – during the event.
- Secondary consequences are experienced in the following days and weeks.

Responses to natural disasters are categorised as immediate and long-term (see **Figure 3**).

Primary consequences	Secondary consequences
• 6 300 killed – most in storm surge • Over 600 000 displaced • 40 000 homes destroyed or damaged • Wind damage to buildings, power lines and crops • Over 400 mm of rain caused widespread flooding	• 14 million affected including 6 million jobs lost • Heavy rain caused landslides – blocking roads and aid access • Shortages of power, water, food, and shelter, leading to outbreaks of disease • **Infrastructure** damaged, including hospitals, schools and power supplies, affecting people's livelihoods and education • Incidents of looting and violence in Tacloban
Immediate responses	**Long-term responses**
• Rapid overseas **relief aid** including from **NGOs (non-governmental organisations)** • US helicopters assisted search and rescue, and delivery of relief aid • Field hospitals helped injured • Over 1 200 evacuation centres set up	• UN, NGOs, and international financial **long-term aid**, building supplies and medical support • Rebuilding of infrastructure • Rice farming and fishing quickly re-established • Homes rebuilt in safer areas • More typhoon shelters built

▲ **Figure 3** Consequences of and responses to natural disasters

📖 Case study: UK drought, 2012

The drought of 2012 was one of the worst in the UK on record – particularly in southern England (**Figure 4**). It was caused by:

- unusually dry winds from Europe causing low rainfall between April 2010 and May 2012
- warmer temperatures causing greater evaporation from reservoirs, lakes, and rivers
- baked, dry soils making it difficult for water to soak in
- high water demand and leakage from pipes.

REVISION TIP

The UK is an example of an **advanced country (AC)** – defined as a country that is wealthy, has a wide range of jobs, and many services. ACs have a high Human Development Index (HDI).

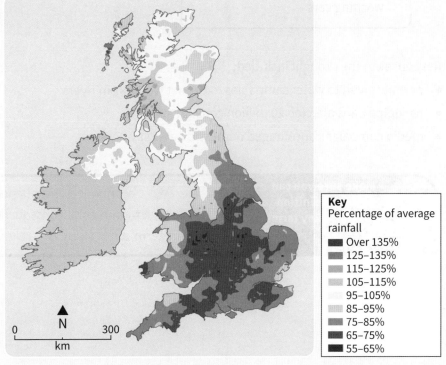

Key
Percentage of average rainfall
- Over 135%
- 125–135%
- 115–125%
- 105–115%
- 95–105%
- 85–95%
- 75–85%
- 65–75%
- 55–65%

0 ____ 300 km
▲ N

▲ Figure 4 UK rainfall, April 2010 to May 2012

Knowledge

3 When does extreme weather become hazardous?

 Case study: UK drought, 2012

Consequences of and responses to the drought

The consequences of a hazard event are often categorised as social, economic, or environmental:

- **Social consequences** affect people.
- **Economic consequences** relate to money – lost revenue, repair costs, and so on.
- **Environmental consequences** affect the natural environment.

Economic – problems for farming:
- water shortages for crops and livestock reduced yields
- dry ground made the harvest difficult in autumn 2011

Consequences of drought

Environmental – problems for the natural environment:
- wildfires in South Wales, Surrey, and the Scottish Borders
- water extraction from rivers affected **ecosystems**

Social – problems for households:
- hosepipe bans banned people from watering gardens or washing cars

Responses to the drought included:

- permits given to water companies to extract water from rivers
- hosepipe bans affected 20 million consumers
- media campaigns encouraged domestic water saving tips.

 Key terms

Make sure you can write a definition for these key terms

AC   economic consequence   ecosystem   EDC
environmental consequence   infrastructure
long-term aid   NGOs   relief aid   social consequence

Learn the answers to the questions below, then cover the answers column with a piece of paper and write down as many answers as you can. Check and repeat.

Questions	Answers
1 What is an emerging and developing country (EDC)?	a country in transition from being a low-income developing country to an advanced country
2 What are primary consequences of a hazard event?	consequences experienced immediately – during the event
3 What are secondary consequences of a hazard event?	consequences experienced in the following days and weeks after an event
4 What is infrastructure?	the basic services needed for a country to operate such as roads, railways, power and water supplies, and telecommunications)
5 What is relief aid?	short-term emergency aid such as from NGOs, to provide food, water, shelter, and medical assistance and supplies
6 What are NGOs?	non-governmental organisations generally independent from governments
7 What is an advanced country (AC)?	a country that is wealthy, has a wide range of jobs, and many services
8 What are social consequences of a hazard event?	consequences directly affecting people
9 What are economic consequences of a hazard event?	consequences relating to money such as lost revenue and repair costs
10 What are environmental consequences of a hazard event?	consequences affecting the natural environment
11 What are ecosystems?	interacting communities of plants and animals and the environment in which they live

Put paper here

Previous questions

Now go back and use the questions below to check your knowledge of previous topics.

Previous questions	Answers
1 What is a tropical storm?	a powerful, rapidly spinning storm that forms 5–15° north and south of the equator
2 What hazards are associated with tropical storms?	strong winds; storm surges; intense rainfall; landslides; and coastal flooding
3 What is the Coriolis effect?	the way the Earth's rotation causes rotating weather systems and tropical storms
4 What is El Niño?	a Pacific Ocean event occurring when weak trade winds, blowing east to west, increase surface temperatures in the eastern Pacific

Put paper here

Practice

Exam-style questions

1 **(a)** Describe **two** primary consequences of a tropical storm. **[2]**

   (b) Describe the social **and** economic impacts of tropical storms. **[4]**

▲ **Fig. 1** – 'Superstorm' Sandy was the second costliest storm in US history

   (c) Study **Fig. 1,** a photograph of coastal flooding in New Jersey, USA, caused by 'Superstorm' (Hurricane) Sandy, October 2012.

   (i) State **one** reason why these coastal properties were so vulnerable to 'Superstorm' Sandy. **[1]**

   (ii) Suggest **two** reasons why the total damage costs of this tropical storm were so high. **[2]**

   (d) Evaluate the social, economic, and environmental impacts of a natural weather hazard event on **either** emerging and developing countries (EDCs) **or** advanced countries (ACs). **[8]**

   (e) Outline the consequences of droughts. **[4]**

   (f) **CASE STUDY – UK-based natural weather hazard event.**

   Name of chosen UK-based natural weather hazard:

   _____

   Explain the causes of your chosen UK-based natural weather hazard. **[6]**

> **EXAM TIP** ◎
>
> **Evaluate** requires you to weigh up the good and bad points to make a judgement. Start by identifying what you are discussing – EDCs **or** ACs – and the type of natural weather hazard event. Due to the high number of marks available, you could use evidence from a located case study.

Questions referring to previous content

2   (a)   Which **one** of the following would cause a tropical storm to intensify?

    A   The storm meeting another weather system

    B   The storm moving over warmer water

    C   The storm changing direction

    D   The storm moving over land

    Write the correct letter in the box. ☐   **[1]**

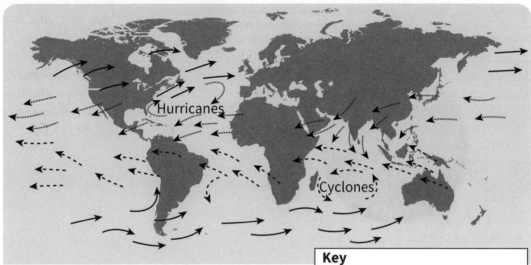

Key
— Westerlies
┈ Trade winds (north-easterly)
--- Trade winds (south-easterly)

▲ *Fig. 2 – Effect of trade winds and westerlies on the paths of tropical cyclones*

(b)   Using **Fig. 2** and your own understanding, explain the global distribution and movement of tropical storms.   **[4]**

(c)   Suggest how climate change might affect the frequency and intensity of tropical storms.   **[4]**

EXAM TIP ◎

Suggest requires you to give an explanation for something when you are unable to be sure.

⚙ Knowledge

4 How do plate tectonics shape our world?

Earth structure

Geologists (scientists who study the Earth and its structure) believe the Earth is made up of many layers (see **Figure 1**).

Crust
- *Oceanic crust* – dense and 5–10 km thick beneath the oceans
- *Continental crust* – less dense and up to 70 km thick under the continents

Mantle
- Hot, dense, molten rock – 2 900 km thick
- The top layer and crust make up the rigid **tectonic plates** of the **lithosphere**
- Temperature and density increases towards the centre

Outer core
- Semi-liquid metallic rock (iron and nickel) – 2 250 km thick

Inner core
- Solid metallic rock – 1 200 km thick
- Temperatures can reach 6 000°C

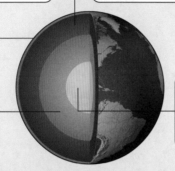

▲ *Figure 1 The internal structure of the Earth*

The Earth's internal energy sources

The extraordinary heat at the core generates **convection currents** within the mantle above. These vast, slow flows of heat rise and spread very slowly within the mantle. They are important, but not solely responsible for the movement of tectonic plates.

Tectonic plate movements

Look at **Figure 2**:

- The Earth's surface consists of irregularly shaped tectonic plates floating on the mantle underneath.
- Conventional explanations of tectonic plate movement suggest mantle convection alone drives the tectonic plates. But constructive boundaries, where **magma** rises may be more significant – new rock 'pushing' the older part of the plate in front (**ridge push**). At the other end, the plate sinks, pulling the rest with it (**slab pull**).

Key
- → Convection currents
- → Direction of plate movement

Magma rises towards the solid surface, is forced sideways, cools, becomes denser, and sinks

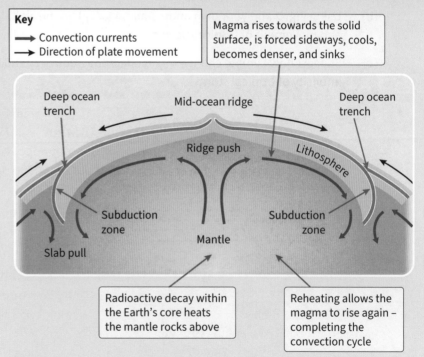

Deep ocean trench

Mid-ocean ridge

Deep ocean trench

Ridge push

Lithosphere

Subduction zone

Subduction zone

Mantle

Slab pull

Radioactive decay within the Earth's core heats the mantle rocks above

Reheating allows the magma to rise again – completing the convection cycle

▲ *Figure 2 The role of convection currents, ridge push, and slab pull in plate movement*

Tectonic plate boundaries

Look at **Figure 3**:

- Tectonic plates slide by each other at conservative boundaries, separate at constructive boundaries, and collide at destructive boundaries.

- It is the movement of the plates relative to each other that explains the major features of the Earth's surface (mountain chains, ocean trenches) and the formation of earthquakes and volcanoes.

WATCH OUT

If you are asked to explain earthquakes, you need to know more than just the ground shaking. An earthquake results from friction and sticking between tectonic plates creating enormous pressures and stresses which build to breaking point.

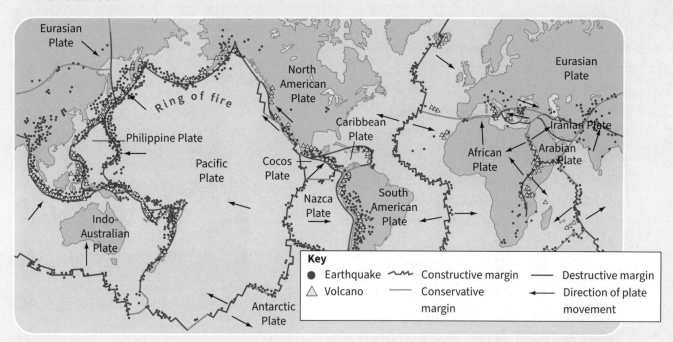

▲ **Figure 3** Tectonic plates, earthquakes, and volcanoes

Conservative boundaries

- Two plates slide past each other at different rates – for example, the San Andreas Fault, California (see **Figure 4**).

- Friction between the plates build stresses and trigger shallow-focus earthquakes when they slip.

- There are no volcanoes because there is no magma.

▲ **Figure 4** Conservative plate boundary

 Key terms Make sure you can write a definition for these key terms

composite volcano   convection current   hotspot   inner core
lithosphere   magma   ridge push   shield volcano
slab pull   tectonic plate

 # ⚙ Knowledge

Constructive boundaries

- The two plates move apart, and magma forces its way to the surface (**Figure 5**).
- As it breaks the crust it causes mild, shallow-focus earthquakes.
- The magma is very hot and fluid, allowing it to flow a long way before cooling. This results in typically broad and flat **shield volcanoes** (for example, Iceland on the Mid-Atlantic Ridge).

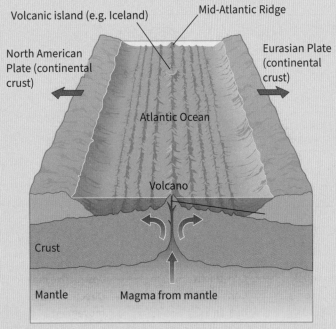

▲ **Figure 5** *Constructive plate boundary*

Collision boundaries

Where two continental plates meet, there is no subduction, so no magma to form volcanoes (**Figure 7**). At these collision boundaries, the crust crumples and lifts to form fold mountains (for example, Himalayas). Powerful shallow-focus earthquakes can be triggered.

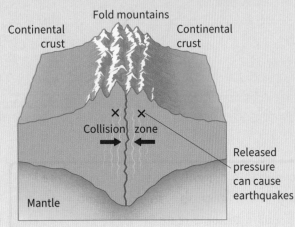

▲ **Figure 7** *Collision boundary*

Destructive boundaries

- Two plates move towards each other – for example, west coast of South America (**Figure 6**).
- The dense oceanic plate is subducted beneath the less-dense continental plate.
- Friction causes strong, deep-focus earthquakes.
- The sinking oceanic plate creates sticky, gas-rich magma – resulting in steep-sided **composite volcanoes** which erupt violently.

▲ **Figure 6** *Destructive boundary*

> **REVISION TIP** ☑
>
> Composite volcanoes have a classic conical volcano shape and summit crater like Mount Fuji in Japan. They form from lava and ash building up the volcano in layers.

Hotspots

- **Hotspots** heat the lower mantle, creating rising plumes of magma.
- If these plumes occur within a plate, they may burn through the lithosphere to create shield volcanoes.
- Hotspots remain stationary, so movement of the overlying plate forms a chain of active and extinct shield volcanoes – for example, the Hawaiian Islands, in the centre of the Pacific plate.

Learn the answers to the questions below, then cover the answers column with a piece of paper and write down as many answers as you can. Check and repeat.

Questions | Answers

	Questions	Answers
1	What is the lithosphere?	the rigid outer layer of the Earth consisting of the crust and upper mantle
2	What is the mantle?	2 900 km thick, the largest of the Earth's layers by volume made of mostly hot, dense, molten rock
3	What is the outer core?	the outer ring of the centre of the Earth – consisting of semi-liquid iron and nickel
4	What is the inner core?	the solid, hot, very dense centre of the Earth
5	How hot is the inner core?	up to 6 000°C
6	What are tectonic plates?	seven major and several minor irregularly shaped sections of the lithosphere 'floating' on the mantle beneath
7	What are convection currents?	flows of heat rising from the Earth's core, spreading, cooling, and sinking again
8	What is a hotspot?	places where magma rises in a plume in the mantle
9	What is a conservative plate boundary?	where two tectonic plates slide past each other at different rates
10	What is a constructive plate boundary?	where two tectonic plates move apart, creating new oceanic plate
11	What is a destructive plate boundary?	where two plates move towards each other, destroying oceanic plate

Put paper here

Previous questions

Now go back and use the questions below to check your knowledge of previous topics.

Previous questions | Answers

	Previous questions	Answers
1	What are primary consequences of a hazard event?	those experienced immediately – during the event
2	What are secondary consequences of a hazard event?	those experienced in the following days and weeks
3	What is the atmosphere?	the layer of gases above the Earth's surface – in short, the air that surrounds the Earth
4	What is latitude?	how far north or south a location on the Earth's surface is from the equator, measured in degrees

Put paper here

Practice

Exam-style questions

1 **(a)** Describe the structure of the Earth's interior. [4]

(b) Identify **one** difference between oceanic and continental crust. [1]

EXAM TIP

Describe requires you to give the main characteristics of something. (No explanation is needed.)

Juan De Fuca Plate
North American Plate
Eurasian Plate
Arabian Plate
African Plate
Philippine Plate
Pacific Plate
Caribbean Plate
Cocos Plate
Pacific Plate
Nazca Plate
South American Plate
Indo-Australian Plate
Fiji Plate
Scotia Plate
Antarctic Plate

— Plate boundary
→ Plate movement

▲ *Fig. 1 – The Earth's major tectonic plates*

(c) Study **Fig. 1**, a map of the Earth's major tectonic plates.

    (i) State which plate the UK is on. [1]

    (ii) Identify **two** plates that are separating. [1]

    (iii) Identify **two** plates that are colliding. [1]

(d) State the type of tectonic plate margin where subduction happens. [1]

(e) Explain the likely causes of tectonic plate movement. [4]

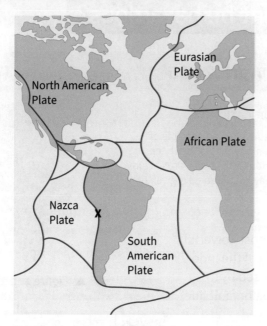

▲ *Fig. 2 – Selected tectonic plate boundaries*

2   **(a)**   Study **Fig. 2**, selected tectonic plate boundaries.

Select the correct description of plate boundary **X**.

   A   conservative

   B   constructive

   C   destructive

   D   collision

   Write the correct letter in the box. ☐   [1]

(b)   Explain the term 'hotspot'.   [2]

(c)   Explain the source of the Earth's internal energy (heat).   [2]

(d)   Explain why some tectonic plate boundaries are more hazardous than others.   [6]

(e)   Explain the differences between the types of volcanoes found at constructive and destructive plate boundaries.   [4]

(f)   Explain how earthquakes are caused at destructive plate boundaries. [2]

(g)   Describe the properties of **two** of the Earth's internal layers.   [4]

> **EXAM TIP**
>
> **Explain** requires you to give reasons why something happens.

Questions referring to previous content

3   **(a)**   Outline the differences between primary and secondary consequences of a natural hazard event.   [2]

(b)   Outline the current and likely future significance of drought as a natural hazard.   [4]

Knowledge

5 How can tectonic movement be hazardous?

📖 Case study: Nepal earthquake, April 2015

Nepal (see **Figure 1**) is an example of a **low-income developing country (LIDC)**. Nepal's HDI is ranked 142nd out of 189 countries, and its gross national income (GNI) ranked 163rd out of 192 countries.

SPECIFICATION TIP

You need a named example of a tectonic event that has been hazardous for people. A case study you may have studied is given here.

Nepal

▲ *Figure 1* Location of Nepal

Causes

The shallow-focus 7.8 magnitude earthquake was the most powerful to hit Nepal in over 80 years. Nepal sits on the boundary of the Indo-Australian and Eurasian Plates. The earthquake was caused by a sudden thrust, or release of built-up stress along this major fault line. Aftershocks continued in the days and weeks that followed.

REVISION TIP

An LIDC is poor, with a narrow range of jobs and few services. LIDCs have a low Human Development Index (HDI).

WATCH OUT

Earthquake **magnitude** is measured on the logarithmic Richter scale. Each number is ten times greater than the one before, so a small increase in value represents an earthquake of much greater power.

▶ **Figure 2** *Searching for survivors in Kathmandu, Nepal*

Consequences and responses

	Primary	Secondary
Consequences	• 9 000 killed, 20 000 injured and 3 million homeless • Widespread destruction of buildings and infrastructure • Power, water, sanitation, and communications cut • US$5 billion damage	• Communities cut off by landslides and **avalanches** – hampering relief efforts • Avalanches on Mount Everest killed at least 19 people • An avalanche in the Langtang region left 250 people missing • Flooding threatened following a landslide blocking the Kali Gandaki River – many people evacuated
	Immediate	**Long-term**
Responses	• International and Nepalese volunteer search and rescue teams rescued 16 survivors (see **Figure 2**) • The NGO World Vision International provided emergency food kits for 8000 people • Relief aid included helicopters for search, rescue, and supply drops in remote areas • 300 000 people migrated from Kathmandu to seek shelter and support from family and friends	• New National Disaster Risk Reduction Policy (2018) to increase future resilience • Most roads repaired and landslides cleared by late 2015 • 212 000 new homes constructed by September 2020, by the Nepal government as part of the Earthquake Housing Reconstruction Project • UNESCO is working with the government to restore 700 damaged temples, palaces, and museums

▲ **Figure 3** *Consequences of and responses to the Nepal earthquake*

Mitigation of tectonic hazards

Mitigation involves reducing the impact of a hazard by **monitoring**, **prediction**, **protection**, and **planning**.

Monitoring: earthquakes can occur without warning. A network of **seismometers** (seismographs) monitors and records them. Tsunami monitoring systems use floating ocean buoys to detect early tsunami waves following an earthquake. Warnings are then issued using sirens, TV, and media alerts.

Prediction: accurate predictions are impossible due to a lack of clear warning signs. But historical records can help identify locations likely to be at risk.

Earthquake mitigation strategies

Protection: earthquake-resistant engineering of infrastructure and buildings can significantly reduce risk (see **Figure 4**). Seawalls can provide protection from some tsunamis.

Planning: hazard mapping is used to identify lower risk areas to locate high-value buildings such as hospitals and power stations.

Monitoring: all active volcanoes are now monitored using high-tech scientific equipment including:
- **seismometers** (seismographs) to detect and record microquakes
- tiltmeters to monitor deformation of the ground as magma rises
- instruments to monitor radon and sulphur gas emissions.

Prediction: monitoring can bring largely accurate prediction and the ability for people to be safely evacuated.

Volcanic eruption mitigation strategies

Protection: earth embankments have been used to divert lava flows. Weirs and small dams can be used to control lahars (mudflows of ash and water).

Planning: hazard mapping is used to identify areas to control development, and plan evacuation routes.

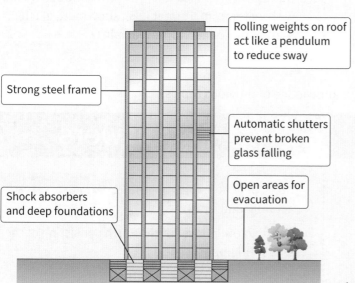

Rolling weights on roof act like a pendulum to reduce sway

Strong steel frame

Automatic shutters prevent broken glass falling

Open areas for evacuation

Shock absorbers and deep foundations

Key terms — Make sure you can write a definition for these key terms

LIDC   magnitude   mitigation   monitoring   planning   prediction   protection   seismometer

◀ **Figure 4** Features of a building designed to withstand earthquakes

Retrieval

Learn the answers to the questions below, then cover the answers column with a piece of paper and write down as many answers as you can. Check and repeat.

Questions / Answers

	Questions	Answers
1	What is meant by earthquake magnitude?	the size or strength of an earthquake measured on the Richter scale
2	What is an avalanche?	a rapid mass movement of snow, ice slabs, rock debris, soil, and vegetation
3	What is meant by mitigation?	action taken to make something less severe to reduce the impact of a hazard
4	What is meant by tectonic hazard monitoring?	ongoing observations and detection by instruments of the hazard
5	What is meant by tectonic hazard prediction?	forecasting a hazard in advance
6	What is the purpose of tectonic hazard prediction?	to allow warnings to be given, and evacuations organised, particularly for volcanic eruptions
7	What is meant by tectonic hazard protection?	the engineering structures built in preparation of the hazard
8	What are examples of tectonic hazard protection?	earthquake-resistant buildings and infrastructure, seawalls, and earth embankments to divert lava flows and lahars
9	What is meant by tectonic hazard planning?	all preparations made in advance of the hazard to enable communities to both respond to it and recover from it
10	What is a seismometer (seismograph)?	an instrument used to record the motion of the ground during an earthquake
11	What is hazard mapping?	mapping to identify areas that are affected by, or vulnerable to, a particular hazard
12	What is a lahar?	mudflow composed mainly of volcanic ash mixed with water from a crater lake, snowmelt, glacier melt or prolonged torrential rain

Put paper here

Previous questions

Now go back and use these questions to check your knowledge of previous topics.

Previous questions / Answers

	Previous questions	Answers
1	What are convection currents?	flows of heat rising from the Earth's core, spreading, cooling, and sinking again
2	What is the lithosphere?	the rigid outer layer of the Earth consisting of the crust and upper mantle
3	What is La Niña?	a Pacific Ocean event occurring when strong trade winds, blowing east to west, reduce surface temperatures in the eastern Pacific

Put paper here

28   **5** How can tectonic movement be hazardous?

Exam-style questions

▲ **Fig. 1** – A photograph of buildings destroyed by an earthquake in Nepal

▲ **Fig. 2** – A photograph of ash-covered ruins in Plymouth, Montserrat

1   **(a)**   Using **Fig. 1** or **Fig. 2** and your own knowledge describe **two** primary consequences of **either** earthquakes **or** volcanic eruptions. Tick the box of the tectonic hazard you have chosen.

☐ Earthquakes   ☐ Volcanic eruptions   **[2]**

(b)   Outline **two** factors determining the consequences of tectonic hazards.   **[2]**

> **EXAM TIP**
>
> **Outline** requires you to summarise the key points.

(c)   Explain why poorer people, in low-income developing countries (LIDCs) and emerging and developing countries (EDCs), are more vulnerable to tectonic hazards.   **[3]**

	Hazard A	Hazard B
Number of deaths in first 24 hours	172	16 304
Number of deaths in following 30 days	13	35 248
Estimated cost of damage (US$)	28 billion	6.2 billion

▲ *Table 1*

(d)   Study **Table 1**, which shows the impacts of two tectonic hazards.

(i)   Which hazard most likely occurred in an advanced country (AC)?   **[1]**

(ii)   State **one** reason for your answer to (i).   **[1]**

(iii)   Referring to both ACs and LIDCs or EDCs, suggest reasons why the number of deaths might increase throughout the month following a hazard event.   **[3]**

(e)   Suggest **two** reasons why the impacts of tectonic hazards are often worse in LIDCs and EDCs.   **[4]**

> **EXAM TIP**
>
> **Explain** requires you to give reasons why something happens.

(f)   Explain the difference between primary and secondary consequences in tectonic hazards.   **[4]**

(g)   **CASE STUDY – a tectonic event that has been hazardous for people**

Name of chosen tectonic hazard: _____

Explain the causes **and** consequences of your chosen tectonic hazard. **[6]**

▲ **Fig. 3** – A photograph of Tokyo-Yokohama Metropolitan Area, Japan

Japan is one of the richest countries in the world. It has a highly developed economy and is a world leader in technology. Japan's workforce is known for its efficiency. The Tokyo-Yokohama Metropolitan Area is the world's biggest megacity. It is also a multi-hazard environment vulnerable to typhoons and tectonic hazards.

2   **(a)**   Study **Fig. 3** and the text extract.

        (i)   State **two** advantages Japan has in preparation for
            tectonic hazards.   **[2]**

        (ii)   Explain how buildings in the Tokyo-Yokohama Metropolitan
            Area might have been designed to reduce the effects of **either**
            earthquakes **or** volcanic eruptions. Tick the box of the tectonic
            hazard you have chosen.

            ☐ Earthquakes   ☐ Volcanic eruptions   **[3]**

        (iii)   Explain how planning for tectonic hazards might help to reduce
            the effects of **either** an earthquake **or** a volcanic eruption in the
            Tokyo-Yokohama Metropolitan Area. Tick the box of the tectonic
            hazard you have chosen.

            ☐ Earthquakes   ☐ Volcanic eruptions   **[4]**

    (b)   Explain what is meant by tectonic hazard management.   **[2]**

    (c)   Outline **two** examples of tectonic hazard protection.   **[2]**

    (d)   **Either** explain the limitations and possibilities of earthquake
        prediction **or** explain ways in which volcanic eruptions can be
        predicted. Tick the box of the tectonic hazard you have chosen.

        ☐ Earthquakes   ☐ Volcanic eruptions   **[4]**

Questions referring to previous content

3   **(a)**   'Short-term relief inevitably follows all tectonic hazard events.'
        Explain what this involves.   **[3]**

    (b)   Evaluate the extent to which the impacts of **either** earthquakes **or**
        volcanic eruptions can be reduced by preparation and relief efforts.
        Tick the box of the tectonic hazard you have chosen.

        ☐ Earthquakes   ☐ Volcanic eruptions   **[8]**

> **EXAM TIP**
>
> **Evaluate** requires you weigh up the good and bad points to make a judgement.

6 What evidence is there for climate change?

The causes of natural climate change

Evidence of natural climate change

We know that climates have changed throughout geological time. For example, fluctuations throughout the last 2.6 million years (the **Quaternary period**) explain glacial periods and warmer interglacial periods. We can see these changes in:

Ice cores from Antarctica and Greenland	Air bubbles from the time the snow fell now trapped in the ice and analysed for carbon dioxide (CO_2) content: Higher CO_2 = warmer temperatures
Landforms shaped by ice during cold glacial periods	Deep U-shaped valleys – now with 'misfit' streams and hollows filled by lakes
Tree rings – each representing a year's growth	Wide rings show growth during warmer and wetter periods – narrow rings show harsh conditions like cold or drought. Fossils of trees in peat bogs go back thousands of years
Historical sources like diaries, old photos, paintings, and harvest records	In the 17th century, the River Thames froze over during an especially cold period; however, accounts like these can be vague, incomplete, or unreliable

Orbital changes – Milankovitch cycles

Three distinct cycles, called **Milankovitch cycles**, decrease or increase the distance from the sun (**Figure 1**).

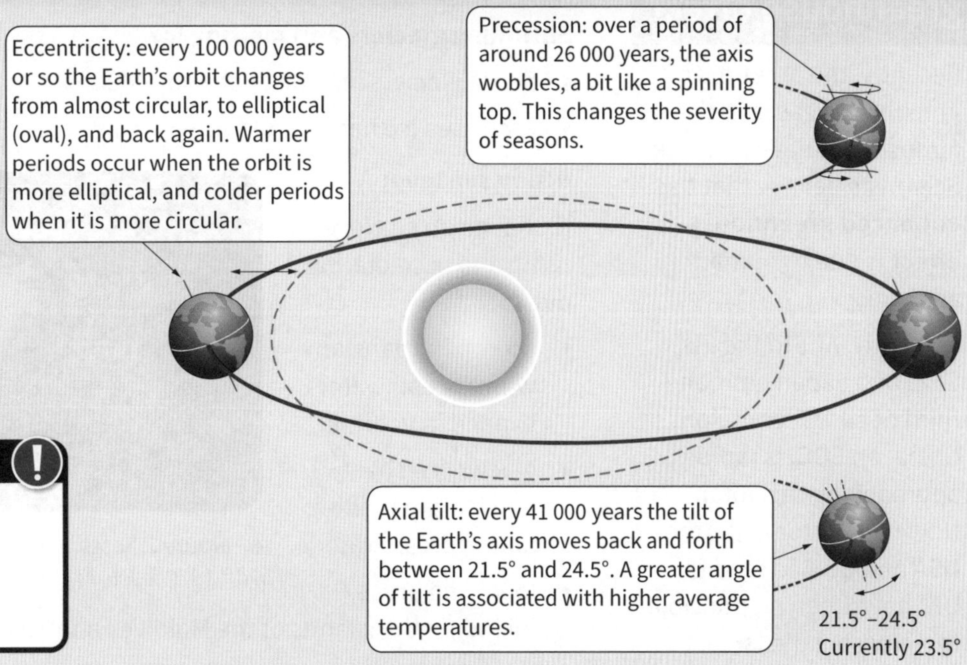

Eccentricity: every 100 000 years or so the Earth's orbit changes from almost circular, to elliptical (oval), and back again. Warmer periods occur when the orbit is more elliptical, and colder periods when it is more circular.

Precession: over a period of around 26 000 years, the axis wobbles, a bit like a spinning top. This changes the severity of seasons.

WATCH OUT ❗

Decreasing distance from the Sun results in natural climate warming. Increasing distance from the Sun results in natural climate cooling.

Axial tilt: every 41 000 years the tilt of the Earth's axis moves back and forth between 21.5° and 24.5°. A greater angle of tilt is associated with higher average temperatures.

21.5°–24.5°
Currently 23.5°

▲ **Figure 1** Milankovitch cycles

Knowledge

6 What evidence is there for climate change?

Solar activity

The Sun has dark patches called **sun spots**, which are intense solar storms on its surface caused by magnetic activity inside the Sun. More sun spots mean that more solar energy is being fired out towards Earth in explosive flares. Over a period of around 11 years, the number of sun spots varies, increasing or lowering Earth temperatures.

Volcanic activity

Volcanic ash can block out the Sun, reducing temperatures on Earth. Sulphur dioxide is also ejected, which becomes droplets of sulphuric acid in the air. These act like mirrors to reflect solar radiation back into space.

The natural greenhouse effect

The natural greenhouse effect keeps the Earth warm enough to support life. It works like a glass greenhouse:

- Greenhouse gases (CO_2, methane, water vapour, and nitrous oxide) trap heat that would otherwise escape into space.
- It allows short-wave radiation (light) from the Sun through to the Earth.
- It traps some of the long-wave radiation (heat) that would otherwise be radiated back into space.

What impacts are humans having on the atmosphere?

The enhanced greenhouse effect

Recently, the amounts of greenhouse gases in the atmosphere have increased. Scientists believe that this **enhanced greenhouse effect** is due to human activities.

Currently, ACs in the EU, USA, and Japan emit one-third of all CO_2 emissions. China, an EDC, is rapidly approaching this total. However, historically, the USA and EU ACs (and the UK) have been responsible for releasing the largest shares of total emissions.

Evidence for current climate change

Shrinking glaciers and melting ice
- Some glaciers may disappear by 2035.
- Arctic sea ice has thinned by 65% since the mid-1970s (see **Figure 2**).

Rising sea level
Global mean sea level is rising and accelerating due to:
- thermal expansion – warm ocean waters expand in volume
- glacier, ice sheet, and ice cap melting adding fresh water
- low-lying areas, including the islands of the Maldives and Tuvala, are vulnerable.

▲ **Figure 2** Satellite image of sea ice levels in 2012, with 1979 levels in yellow

Seasonal changes
- Tree flowering and bird migration is advancing.
- Bird nesting is earlier than in the 1970s.

What human activities contribute to greenhouse gases?

There are many human sources of greenhouse gases, including sewage treatment, and emissions from landfill sites, coal mines, and natural gas pipelines.

Use of fossil fuels

- Most CO_2 comes from burning **fossil fuels** in industry and power stations. Transport and farming also contribute.

- Since 1960, CO_2 emissions from fossil fuels have increased rapidly:

▲ *Global fossil fuel carbon dioxide emissions, 1960–2018*

Human activities contributing to greenhouse gases

Agriculture

- Agriculture accounts for about 30% of global greenhouse gas emissions.

- Livestock such as cattle emit vast volumes of methane.

- Paddy rice cultivation releases methane.

- 75% of all nitrous oxide comes from manure and nitrogen-rich fertilisers.

Deforestation

- **Deforestation** involves cutting down or burning trees, usually to clear land for farming, settlement, or industry.

- 70% of deforestation is to create grazing land for commercial livestock.

- Deforestation in tropical regions such as rainforests accounts for 20% of global greenhouse gas emissions.

- Through photosynthesis, trees naturally convert atmospheric CO_2 into (stored) carbon. But deforestation releases the CO_2 back into the atmosphere.

Global impacts of climate change

Global impacts of climate change

- More extreme weather events, such as droughts, floods, heatwaves, and wildfires

- Stronger tropical storms

- More heat-related illness and disease

- Reduced crop yields and water security

- Changing ecosystems and animal habitats

- Flooding of low-lying coastal areas

- 'Climate refugees' as people evacuate areas no longer habitable

- Desertification

⚙ Knowledge

6 What evidence is there for climate change?

The impacts of climate change within the UK

The UK's climate is changing:

- Average temperature is increasing.
- Winters are becoming warmer and wetter.
- Summers are becoming warmer and drier.
- The changes are expected to be greatest in the south of the UK – see **Figure 3**.

	Social impacts	Economic impacts	Environmental impacts
Negative impacts	• Water shortages • Elderly vulnerable to heatwaves • Coastal homes vulnerable to sea level rise and cliff erosion • Extreme rainfall events causing **flash flooding**	• Agricultural land lost to coastal flooding and/or managed retreat • Coastal industries (e.g. Teeside) vulnerable to sea level rise • Coastal defences will need upgrading	• Coastal and salt marsh flooding and erosion • Wildlife species will struggle to survive if the seasons do not provide their food supply
Positive impacts	• Heating costs will reduce • Fewer cold-related deaths in winter	• Increased summer tourist activity generating revenue in historic places, national parks, and coastal resort	• Some trees and plants will flower earlier • New crops such as citrus fruits could be cultivated in southern England

▲ **Figure 3** Social, economic and environmental impacts of climate change in the UK

What of the future?

Many of us, including scientists and politicians, are worried about global warming. We look to the United Nations' Intergovernmental Panel on Climate Change (IPCC) for accurate data to:

- understand and explain what is happening now
- forecast what may happen in future
- advise on how the causes of climate change can be managed (mitigated) and adapted to.

The IPCC estimates that average global temperatures could rise between 1.1 and 6.4°C, and that sea levels could rise between 30 cm and 1 metre by 2100. But without certainty on future population growth, economic development, and **renewable energy** trends – not least changes in people's lifestyles – the only certainty is that less fossil fuel dependency and much more recycling, energy **conservation** and tree planting will help to avoid the worst scenarios.

Key terms Make sure you can write a definition for these key terms

conservation   deforestation   enhanced greenhouse effect   flash flooding   fossil fuel
Milankovitch cycle   Quaternary period   renewable energy   sun spot

 # Retrieval

Learn the answers to the questions below, then cover the answers column with a piece of paper and write down as many answers as you can. Check and repeat.

Questions | Answers

Questions	Answers
1 What is the Quaternary period?	the geological time period of the most recent 2.6 million years
2 How do ice cores provide evidence of past climate change?	trapped air bubbles are analysed for CO_2: higher volumes suggest warmer past temperatures
3 What can tree rings tell us about past climate change?	wide rings indicate warmer, wetter periods and narrow rings indicate cold or drought
4 What are Milankovitch cycles?	gradual orbital changes that affect the Earth's distance from the Sun
5 What are Sun spots?	dark patches on the Sun's surface, caused by magnetic energy inside the Sun, which can lead to increased temperatures on Earth
6 How can volcanic eruptions change the Earth's climate?	they lower temperatures due to volcanic ash and reflective droplets of sulphuric acid in the atmosphere
7 What is the natural greenhouse effect?	greenhouse gases trap heat from the Sun that would normally escape into space, warming the Earth
8 What is the enhanced greenhouse effect?	human activity adds more greenhouse gases to the atmosphere, causing the planet to warm
9 What is the evidence for current climate change?	shrinking glaciers and melting ice; rising sea levels due to thermal expansion, and glacier and ice cap melting adding fresh water; and seasonal changes
10 What impact will climate change have on low-lying coastal areas?	they are vulnerable to flooding due to rising sea levels
11 What impact will climate change have on food and water availability?	reduced crop yields and increased water scarcity
12 What are 'climate refugees'?	people forced to move away from areas that are no longer habitable due to climate change

Put paper here

Previous questions

Now go back and use these questions to check your knowledge of previous topics.

Previous questions | Answers

Previous questions	Answers
1 What is meant by mitigation?	action taken to make something less severe to reduce the impact of a hazard
2 What is hazard mapping?	mapping to identify areas that are affected by, or vulnerable to, a particular hazard
3 What is relief aid?	short-term emergency aid to provide food, water, shelter, and medical assistance and supplies

Put paper here

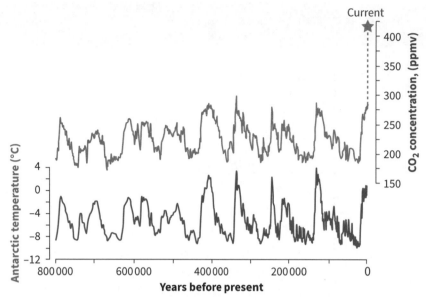

▲ **Fig. 1** – *Antarctic ice core data*

1   **(a)**   Study **Fig. 1**, graphs showing Antarctic ice core data. The peaks are
warm interglacial periods, and the troughs are cold, glacial periods
(ppmv = parts per million by volume).

        (i)   Describe the variations in the temperature graph.   **[2]**

        (ii)   Compare the CO_2 graph to the temperature graph.   **[2]**

    (b)   **(i)**   Explain how ice core data can help indicate past climates.   **[2]**

        (ii)   Explain **two** other sources of evidence for past climate change.   **[4]**

    (c)   Explain the causes of contemporary sea level rise.   **[4]**

    (d)   Outline the social, economic, and environmental impacts of
climate change in the UK.   **[6]**

2   **(a)**   Explain the enhanced greenhouse effect.   **[4]**

    (b)   Outline why climate scientists are uncertain about projected
increases in average global temperatures.   **[2]**

    (c)   Describe the evidence for current climate change.   **[4]**

    (d)   'The global impacts of climate change could be alarming.' Justify
this statement.   **[8]**

> **EXAM TIP**
>
> **Compare** requires you to
> describe similarities and
> differences between two or
> more things.

> **EXAM TIP**
>
> **Justify** means give
> evidence to support your
> ideas. Make sure you
> explain each of the possible
> expected global impacts.
> This is an 8-mark question,
> so you need to be detailed!

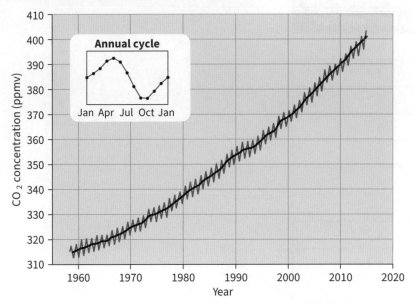

▲ **Fig. 2** – *Increases in global carbon dioxide (CO_2) since 1965*

3 **(a)** Study **Fig. 2**, a graph showing increases in global carbon dioxide (CO_2) since 1965.

    (i) Describe the variations in the global CO_2 graph. **[2]**

    (ii) Suggest **one** reason for the annual cycle. **[1]**

(b) Explain **two** ways in which climate has changed naturally in the past. **[4]**

(c) Describe the global impacts of climate change. **[4]**

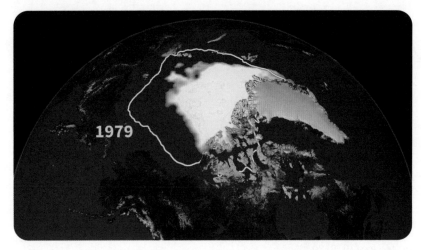

▲ **Fig. 3** – *Arctic sea ice retreat since 1979. September 2020 recorded the second smallest ever concentration (extent) of Arctic sea ice*

4 **(a)** Study **Fig. 3**, a GIS satellite image of Arctic sea ice retreat since 1979.

    (i) Describe the change in Arctic sea ice coverage since 1979. **[2]**

    (ii) Suggest **one** advantage and **one** disadvantage of this change. **[2]**

Exam-style questions

Table 1

Year	Minimum Arctic sea ice extent (millions km²)
2006	5.9
2007	4.3
2008	4.7
2009	5.3
2010	4.9
2011	4.6
2012	3.6
2013	5.2
2014	5.2
2015	4.6
2016	4.5
2017	4.8
2018	4.8
2019	4.4
2020	3.9

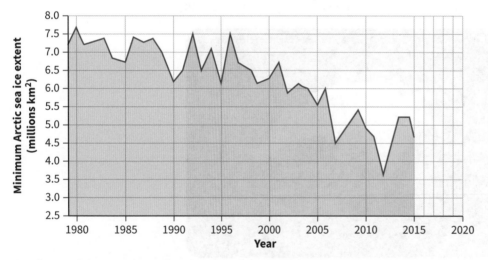

▲ **Fig. 4** - Minimum extent of Arctic sea ice (1979–2020)

(b) **(i)** Use **Table 1** to complete the line graph in **Fig. 4**. **[2]**

(ii) Plot a trend line to show the decrease in Arctic sea ice 1979–2020. **[1]**

(iii) Describe the trend of Arctic sea ice shrinkage (1979–2020). **[2]**

(iv) Suggest reasons for the trend of Arctic sea ice shrinkage (1979–2020). **[2]**

(c) Describe how volcanic eruptions can cause climate change. **[2]**

> **LINK**
>
> To understand the skill of constructing and reading a line graph, and plotting a trend line, refer to the Geographical skills section pages 191–193.

COP26: Keeping 1.5 alive?

COP26, the 26th annual UN climate 'Conference of the Parties', in Glasgow in 2021, was seen as crucial in keeping up international pressure to ensure that the 2015 Paris Agreement pledges on limiting climate change are reinforced. The goal is to keep cutting carbon emissions until they reach 'net zero' by mid-century.

The COP26 'Glasgow Climate Agreement', although not legally binding on the participating countries, aims to keep temperature rises within 1.5°C, and so prevent a 'climate catastrophe'. To achieve this several key commitments were negotiated. For example, to:

- stop deforestation by 2030
- cut 30% of methane emissions by 2030
- significantly increase 'climate aid' donations from developed countries to developing countries to allow them to cope with the effects of climate change, and make the switch to clean energy
- phase-out subsidies that artificially lower the price of coal, oil, or natural gas
- phase-down (not phase-out) coal.

Not all countries agreed to the commitments, as some wanted to protect their own interests and priorities. This explains the last-minute Indian and Chinese insistence of coal 'phase-down' rather than the 'phase-out' demanded and expected by most.

However cynical some may be of catchy slogans such as 'keeping 1.5 alive', what cannot be ignored is that annual COPs headline the impacts of climate change, and global responses to it.

▲ **Fig. 5** – COP26 'Glasgow Climate Agreement Pact'

(d) Study **Fig. 5**, an extract about COP26. With reference to your understanding of the impacts of climate change, justify if COP26 was right to 'keep 1.5 alive'. [8]

Questions referring to previous content

5 **(a)** Define hazard mitigation. [2]

(b) Outline the distinction between a destructive and a collision plate boundary. [2]

> **EXAM TIP**
>
> This is a high-mark question, so read the extract carefully, and make sure you refer to it in your answer. You may also have strong opinions yourself. But make sure you evidence them.

Knowledge

7 What makes a landscape distinctive?

What makes a landscape?

Landscapes are what we see when we view the surface of the Earth – whether natural or built. There are five main elements to any landscape.

WATCH OUT (!)

Make sure you know the difference between the UK (made up of England, Scotland, Wales, and Northern Ireland) and the British Isles (which also include the Republic of Ireland).

Natural: geology (rock types), landforms (e.g. mountains and valleys), and physical processes

Water: rivers, lakes, and adjoining sea

Human: land uses, the built environment and infrastructure

Landscape elements

Biological: living flora (plants) and fauna (animals)

Transitory (temporary): weather and the seasons

Upland and lowland landscapes in the UK

In **Figure 1** the relief map of the UK can be divided into lowlands and uplands. The flat and rolling lowlands are mainly found in southern England, south of an imaginary line from Flamborough Head in East Yorkshire to the Bristol Channel. The mountainous uplands in northern England, Wales and Scotland show dramatic evidence of glaciation during the Quaternary period.

LINK

To understand climate changes in the Quaternary period, refer to page 31.

▶ **Figure 1** Landscape elements in selected lowland and upland landscapes

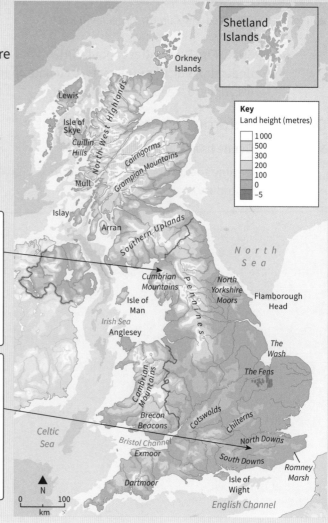

Key
Land height (metres)
- 1 000
- 500
- 300
- 200
- 100
- 0
- −5

The Lake District – an upland landscape:
- Cumbrian upland contains England's highest mountain – Scafell Pike.
- Glaciers created deep U-shaped valleys and hollows now containing lakes, rivers, and fertile land.
- Screes of angular rock fragments created by **freeze-thaw weathering** (water in cracks freezing, expanding, thawing, and contracting).
- Slope processes including rockfalls and landslides.

The Weald – a lowland landscape:
- Gently rolling hills in Sussex and Kent.
- Once a dome of tectonically-folded rock forming an arch (called an anticline).
- **Erosion** (the wearing away of material) has left alternate strata of more resistant chalk, and less resistant clay.
- Chalk is calcium carbonate dissolved by **chemical weathering**.
- During and after the last **Ice Age**, water in the chalk froze, making it **impermeable** and eroded by rivers – but now permeable again leaving dry valleys.

The role of geology

Geology is very important to understanding the UK's physical landscape. The uplands mainly consist of older igneous and metamorphic rocks. The lowlands mainly consist of younger sedimentary rocks.

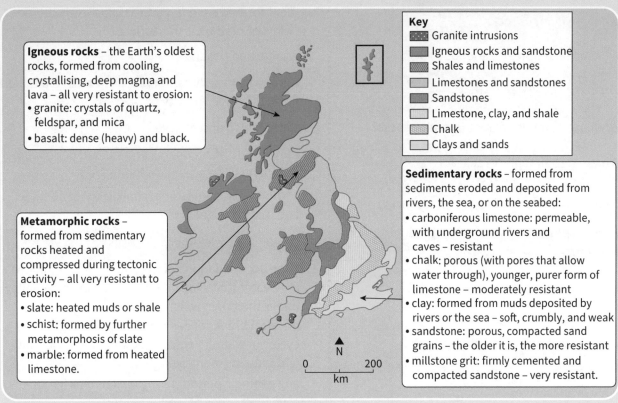

Igneous rocks – the Earth's oldest rocks, formed from cooling, crystallising, deep magma and lava – all very resistant to erosion:
- granite: crystals of quartz, feldspar, and mica
- basalt: dense (heavy) and black.

Metamorphic rocks – formed from sedimentary rocks heated and compressed during tectonic activity – all very resistant to erosion:
- slate: heated muds or shale
- schist: formed by further metamorphosis of slate
- marble: formed from heated limestone.

Key
- Granite intrusions
- Igneous rocks and sandstone
- Shales and limestones
- Limestones and sandstones
- Sandstones
- Limestone, clay, and shale
- Chalk
- Clays and sands

Sedimentary rocks – formed from sediments eroded and deposited from rivers, the sea, or on the seabed:
- carboniferous limestone: permeable, with underground rivers and caves – resistant
- chalk: porous (with pores that allow water through), younger, purer form of limestone – moderately resistant
- clay: formed from muds deposited by rivers or the sea – soft, crumbly, and weak
- sandstone: porous, compacted sand grains – the older it is, the more resistant
- millstone grit: firmly cemented and compacted sandstone – very resistant.

N
0   200
km

▲ **Figure 2** *Characteristics of ten key rocks of the British Isles*

The role of climate

The UK has a mild, maritime climate with:

- lowest temperatures and the highest precipitation in the uplands (over 2 400 mm a year in north-west Scotland)
- lowest precipitation in the east of England (less than 600 mm a year).

Climate has a two-way relationship with the UK's landscape – it is affected by it (e.g. relief rainfall) and also helps create it through weathering processes.

LINK

To understand weathering processes, refer to page 45.

The role of human activity

Human activity has transformed the UK landscape from largely forested at the end of the last Ice Age to agricultural and urbanised today:

- uplands – sparsely populated, but evidence of human activity, for example commercial forestry, sheep farming, hydroelectric power (HEP) and water supply reservoirs, and wind farms
- lowlands – often densely populated, with commercial farming, built-up towns and cities, and extensive service and transport infrastructure.

 Key terms | **Make sure you can write a definition for these key terms**

chemical weathering   erosion
freeze-thaw weathering   Ice Age
igneous rock   impermeable
metamorphic rock   sedimentary rock

WATCH OUT

Make sure you know the difference between climate and weather. Climate refers to average long-term weather conditions. Weather refers to day-to-day atmospheric conditions.

Retrieval

Learn the answers to the questions below, then cover the answers column with a piece of paper and write down as many answers as you can. Check and repeat.

	Questions	Answers
1	What are igneous rocks?	rocks formed from magma and lava as it cooled below or on the Earth's surface
2	What are examples of igneous rocks?	granite and basalt
3	What are metamorphic rocks?	formed from sedimentary rocks heated and folded during tectonic activity
4	What are examples of metamorphic rocks?	slate, schist, and marble
5	What are sedimentary rocks?	rocks made of sediments eroded and deposited from rivers, the sea, or on the seabed
6	What are examples of sedimentary rocks?	carboniferous limestone, chalk, clay, sandstone, and millstone grit
7	Which types of rocks are very resistant to erosion?	igneous and metamorphic rocks
8	What are glaciers?	large accumulations of ice, snow, rock, sediment, and water that slide down pre-existing river valleys under their own weight and gravity
9	What is freeze-thaw weathering?	physical breakdown of rocks following repeated cycles of water in cracks freezing (and expanding) and thawing (contracting)
10	What is an Ice Age?	any geologic period during which thick ice sheets cover vast areas of land
11	When did the last Ice Age end?	11 700 years ago
12	What is meant by impermeable?	not allowing water through
13	What is a dry valley?	a valley found on permeable rock, such as limestone or chalk – crucially not sustaining permanent river flow

Put paper here

Previous questions — Answers

	Previous questions	Answers
1	How do ice cores provide evidence of past climate change?	trapped air bubbles are analysed for CO_2: higher volumes suggest warmer past temperatures
2	What is the enhanced greenhouse effect?	human activity adds more greenhouse gases to the atmosphere, causing the planet to warm
3	What is an earthquake?	a sudden, violent period of ground shaking caused by the release of pressure between two tectonic plates

Put paper here

7 What makes a landscape distinctive?

Exam-style questions

1 **(a)** **(i)** Define the term 'landscape'. [1]

(ii) Outline the main elements of a landscape. [3]

(b) UK landscapes are made up of different rock types.

(i) Identify one example of a sedimentary rock:

A granite

B slate

C sandstone

D schist

Write the correct letter in the box. ☐ [1]

(ii) Describe **one** characteristic of sedimentary rocks. [1]

(c) Explain **one** way in which rock type influences the relief of the UK. [2]

(d) Compare the role of geology and past processes resulting in named, located, contrasting upland and lowland landscapes in the UK. [8]

> **EXAM TIP**
>
> 8-mark questions are 'level marked'. The examiner judges your answer by level:
> - Level 1 – no detail or examples, with few geographical terms or vocabulary
> - Level 2 – some detail, such as named examples, with some geographical terms or vocabulary
> - Level 3 – detailed, using named examples with relevant geographical terms and vocabulary.

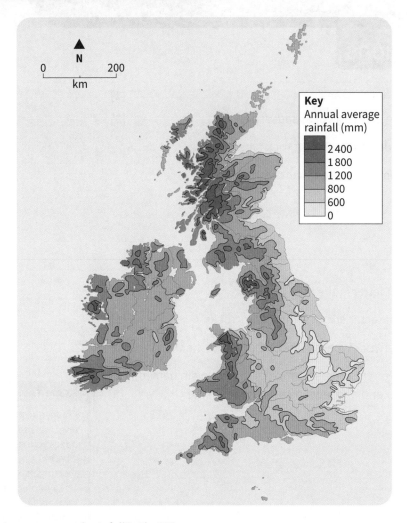

▲ **Fig. 1** – *Average annual rainfall in the UK*

2   **(a)**   Study **Fig. 1,** annual average rainfall in the UK.
Describe the distribution of rainfall shown.   **[3]**

   (b)   Explain **one** way in which human activity has influenced
UK lowland landscapes.   **[2]**

   (c)   Describe the human activities most likely to impact
physical landscapes in the UK.   **[3]**

   (d)   Outline the difference between climate and weather.   **[2]**

Questions referring to previous content

3   **(a)**   Outline the evidence used to determine past climate change.   **[3]**

   (b)   Explain how landscape processes are affected by climate change.   **[4]**

> **EXAM TIP**
>
> Short answer, low mark
> questions (1–4 marks) are
> 'point marked'. You will
> receive a mark for every
> valid point you make,
> including supporting
> examples.

8 What influences the landscapes of the UK?

Physical processes

Landscapes constantly change – sometimes suddenly, like a cliff collapsing, but more usually over thousands of years due to **geomorphic processes**: weathering, mass movement, erosion, transportation, and deposition.

Weathering

Physical (freeze-thaw) weathering: physical breakdown of rocks following repeated cycles of water in cracks freezing (and expanding) and thawing (contracting) – leaving scree on mountainsides

Weathering processes

Biological weathering: caused by plant and tree roots growing in cracks containing water and nutrients, forcing the cracks apart and eventually breaking the rock into pieces

Chemical weathering: any chemical change or decay of solid rock. For example, rain mixes with atmospheric gases (such as CO_2) to form weak acids (such as carbonic acid) which dissolves alkaline rocks such as limestone

Mass movement: sliding and slumping

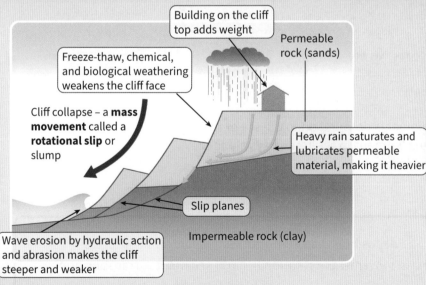

Building on the cliff top adds weight

Freeze-thaw, chemical, and biological weathering weakens the cliff face

Cliff collapse – a **mass movement** called a **rotational slip** or slump

Permeable rock (sands)

Heavy rain saturates and lubricates permeable material, making it heavier

Slip planes

Impermeable rock (clay)

Wave erosion by hydraulic action and abrasion makes the cliff steeper and weaker

▲ *Figure 1 Mass movement on a soft rock coastline*

▲ *Figure 2 Rapidly eroding 'boulder clay' cliffs along the Holderness Coast, East Yorkshire – an example of a soft rock coastline*

⚙ Knowledge

8 What influences the landscapes of the UK?

Erosion

Erosion processes involve the wearing away of the land and removal of the rock debris. There are four main processes involved.

Attrition: abrasion and hydraulic action loosen the sediment (rocks). As the eroded sediment rubs and rolls together, it is worn smaller and smoother

Erosion processes

Hydraulic action: air is forced into cracks by powerfully moving water – forcing the rocks apart

Abrasion: sediment thrown against coastal cliffs or river banks acts like sandpaper, wearing them down

Solution: weak acids in water dissolve alkaline rocks (e.g. chalk or limestone)

REVISION TIP

Make sure that you understand the difference between weathering processes and erosion processes. Despite both breaking down rocks, they are not the same.

Transportation and deposition

Transportation involves the movement of eroded **sediment** from one place to another (see **Figure 3**). There are four processes involved.

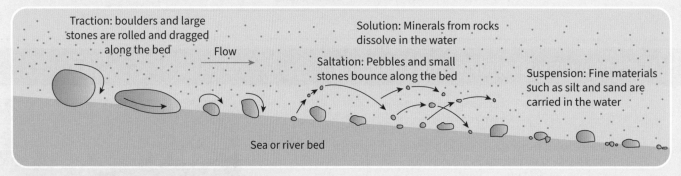

Traction: boulders and large stones are rolled and dragged along the bed

Flow

Solution: Minerals from rocks dissolve in the water

Saltation: Pebbles and small stones bounce along the bed

Suspension: Fine materials such as silt and sand are carried in the water

Sea or river bed

▲ **Figure 3** *Processes of sediment transportation*

Deposition occurs when transported sediment is dropped on to the sea or river bed due to a reduction in energy. This often happens in sheltered bays along the coast, or on the inside bends of river meanders.

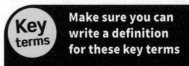

Key terms Make sure you can write a definition for these key terms

deposition   erosion process   geomorphic process
mass movement   rotational slip   sediment   transportation

Learn the answers to the questions below, then cover the answers column with a piece of paper and write down as many answers as you can. Check and repeat.

Questions | Answers

	Questions		Answers
1	What are geomorphic processes?		the physical processes responsible for shaping landscapes
2	What are the five geomorphic processes?		weathering, mass movement, erosion, transportation, and deposition
3	What is a rotational slip?		a mass movement in the form of a curved slump or landslip
4	What is weathering?	Put paper here	the physical, chemical, or biological breakdown of solid rock by the action of weather (e.g. frost or rain) or plants
5	What is meant by mass movements?		the movement of weathered rock or soil down slopes under the force of gravity
6	What are examples of mass movements?		rockfalls, landslides, and cliff collapses
7	What is erosion?	Put paper here	the wearing away and removal of material by a moving force such as a river or breaking wave
8	What are the four processes of erosion?		abrasion, attrition, hydraulic action, and solution
9	What is transportation?		the movement of eroded sediment from one place to another
10	What are the four processes of transportation?	Put paper here	traction (rolling and dragging), saltation (bouncing), carried in suspension, and dissolved in solution
11	What is sediment?		any material eroded from coastal cliffs or river banks
12	What are examples of sediments?	Put paper here	tiny clay particles to larger silt and sand, up to pebbles, cobbles, and boulders
13	What is deposition?		when sediment being transported is dropped due to a reduction in energy

Previous questions | Answers

	Previous questions		Answers
1	Which types of rocks are very resistant to erosion?		igneous and metamorphic rocks
2	What are sedimentary rocks?	Put paper here	rocks made of sediments eroded and deposited from rivers, the sea, or on the seabed
3	What are Milankovitch cycles?		gradual orbital changes that affect the Earth's distance from the Sun

Practice

1. **(a)** Select the correct term for 'the wearing away of the land and removal of the rock debris'.

   A erosion

   B geomorphic processes

   C weathering

   D transportation

   Write the correct letter in the box. ☐ **[1]**

   (b) Explain **two** weathering processes. **[4]**

   (c) Explain the processes involved in erosion. **[6]**

   (d) Explain the mass movement known as a rotational slip or slump. **[4]**

   (e) Describe the processes involved in sediment transportation. **[4]**

> **EXAM TIP**
>
> You can use a sketch to describe the processes if it helps, but remember, the marks will come from your labels and annotations – **not** the quality of the drawing.

Questions referring to previous content

▲ *Fig. 1 – the Watlowes, Malham, Yorkshire Dales National Park*

2. Study **Fig. 1**, which shows the Watlowes, Malham, Yorkshire Dales National Park.

   (a) Select the phrase that would best describe the geology of this area.

   A impermeable metamorphic schist

   B permeable sedimentary limestone

   C impermeable sedimentary clay

   D impermeable igneous granite

   Write the correct letter in the box. ☐ **[1]**

   (b) Identify the feature labelled **A**. **[1]**

   (c) Identify the feature labelled **B**. **[1]**

   (d) State the physical process responsible for **B**. **[1]**

   (e) Identify **one** piece of evidence from the photograph demonstrating human activity in this area. **[1]**

   (f) Suggest **two** likely human activities in this area. **[2]**

> **EXAM TIP**
>
> **Suggest** requires you to explain something when you can't be sure.

Coastal landforms

Headlands and bays

Headlands and bays are features of **discordant coastlines** of different (hard and soft) rock types (**Figure 1**).

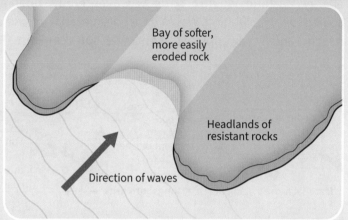

Bay of softer, more easily eroded rock

Headlands of resistant rocks

Direction of waves

▶ *Figure 1* *How headlands and bays form along coastlines*

Caves, arches, and stacks

Weaknesses in rock are vulnerable to erosion by the sea:

- joints are small, usually vertical cracks
- faults are larger cracks from past tectonic movement.

The more joints and faults there are, the weaker the structure is – leading to the formation of coastal landforms (see **Figure 2**).

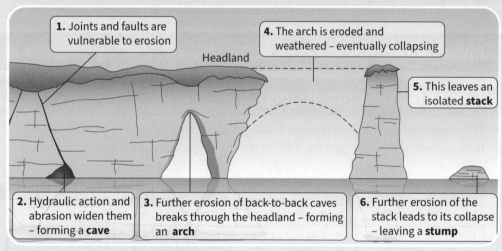

1. Joints and faults are vulnerable to erosion

Headland

4. The arch is eroded and weathered – eventually collapsing

5. This leaves an isolated **stack**

2. Hydraulic action and abrasion widen them – forming a **cave**

3. Further erosion of back-to-back caves breaks through the headland – forming an **arch**

6. Further erosion of the stack leads to its collapse – leaving a **stump**

▲ *Figure 2* *The formation of caves, arches, stacks, and stumps*

▲ *Figure 3* *Cave and arch at Flamborough Head, East Yorkshire*

For example, the hard chalk of Flamborough Head, East Yorkshire, has been eroded via cliff weaknesses (see **Figure 3**). Faults and joints have been exploited by hydraulic action and abrasion to create caves, some of which have broken through to form arches. The coastline here also includes examples of stacks and stumps.

9 Coastal and river landforms

Beaches and spits

A **beach** is a depositional landform. Sandy beaches are commonly formed in sheltered bays. Pebble beaches are usually found on higher-energy coastlines where destructive waves remove finer material, leaving coarser pebbles behind. Waves transport material up and down the beach – and if they approach at an angle, **spits** can form (**Figure 4**).

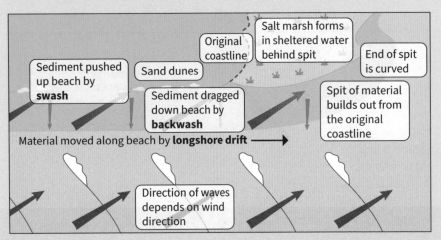

Sediment pushed up beach by **swash**

Sand dunes

Sediment dragged down beach by **backwash**

Original coastline

Salt marsh forms in sheltered water behind spit

End of spit is curved

Spit of material builds out from the original coastline

Material moved along beach by **longshore drift** ⟶

Direction of waves depends on wind direction

▲ *Figure 4 Spit formation*

River landforms

A river from source to mouth

The **long profile** of a river (**Figure 6**) shows its changes in gradient from source to the point where it enters the sea, a lake, or larger river. River landforms and characteristics change with distance downstream (**Figures 5** and **6**).

	Upper course	Middle course	Lower course
River long profile	Steep gradient	Moderate gradient	Gentle gradient
Physical processes	Erosion cuts down vertically due to the fast-flowing river	River erosion now more lateral (sideways)	Deposition, during flood conditions, is the dominant process
Valley **cross profile**	Steep sides – narrow bottom	Sides still steep – floodplain begins	Gentle sides – wide, flat **floodplain**
River landforms	V-shaped valley, interlocking spurs, **waterfalls**, gorges, rapids	Meanders, ox-bow lakes	Alluvium, levees, mudflats, deltas
River characteristics	Narrow, shallow channel, with low but fast-flowing **discharge**. Sediment is coarse and the channel bed is rough.	Wider, deeper channel with higher discharge. Size of sediment decreases, and the channel bed is less rough.	Wide, deep channel, with highest discharge. Sediment is small and the channel bed is much smoother.

▲ *Figure 5 Characteristics of a river's upper, middle, and lower courses*

A river from source to mouth

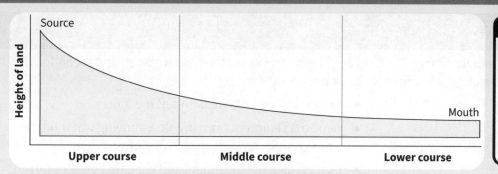

▲ *Figure 6* *Long profile of a river and its characteristics*

Upper course

In a river's upper course, valley sides are steep and the high energy river cuts vertically – winding round areas of more resistant rock to form interlocking spurs (**Figure 7**). Although the river erodes a steep, V-shaped valley, evidence of mass movements, such as rockfalls leaving screes, are usually found.

- Where a river meets a band of soft rock, the soft rock erodes more rapidly until it forms a waterfall (**Figure 8**).

- In time, the hard rock is undercut until it eventually collapses in the water beneath, where abrasion and hydraulic action will make the plunge pool larger.

- The repeating process of undercutting and collapse causes the waterfal to gradually retreat, leaving a steep-sided gorge.

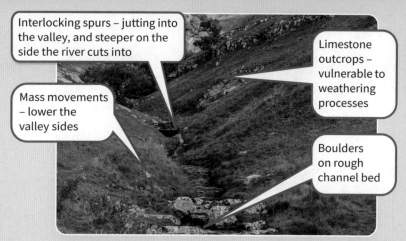

▲ *Figure 7* *Interlocking spurs*

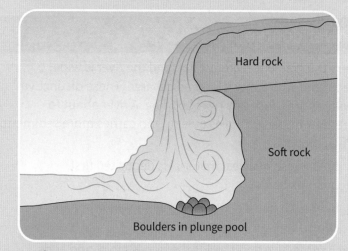

▲ *Figure 8* *A waterfall*

9 Coastal and river landforms

Middle course

Tributaries flowing into the middle course make the river wider and deeper. So, although the gradient of the middle course is gentler, the river is able to:

- carry more load – pebbles, sand, and mud, rather than boulders
- flow faster – over the smoother bed as there is less friction.

Lateral erosion causes the river to widen and meander. Over time, the flow:

- undercuts the outside banks of meanders
- deposits sediment from the slow-moving water on the inside bend – forming a **slip-off slope**
- exaggerates the meanders and widens the valley further
- narrows the neck between meander loops – breaking through to create **ox-bow lakes** (**Figure 9**).

How meanders exaggerate over time

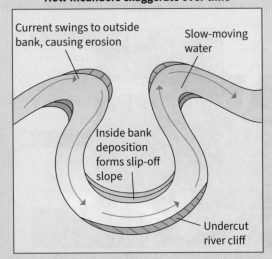

Ox-bow lake

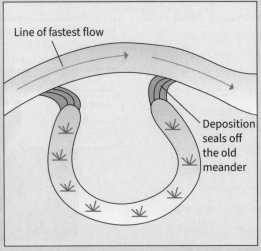

▲ *Figure 9* How the neck of a meander can be broken through to create an ox-bow lake

Lower course

Here the gradient is almost flat, and the river is wide, deep, and with a much larger discharge. These distinctive features are caused by river flooding. A river about to overflow its banks moves quickly and carries more sediment. When it floods:

- the largest, heaviest material is deposited first, building **levees**
- finer silt is carried further – only settling when the spreading waters slow to a halt.

Each successive flood builds the levees more, and adds another layer of **alluvium** to the wide, flat floodplain (**Figure 10**).

> **REVISION TIP**
>
> If your Physical Geography Fieldwork was a rivers geographical investigation, this would be a good time to revise it. Pages 178–179 will help.

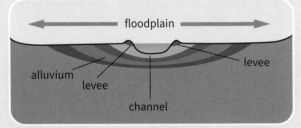

▲ *Figure 10* Features on a floodplain of a river's lower course

---

> **Key terms** Make sure you can write a definition for these key terms
>
> alluvium   cross profile   discharge
> discordant coastline   levee   long profile   longshore drift
> ox-bow lake   plunge pool   slip-off slope   spit

Learn the answers to the questions below, then cover the answers column with a piece of paper and write down as many answers as you can. Check and repeat.

Questions / Answers

	Questions	Answers
1	What is a discordant coastline?	a coastline alternating between bands of hard (resistant) and soft (less resistant) rocks, so the rock strata are at right angles to the coast
2	What is a coastal cave?	an extended crack at the base of a cliff creating a natural underground chamber
3	What is a beach?	a depositional landform made of sand or pebbles
4	What is longshore drift?	the zig-zag movement of sediment along the coast caused by waves going up a beach at an angle and returning (through gravity) at right angles
5	What is a spit?	a ridge of sand or shingle, formed by longshore drift, extending out along a coast
6	What is the long profile of a river?	the changing gradient of a river from its source to where it enters the sea, a lake, or larger river
7	What is a waterfall?	a drop where a river flowing over a band of hard rock meets and erodes a band of soft rock
8	What is discharge?	the volume of water flowing in a river, measured in cubic metres per second (cumecs)
9	What is an ox-bow lake?	a crescent-shaped lake formed when a river meander is cut off from the river and isolated
10	What are levees?	raised river embankments built by material deposited when the river floods
11	What is a floodplain?	flat land, along the sides of a river, formed by deposits of alluvium when the river floods

Put paper here

Previous questions / Answers

	Previous questions	Answers
1	What are geomorphic processes?	the physical processes responsible for shaping landscapes
2	What are the five geomorphic processes?	weathering, mass movement, erosion, transportation, and deposition
3	What is transportation?	the movement of eroded sediment from one place to another
4	What are the four processes of transportation?	traction (rolling and dragging), saltation (bouncing), carried in suspension, and dissolved in solution

Put paper here

Practice

Exam-style questions

1 (a) Explain **two** processes of coastal erosion. [4]

EXAM TIP

Explain requires you to give reasons why something happens.

   (b) Explain the process of longshore drift. [3]

   (c) Explain the formation of a spit. [4]

   (d) Explain the formation of the distinctive coastal landforms most likely to be found on a resistant rock headland. [6]

2 (a) Which is most characteristic of the upper course of a river?

       A   steep V-shaped valley

       B   wide flood plain

       C   smooth river bed

       D   high river discharge

       Write the correct letter in the box. ☐ [1]

▲ **Fig. 1** – The valley of the River Wharfe in its middle course

   (b) Study **Fig. 1,** the valley of the River Wharfe in northern England, in its middle course.

       (i)   Identify the feature labelled **A**. [1]

       (ii)   Identify the feature labelled **B**. [1]

       (iii) Identify the feature labelled **C**. [1]

       (iv)   Identify the physical processes responsible for **D**. [2]

       (v)   State **one** piece of evidence from the photograph demonstrating human activities in his area. [1]

EXAM TIP

State requires you to give a simple word or statement.

   (c) Explain **two** processes of river erosion. [4]

   (d) Describe how a river transports it sediment. [4]

   (e) (i)   Define the term levees. [1]

       (ii) Explain how levees are formed. [2]

   (f) Explain the processes that lead to the formation of an ox-bow lake. [3]

(g) Examine the role of different physical processes in the formation of a waterfall.

[6]

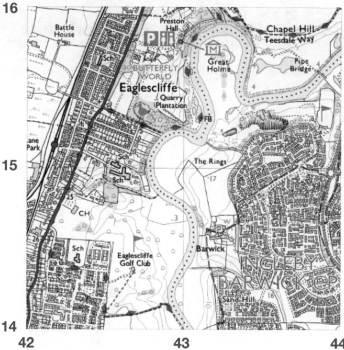

▲ *Fig. 2 – 1:25 000 OS map extract of the River Tees near Stockton-on-Tees*

3 **(a)** Study **Fig. 2,** a 1:25 000 OS map extract of the River Tees near Stockton-on-Tees.

    (i) State the 4-figure grid reference for Barwick. [1]

    (ii) Identify the land use in 42 14 for leisure purposes. [1]

    (iii) State the 6-figure reference for Battle House. [1]

    (iv) Identify the features at 432 159. [1]

    (v) Suggest how and why the feature in **(iv)** might change in the next 50 years. [2]

    (vi) Describe the relief of the area shown on the map extract. [4]

(b) Explain why the lower course of a river valley has a different cross profile from the upper course. [4]

(c) Examine the role of sub-aerial processes (weathering, mass movement, and erosion) in affecting the shape of river valleys. [8]

Questions referring to previous content

4 **(a)** Define the term geomorphic processes. [1]

(b) Outline the two-way relationship climate has with the UK's landscape. [2]

Knowledge

 Case study: A coastal landscape – Holderness, East Yorkshire

Figure 1 shows the Holderness coast, a stretch of coastline in eastern England. It includes:

- Flamborough Head in the north – a chalk headland with many typical landforms of coastal erosion

- Bridlington Bay to Spurn Head – a zone of erosion and sediment transportation with one of the most rapid rates of erosion in Europe

- Spurn Head – a classic spit formed at the estuary of the River Humber.

Geomorphic processes along the coastline

- Chalk stretches from the Lincolnshire Wolds in the south to Flamborough Head.

- During the last Ice Age, ice advanced over the area, depositing boulder clay (glacial till).

- Prevailing winds ensure powerful waves from the north-east.

- Longshore drift operates from north-west to south-east.

- Geomorphic processes, including freeze-thaw weathering and mass movements (particularly rotational slips), are very active on the boulder clay cliffs.

- Narrow beaches make the cliffs vulnerable and worsen coastal erosion – at rates between 1 m and 10 m per year.

Coastal management strategies

The Holderness coast is known mainly for agriculture, tourism, and the Easington Gas Terminal. The coast needs to be managed, but different **stakeholders** have different views how to do this. Coastal residents may want 'hard' engineering while environmentalists may prefer 'soft' engineering.

Managing the coast can be expensive, controversial, and requires evaluating the social, economic, and environmental costs of a project before deciding whether to go ahead (a **cost-benefit analysis**).

> **SPECIFICATION TIP**
>
> You need a named example of a coastal landscape. A case study you may have studied is given here.

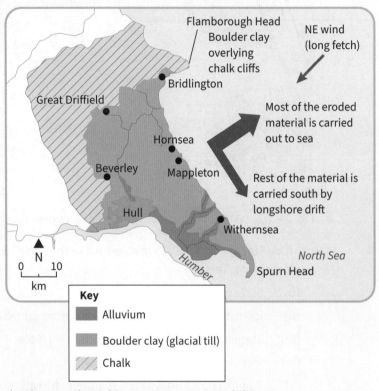

▲ **Figure 1** The Holderness coast, East Yorkshire

> **REVISION TIP**
>
> For any study of coastal management, make sure that you can discuss both the advantages and disadvantages of the strategies adopted.

There are three main approaches:

1 **Hard engineering** – building artificial structures using concrete and steel.

2 **Soft engineering** – smaller structures, using natural materials.

3 Integrated Coastal Zone Management (ICZM) – long-term, **sustainable**, **management** of a whole stretch of coastline as one area. ICZM involves the drawing up of Shoreline Management Plans (SMPs) to consider the following options:

- **hold the line** – using sea defences to stop erosion
- **strategic realignment** – letting the coast erode and moving/compensating people affected
- do nothing – let nature take its course.

> **WATCH OUT** !
>
> 'Strategic realignment' is also known as 'strategic retreat' or 'managed retreat'. All three terms mean the same thing!

	Method	Description	Disadvantages (Costs)	Advantages (Benefits)
Hard engineering	Sea walls (e.g. Hornsea and Withernsea)	Stone or concrete walls, at cliff foot or beach top – often with a curved face to reflect waves back to sea	• Very expensive to build • Do not look natural • Create strong, eroding backwash beneath	• Prevent erosion • Prevent flooding • Often have a promenade to walk along
	Revetments (e.g. Hornsea)	Sloping wooden, concrete or rock structures at cliff foot or beach top	• Do not look natural • Need high levels of maintenance	• Inexpensive to build • Break up wave energy
	Rip-rap (rock armour) (e.g. Hornsea (see **Figure 4**), Withernsea, Mappleton, and Easington Gas Terminal)	Large rocks placed at cliff foot or beach top	• Does not blend in with local geology • Dangerous to clamber over • Attract vermin	• Cheap • Easy to construct and maintain • A permeable barrier – breaking up waves and absorbing their energy
	Gabions (e.g. Hornsea)	A wall of wire cages filled with rocks, at cliff foot	• Does not look natural • Not very strong • Wire cages corrode over time	• Cheap, easy to build • A permeable barrier – absorbing wave energy
	Groynes (e.g. Hornsea (see **Figure 5**) and Withernsea)	Timber or rock structures (built at right angles to the coast) to trap sediment transported along the coast by longshore drift	• Unnatural – can be unattractive • Starve beaches further down the coast of sediment – 'terminal groyne syndrome' – leading to their greater erosion	• Inexpensive to build • Work with natural processes to build up the beach • Increase tourist potential

▲ **Figure 2** *Examples of hard engineering management strategies*

10 Coastal landscapes

	Method	Description	Disadvantages (Costs)	Advantages (Benefits)
Soft engineering	Beach nourishment	The addition of sand or pebbles (dredged from offshore) to an existing beach	• Needs constant maintenance because of natural processes of erosion and longshore drift	• Cheap and easy to maintain • Looks natural • Increases tourist potential
	Cliff regrading	Reducing the angle of a cliff to improve stability	• Causes the cliff to retreat	• Most effective on soft rock (e.g. clay)
	Cliff drainage	Drainage removes water to prevent slumping	• Drained cliffs can dry out leading to collapse (rockfalls)	• Drainage is cost-effective
	Dune stabilisation	Marram grass planted to stabilise dunes	• Time consuming to plant	• Cheap • Sustainable • Maintains wildlife habitats

▲ **Figure 3** *Examples of soft engineering management strategies*

▲ **Figure 4** *Significant erosion beyond the last line of rock armour at Hornsea illustrates its simple effectiveness*

▲ **Figure 5** *The last groyne protecting the beach at Hornsea: note the lower, sand-starved beach on the south (right-hand) side*

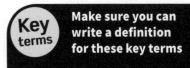

Make sure you can write a definition for these key terms

cost-benefit analysis   hard engineering   hold the line
soft engineering   stakeholder   strategic realignment
sustainable management

Learn the answers to the questions below, then cover the answers column with a piece of paper and write down as many answers as you can. Check and repeat.

Questions / Answers

	Questions	Answers
1	Who or what are stakeholders?	individuals, groups, or organisations affected by, or having an interest in, an issue
2	What is a cost-benefit analysis?	evaluating the social, economic, and environmental costs of a project before deciding whether to go ahead
3	What is hard engineering?	building physical structures to deal with natural hazards
4	What are examples of coastal hard-engineering approaches?	sea walls, revetments, rip-rap (rock armour), gabions, and groynes
5	What is soft engineering?	adapting to natural hazards and working with nature to limit damage
6	What are examples of coastal soft engineering approaches?	beach nourishment, cliff regrading, cliff drainage, and dune stabilisation
7	What is meant by Integrated Coastal Zone Management (ICZM)?	long-term, sustainable, planning for a whole stretch of coastline as one area
8	What is a Shoreline Management Plan (SMP)?	the specific plan adopted in ICZM – whether holding the line, strategic realignment, or letting nature take its course
9	What is meant by sustainable management?	meeting the needs of people now, and in the future, while limiting harm to the environment
10	What is meant by 'holding the line'?	a term used in SMPs to indicate where sea defences will be used to stop erosion
11	What is meant by 'strategic realignment'?	a term used in SMPs to indicate where the coast will be allowed to erode and people directly affected will be relocated or compensated

Put paper here

Previous questions / Answers

	Previous questions	Answers
1	What is longshore drift?	the zig-zag movement of sediment along the coast caused by waves going up a beach at an angle and returning (through gravity) at right angles
2	What is a spit?	a ridge of sand or shingle, formed by longshore drift, extending out along a coast
3	What is the long profile of a river?	the changing gradient of a river from its source to the point where it enters the sea, a lake, or larger river
4	What is alluvium?	all deposits laid down by rivers, especially in times of flood

Put paper here

Exam-style questions

1 **(a)** Study the table below, which shows the change in global mean sea level (mm) 1940–2020.

Year	Change in mean sea level compared to 1993–2008 average (mm)
1940	−110
1960	−70
1980	−40
2000	0
2020	+70

(i) Calculate the range in the changing global mean sea level 1940–2020. **[1]**

(ii) State the median value. **[1]**

(iii) Use the data in the table to complete the line graph showing changes in global mean sea levels. **[2]**

EXAM TIP

Calculate means you need to work out an answer.

LINK

To understand line graphs, refer to page 192.

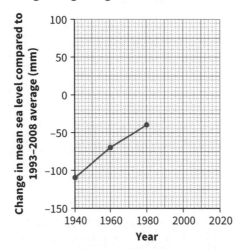

(iv) Describe the changes in global mean sea levels. **[2]**

(b) (i) Describe **two** soft engineering coastal management strategies. **[4]**

(ii) For **one** of the named soft engineering coastal management strategies, state **one** advantage and **one** disadvantage. **[2]**

(c) Explain **one** hard engineering strategy used to reduce coastal erosion **[2]**

(d) Explain why erosion is rapid on some coastlines, but very slow on others. **[8]**

(e) **CASE STUDY – A coastal landscape in the UK.**

Name of chosen coastal landscape in the UK: _____

Discuss the impact of management on your chosen coastal landscape. **[6]**

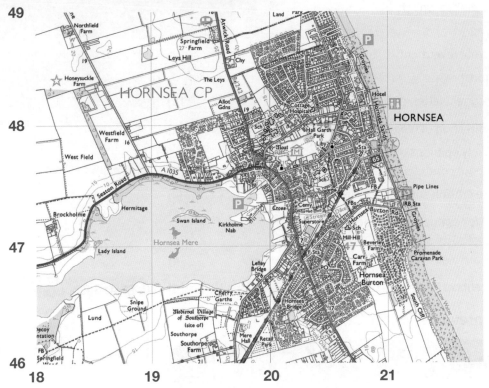

▲ *Fig. 1 – 1:25 000 OS map extract of Hornsea, East Yorkshire*

LINK

To understand Ordnance Survey maps, refer to page 189. Symbols for OS maps are given on page 199.

2 **(a)** Study **Fig. 1**, an OS map extract of Hornsea, East Yorkshire.

    (i) State the 4-figure grid reference for Hornsea Bridge and Hornsea Burton. **[1]**

    (ii) Name the public facility found at 209 478. **[1]**

    (iii) State the 6-figure reference for the Cottage Hospital. **[1]**

    (iv) Identify **three** tourist services in Hornsea and state the 4 or 6-figure reference for each. **[3]**

▲ *Fig. 2 – Coastal defences at Hornsea*

(b) Study **Fig. 2**, which shows coastal defences at Hornsea, East Yorkshire. The photograph was taken at 213 471.

    (i) Identify in what compass direction the camera was pointing. **[1]**

    (ii)   Select the coastal defence **not** shown in the photo.

        A   concrete sea wall

        B   groyne

        C   concrete revetment

        D   gabions

        Write the correct letter in the box. ☐   **[1]**

    (iii)   State the direction of longshore drift.   **[1]**

    (iv)   Suggest likely opinions of the stakeholders on the cliff top, about coastal protection.   **[2]**

    (v)   Explain the erosion south of the last defence.   [4]

(c)   Explain the need for evaluating the social, economic, and environmental costs of a project (cost-benefit analysis) before decisions are made regarding coastal management.   **[4]**

(d)   Evaluate the benefits of Integrated Coastal Zone Management.   **[4]** ◀

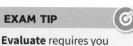

EXAM TIP

Evaluate requires you weigh up the good and bad points to make a judgement.

Questions referring to previous content

▲ **Fig. 3** – *The impact of coastal erosion at Flamborough Head, East Yorkshire*

3   **(a)**   Study **Fig. 3,** the impact of coastal erosion on cliff weaknesses at Flamborough Head, East Yorkshire.

    (i)   Select the type of rock that best describes the geology of this headland.

        A   porous sandstone

        B   hard chalk

        C   soft clay

        D   dense granite

        Write the correct letter in the box. ☐   **[1]**

    (ii)   State **two** processes of erosion acting on this headland.   **[2]**

    (iii)   Suggest **two** changes to these features over the next 1 000 years.   **[4]**

11 River landscapes

📖 Case study: A river basin - the River Wye

The River Wye is the fifth-longest in the UK, flowing from the Plynlimon Hills in central Wales to join the River Severn at Chepstow (**Figure 1**).

Geomorphic processes along the river

- Impermeable shales and gritstones are commonly found in the upper course.

- Alternating bands of hard and soft rock near Rhayader result in a series of 'white water' rapids (popular for kayaking).

- Weak mudstone and sandstone south of Hereford have been easily eroded into a wide, flat valley.

- Carboniferous limestone between Goodrich and Chepstow has been eroded into the steep-sided Wye Valley gorge.

- Average annual rainfall near the source exceeds 2 400 mm. This, the impermeable geology, and limited moorland vegetation, lead to high discharge and the potential for flooding downstream.

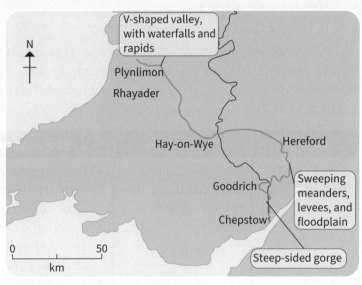

▲ **Figure 1** The River Wye basin

- Geomorphic processes, including freeze-thaw weathering and mass movements are active.

The impact of human activity and river management

The River Wye basin is known mainly for agriculture and tourism. The river passes through several large settlements, and the risk of flooding is taken seriously. Hereford, for example, has several management strategies in place to protect the city from flooding (**Figure 1**).

Physical and human factors affecting flood risk

Time of year
- River discharge is lower in summer with less rain and higher temperatures causing evaporation. More rainwater soaks into the ground – **infiltration**.
- Winter snow delays surface run-off – but rapid snowmelt can lead to flooding.

Ground conditions
- Recent rainfall may have already saturated the soil, so flooding is more likely.
- Heavy (storm) rainfall quickly saturates the soil.
- Permeable geology and soils (e.g. sandstone) encourage infiltration, but impermeable ground encourages rapid surface run-off.

Relief and river basin shape
- Steep slopes encourage run-off – flatter ground allows water to collect in lakes and ponds.
- Long, thin **river basins** have a low flood risk – but circular ones shorten channel distances, and so more water arrives at the same time.

Land use
- Woodland and agricultural crops intercept rainfall – reducing run-off and flood risk.
- Deforestation reduces **interception** – so more rainfall reaches the ground.
- Urban development adds impermeable concrete, tarmac surfaces, and efficient drains leading to rivers – increasing flood risk.

Knowledge

11 River landscapes

Managing flood risk

Remember, flood risk can vary depending on a range of physical and human factors.

Climate change will bring the following to the UK:

- more extreme weather events – including heavy rainstorms and high winds
- higher tides and storm surges
- more severe flooding.

In consequence, there is increasing debate about how to manage flood risks. Flood protection is carried out by the Environment Agency, who must choose between hard- and soft-engineering solutions following a cost-benefit analysis (**Figures 1** and **2**).

REVISION TIP

Remember – once rainwater infiltrates the soil, it is either **transpired** by plants (taken up through roots and then evaporated via pores in leaves), or reaches the river via **throughflow** and **groundwater flow**. Make sure you understand these processes.

Method	Description	Disadvantages (Costs)	Advantages (Benefits)
Flood walls (e.g. Hereford)	High walls built alongside rivers to increase their capacity	• Costs depend on the building materials used (e.g. attractive local stone can be expensive) • Concrete is often seen as unsightly and prone to vandalism • Increase flood risk downstream	• A 'one-off' solution – once built, they're permanent • Useful in city centres where space is limited • Disperse water quickly
Levees	Normally built some distance from the river (including increasing height of existing levees) to increase river capacity	• Expensive because of land required • Can eventually fail following erosion, slumping, or by the river overflowing • Increase flood risk downstream	• Reduced risk of flooding allows people to live and/or farm beside rivers • Look natural
Dredging	Deepening and widening rivers to increase capacity. Concrete lining speeds river flow further	• Must be re-done annually • Concrete lining is expensive and harmful to river ecosystems • Speeding up flow increases flood risk downstream	• Cheap • Concrete lining is cheap to maintain
Flood relief channels (diversion spillways)	Creating extra channels to divert excess water from high-risk areas (e.g. city centres)	• Expensive because of land required • Could cause flooding elsewhere – the water must go somewhere	• Protects high-risk, high-value, built-up areas • New aquatic habitats created

▲ **Figure 1** Hard strategies used in flood protection

Key terms

Make sure you can write a definition for these key terms

dredging   evapotranspiration   groundwater flow   infiltration   interception   river basin   throughflow   transpiration

Method	Description	Disadvantages (Costs)	Advantages (Benefits)
Demountable flood barriers (**Figure 3**)	Steel or aluminium barriers erected when a flood is forecast, then taken down afterwards	• Very expensive • 'One-off' costs depend on the materials used	• Unsightly look is temporary
Floodplain retention	Floodplain lowered, cleared of most development, and restored with grassland and shrubs	• Clearance of existing development has costs, as does removal of levees	• Affordable, sustainable solution • Increased capacity to store floodwater • Looks natural • May create new wetland habitats
Floodplain zoning (e.g. Hereford)	Restricting different land uses to certain locations on the floodplain (e.g. pasture nearest the channel – playing fields further away)	• No costs beyond planning/political administration • Restricts economic development	• Low-cost, sustainable solution • Natural floodplains act as an effective, natural soakaway • Conserves natural habitats
Afforestation (e.g. Wye basin)	Planting trees to increase interception and reduce throughflow and surface run-off	• Variable depending on the cost of land required • Loss of potential farmland	• Relatively inexpensive, sustainable solution • **Evapotranspiration** gets rid of water that would otherwise end up in the river channel • Creates habitats for wildlife
River channel restoration	Returning rivers to their natural state by removing past hard engineering protection, restoring meanders, and planting trees	• Expensive clearance of existing flood walls, embankments, and development • Slows river flow, so floods will occur	• Sustainable solution • Looks natural • Wetland ecology supports range of wildlife habitats • Reduces flooding downstream

▲ *Figure 2* Soft engineering strategies used in flood protection

◀ *Figure 3* Erecting demountable flood barriers along the River Severn at Bewdley, Worcestershire

Retrieval

Learn the answers to the questions below, then cover the answers column with a piece of paper and write down as many answers as you can. Check and repeat.

Questions | Answers

#	Question	Answer
1	What are rapids?	turbulent river flow where thinner layers of soft and hard rock have eroded unevenly
2	What is a river basin?	the area of land from which one river and its tributaries collects its water
3	What is interception?	vegetation leaves and branches capture rainfall – some evaporates, the rest drips onto the soil
4	What is groundwater flow?	water seeping slowly through saturated rocks underground towards the river
5	What is throughflow?	water seeping through pores or air spaces in the soil towards the river
6	What is transpiration?	the evaporation of water out of pores in plant leaves
7	What is dredging?	the digging out of rivers and drainage ditches to make them deeper
8	What is the consequence of not dredging?	silt accumulates on the bed – reducing water carrying capacity, and so increasing flood risk
9	What is evapotranspiration?	the loss of moisture from vegetation through evaporation and transpiration

Put paper here

Previous questions | Answers

#	Question	Answer
1	Who or what are stakeholders?	individuals, groups, or organisations affected by, or having an interest in, an issue
2	What is a cost-benefit analysis?	evaluating the social, economic, and environmental costs of a project before deciding whether to go ahead
3	What is hard engineering?	building physical structures to deal with natural hazards
4	What is soft engineering?	adapting to natural hazards and working with nature to limit damage

Put paper here

Exam-style questions

1 **(a)** State **two** physical factors affecting the risk of river flooding. [2]

   (b) Suggest **two** reasons why flood risks in the UK are rising. [4]

   (c) Explain the need for evaluating the social, economic, and environmental costs of a project (cost-benefit analysis) before decisions are made regarding river flood management. [4]

   (d) (i) Describe **two** soft engineering river flood management strategies. [4]

   (ii) For **one** of the named soft engineering river flood management strategies, state **one** advantage and **one** disadvantage. [2]

   (e) **CASE STUDY – the landscape of a UK river basin.**

   Name of chosen river basin in the UK: _____

   Explain the influence of geology in the formation of river landforms within your chosen river basin. [6]

> **EXAM TIP**
>
> **State** requires you to give a simple word or statement.

> **EXAM TIP**
>
> **Describe** requires you to give the main characteristics of something. (No explanation is needed.)

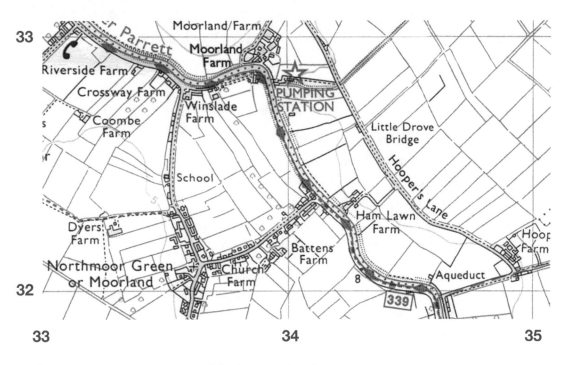

▲ *Fig. 1 – 1:25 000 OS map extract of the Somerset Levels*

Exam-style questions

▲ **Fig. 2** – Aerial photo of flooding in Moorland, Somerset, in 2014

LINK

To understand Ordnance Survey maps, refer to page 189. Symbols for OS maps are given on page 199.

2   **(a)**   Study **Figs. 1** and **2**. **Fig. 1** is a 1:25 000 map extract of the Somerset Levels. **Fig. 2** shows flooding in Moorland, Somerset (2014).

       (i)   State evidence from the map indicating that this area is very flat and low-lying.   **[2]**

       (ii)   Suggest reasons why this area has so many drainage ditches.   **[2]**

       (iii)   Explain the evidence for most of this area being farmland.   **[2]**

       (iv)   Identify the feature at 341 328.   **[1]**

       (v)   Identify in what compass direction the camera was pointing.   **[1]**

       (vi)   State the name of the farm marked A.   **[1]**

       (vii)   Describe what has been done to stop this property from flooding.   **[2]**

       (viii)   Describe the extent of flooding in the photograph.   **[2]**

       (ix)   Describe the likely social, economic, and environmental impacts of flooding on the residents of Moorland.   **[4]**

   (b)   State **two** human factors increasing the risk of river flooding.   **[2]**

   (c)   'Soft engineering approaches to river flood management are increasingly adopted as more affordable, sustainable solutions.' Justify this claim.   **[8]**

3   **(a)**   Suggest reasons why the lower courses of rivers represent increasing flood risks.   **[4]**

   (b)   Explain why soft engineering is increasingly preferred to hard engineering when managing river flood risk.   **[4]**

EXAM TIP

With questions involving both photos and maps, always take your time to orient the photo on the map. Looking for evidence in the foreground and background will help you do this. In this instance, the church is at the road junction in the centre of the village.

EXAM TIP

Justify means you must decide whether you agree with the statement. Give your answer and then give evidence to support your ideas, especially if you have any located case study evidence in support. Remember to acknowledge any disadvantages too.

▲ **Fig. 3** – Restoration of the River Skerne in Darlington, northern England

The River Skerne, Darlington

A good example of river restoration is the River Skerne in Darlington (see **Fig. 3**). Between 1850 and 1945, the river was straightened and the floodplain was narrowed to allow for the city's ironworks and heavy engineering industry. Further widening and deepening of the river channel was undertaken in the 1950s and 1970s. By 1995, de-industrialisation had left the river a polluted wasteland, with much of the floodplain raised by old industrial waste tipping.

(c) Study **Fig. 3** and the text extract.

Evaluate river restoration and other soft engineering strategies as suitable solutions for river flood management in the UK in the 21st century. **[8]**

Questions referring to previous content

4 **(a)** Define the term 'mass movement'. **[1]**

(b) State **two** examples of mass movements. **[2]**

> **EXAM TIP** ◎
>
> **Evaluate** requires you weigh up the good and bad points to make a judgement. For this question, make sure you refer to specific aspects of Figure 3 and the text extract in your answer.

12 Why are natural ecosystems important?

What are ecosystems?

An ecosystem is a complex natural system made up of plants (flora), animals (fauna), and the environment. Ecosystems occur on land and in the oceans (e.g. **coral reefs**), and at different scales from small (e.g. pond) to global (e.g. tropical rainforest).

Within an ecosystem there are complex relationships between the living (biotic) features (e.g. plants, animals, and fish) and the non-living (abiotic) environmental factors (e.g. climate, soil, and light).

Producers (e.g. plants) convert energy from the Sun by **photosynthesis** into carbohydrates (sugars) for growth

Animals take in oxygen from the atmosphere and return CO_2

Plants take in CO_2 from the atmosphere and return oxygen

Processes and interactions within ecosystems

Water is returned to the atmosphere via respiration, evaporation, and transpiration

Consumers get their energy from eating producers and other consumers, creating direct links within ecosystems in complex **food webs**

Water (from precipitation) moves through the soil, plants, and animals

Dead plant and animal material is broken down by **decomposers** (e.g. bacteria and fungi) to add to nutrients within the soil

Nutrients are used by plants in a process called **nutrient cycling**

Weathering of rock provides soil nutrients (e.g. phosphates and magnesium)

The nutrient cycle

Within every ecosystem there are stores and flows of nutrients, water, and energy. These stores and flows are explained by the nutrient cycle (**Figure 1**).

LINK

To understand nutrient cycling, refer to page 75.

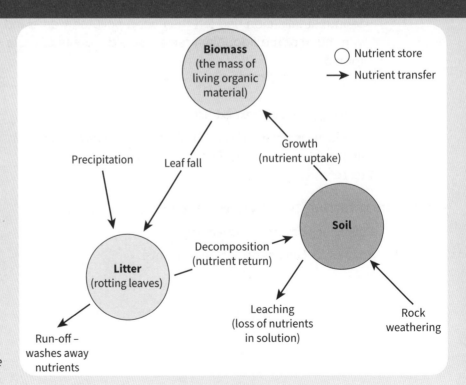

▶ *Figure 1 The nutrient cycle*

Biomes

Global-scale ecosystems are called **biomes**. Biomes are usually dominated by one type of vegetation. They form broad belts usually parallel to lines of latitude (**Figure 2**), because their climate and characteristics are determined by the Sun's energy and global atmospheric circulation.

Tundra – located between the Arctic Circle and about 60°–70° north. Cold, windy, and dry conditions support low-growing plants easily damaged by human activities such as oil exploitation and tourism.

Temperate deciduous and coniferous forests – located roughly 50°–60° north. Deciduous trees shed their leaves in winter. Coniferous evergreens do not shed their leaves and are better suited to the colder climates of the north.

Temperate grassland – located 30°–40° north and south of the equator, and always inland. Warm, dry, summers, and cold winters support grasses for grazing animals.

Mediterranean – around the Mediterranean Sea and also isolated locations south of the equator. Hot, sunny, dry summers, and mild winters support olive groves and citrus fruits.

Hot desert – covering 14% of the Earth's land surface. High daytime temperatures, low night-time temperatures, and very low rainfall limit the plants and animals that can adapt to living here.

Coral reefs – clear, shallow, warm water areas (mean annual temperature 18°C).

Polar regions – around the North and South poles. Low temperatures (below –50°C) and dry conditions mean there is little plant and animal life.

Tropical grassland (savannah) – located between 15°–30° north and south of the equator. Wet and dry seasons support large herds of grazing animals and their predators.

Tropical rainforest – covering 6% of the Earth's land surface mainly close to the equator. High temperatures and heavy rainfall create ideal conditions for vegetation. More than half of all plant and animal species come from here.

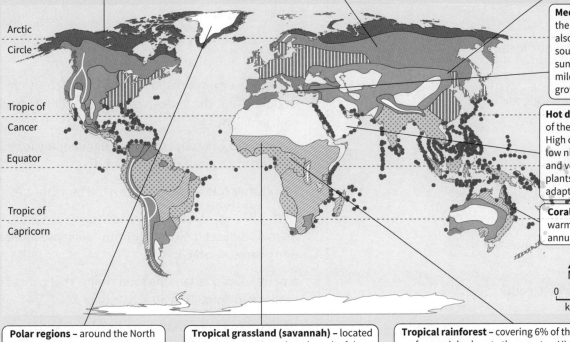

Arctic Circle · Tropic of Cancer · Equator · Tropic of Capricorn

N
0   100
km

Key
- ▧ Tundra
- ▨ Coniferous forest (taiga)
- ▤ Temperate deciduous forest
- ▥ Temperate grassland
- ▧ Mediterranean
- ☐ Desert
- ⠿ Tropical rainforest
- ▨ Tropical grassland (savannah)
- ☐ Other biomes, (e.g. polar, ice, mountains)
- • Coral reefs

▲ *Figure 2 The distribution and characteristics of global biomes*

LINK

To understand how the Sun's energy and global atmospheric circulation affect climates and rainfall distributions, refer to page 2.

REVISION TIP

Remember:
- temperature affects the length of the growing season
- precipitation provides water
- sunshine hours and intensity affect photosynthesis and so plant growth.

Key terms
Make sure you can write a definition for these key terms

biomass   biome   consumer   coral reef
decomposer   ecosystem   fauna   flora   food web
nutrient cycling   photosynthesis   producer

Retrieval

Learn the answers to the questions below, then cover the answers column with a piece of paper and write down as many answers as you can. Check and repeat.

Questions — Answers

#	Questions	Answers
1	What is an ecosystem?	a community of plants and animals and the physical environment in which they live
2	What is a biome?	a global-scale ecosystem
3	What are coral reefs?	large amounts of coral, which grow in clear, shallow warm water areas
4	What are biotic features?	living components of an ecosystem or biome (e.g. plants, animals, and fish)
5	What are abiotic features?	non-living environmental factors in an ecosystem or biome (e.g. the atmosphere, water, climate, rock, soil, and light)
6	What is photosynthesis?	the process whereby plants use light energy from the Sun to produce their own food
7	What are producers?	plants that convert energy from the Sun into sugars for growth
8	What are consumers?	animals that get their energy from eating producers and other consumers
9	What is a food web?	a network of overlapping food chains that connects plants and animals in an ecosystem
10	What are decomposers?	bacteria and fungi that cause the decay and breakdown of dead plants, animals, and excrement
11	What do decomposers add to the soil?	nutrients
12	What is nutrient cycling?	nutrients moving between biomass, litter, and soil as part of a continuous cycle which keeps both plants and soils healthy

Put paper here

Previous questions — Answers

#	Previous questions	Answers
1	What is transpiration?	the evaporation of water out of pores in plant leaves
2	What is evapotranspiration?	the loss of moisture from vegetation through evaporation and transpiration
3	What is sediment?	any material eroded from coastal cliffs or river banks
4	What are some examples of sediments?	silt, sand, pebbles, cobbles, and boulders

Put paper here

12 Why are natural ecosystems important?

Practice

Exam-style questions

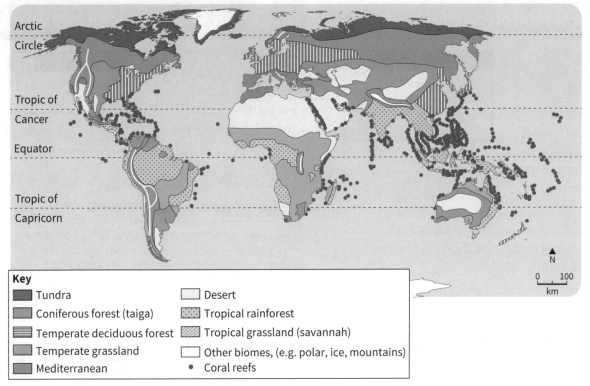

Key

▓ Tundra	☐ Desert
▒ Coniferous forest (taiga)	⠿ Tropical rainforest
≡ Temperate deciduous forest	▨ Tropical grassland (savannah)
▒ Temperate grassland	☐ Other biomes, (e.g. polar, ice, mountains)
▨ Mediterranean	• Coral reefs

▲ **Fig. 1** – *Global distribution of biomes*

1 (a) Study **Fig. 1**, the global distribution of biomes.

    (i) Identify which statement is true.

        A Temperate deciduous forest can be found along the Tropic of Capricorn.

        B Coral reefs are mainly found between the Tropics.

        C Taiga biomes are found in the northern hemisphere only.

        D Tropical rainforests are found north of the Tropic of Cancer.

        Write the correct letter in the box. ☐ [1]

    (ii) Describe the distribution of tropical rainforests. [2]

    (iii) Explain the relationship between latitude and biome distribution. [4]

  (b) Outline the main characteristics of coral reefs. [3]

  (c) Explain the term 'photosynthesis'. [2]

  (d) Explain **two** interactions between the abiotic and biotic features of biomes or ecosystems. [4]

  (e) Outline what is meant by nutrient cycling. [2]

Questions referring to previous content

2 (a) Outline what is meant by an ICZM approach to coastal management. [2]

  (b) Outline the **three** options most associated with Shoreline Management Plans (SMPs). [3]

> **EXAM TIP**
>
> A good tip with multiple choice questions is to examine each option in turn and eliminate each response that is clearly wrong. This narrows you down to the correct answer. Always check your decision before writing your answer!

> **EXAM TIP**
>
> **Outline** requires you to summarise the key points. So, briefly summarise what coral reefs are, their significance, and where they are found.

> **EXAM TIP**
>
> **Explain** requires you to give reasons why something happens – so think about how these features are linked.

13 Why do tropical rainforests matter?

The tropical rainforest climate

Tropical rainforests grow well in equatorial climates where:

> **LINK**
>
> To understand the distribution and key characteristics of tropical rainforests, refer to page 71.

- temperatures are high throughout the year (averaging 27°C) because the Sun is mostly overhead
- rainfall is high (usually over 2 000 mm a year) because of rising air and low pressure at the equator creating clouds and triggering heavy convectional rain
- there is a wet season of intense rainfall.

Tropical rainforest biodiversity

Tropical rainforests cover only 6% of the Earth's surface yet support more than 50% of all living organisms – a huge **biodiversity** of plants, micro-organisms, fungi, insects, birds, and animals, with complex food webs.

> **LINK**
>
> Food webs were introduced on page 70.

> **REVISION TIP**
>
> Despite huge biodiversity in tropical rainforests, there is a delicate balance between species. Any disruptive event will reduce the biodiversity. If disease kills a plant species, then the consumers that eat it will suffer too – and so on up the food chain.

How have plants adapted to living in the tropical rainforest?

The vertical layers of a tropical rainforest (its **stratification**) allow vegetation to adapt to competition for sunlight and shortages of available nutrients (see **Figure 1**).

Emergent trees (35–50 m) Hardy, exposed trees with straight branchless trunks receive the most sunlight.

Under canopy (10–20 m) Shaded, smaller trees wait to take advantage of the next available space in the sunlight. Interlocking branches and woody vines (lianas) form green corridors along which lightweight animals can travel.

Canopy (20–35 m) The most productive layer as each mushroom-shaped crown has an enormous surface of dark, waxy leaves that aid photosynthesis. **Drip tips** on leaves help them shed water quickly and efficiently.

Shrub and ground layer (0–10 m) Limited to ferns, woody plants, and younger trees because of lack of sunlight. Bacteria and fungi rapidly decompose the fallen leaves, dead plants, and animals. Thick **buttress roots** help to spread the weight of the towering trees above.

Soils Rapid nutrient cycling supports new growth. If the rainforest is cleared, soils suffer extreme **leaching** and rapidly lose their stored nutrients.

▲ **Figure 1** Stratified structure of a tropical rainforest

How have animals adapted to living in the tropical rainforest?

Camouflage: enables creatures to blend into the natural environment, concealing themselves from potential prey (e.g. green-eyed frogs looking like tree bark)

Mimicry: pretending to be something else (e.g. grasshoppers looking and behaving like stinging wasps)

Animal rainforest adaptations

Limiting diets: (e.g. toucans only consuming fruits that other birds and animals cannot access)

Habitat adaptation: (e.g. sloths, with long arms and claws, living in treetops)

Bright colours and poisons: to warn predators to avoid them (e.g. spiders and snakes)

Why aren't rainforest soils fertile?

Tropical rainforest soils are typically old, deep, iron-rich, and red in colour. Despite supporting lush vegetation, they are not fertile – they are prone to rapid leaching where minerals are lost in solution, and nutrient cycling is so rapid (see **Figure 2**).

Most nutrients are stored in the biomass – the lush vegetation. Few nutrients are stored as litter, due to rapid decomposition by fungi and bacteria. Similarly, few nutrients are stored in the soil, due to leaching and the rapid uptake by plants.

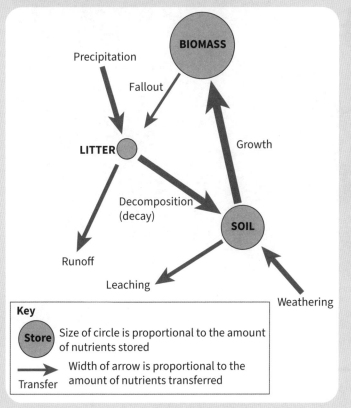

▲ *Figure 2 The nutrient cycle in a tropical rainforest*

The water cycle

Rainforest vegetation plays an important role in the water cycle:

- The tree canopy layers intercept the heavy rainfall.

- Most of this water is returned to the atmosphere through evaporation and transpiration.

- This evapotranspiration leads to further cloud formation and convectional rainfall.

- Deforestation results in less water being cycled – and can lead to droughts.

13 Why do tropical rainforests matter?

The value of tropical rainforests

Goods are the products we can directly take from the rainforest – such as food, wood and fibres, rubber, and medicines.

Services are the specific roles that the rainforest performs – such as providing habitats for flora and fauna, and income for indigenous people through agriculture and tourism.

Around 50 million **indigenous people** live sustainably in the world's tropical rainforests by **shifting cultivation** (see **Figure 3**)

Around 25% of the world's medicines come from rainforest plants and animals

The value of tropical rainforests

Tropical rainforests provide hardwoods (for furniture), nuts, fruits, rubber, and rich mineral resources

Tropical rainforests have extraordinary biodiversity, provide clean water, and – through acting as a **carbon sink** – help to cool the climate

Crops grown among stumps need regular weeding in the hot, humid conditions

Huts made of timber, branches, and leaves

Surrounding trees give shelter from the driving rain

Ashes spread to add nutrients to the soil

Living roots hold soil together – and allow the trees to regrow

Trees cut to shoulder height (easier to chop)

Clearing abandoned after 5–6 years to allow the vegetation and soils to recover

▲ *Figure 3 Shifting cultivation (also called slash and burn farming)*

 **Key terms** | **Make sure you can write a definition for these key terms**

biodiversity   buttress roots   carbon sink
drip tip   indigenous people   leaching
shifting cultivation   stratification

Learn the answers to the questions below, then cover the answers column with a piece of paper and write down as many answers as you can. Check and repeat.

Questions / Answers

	Questions	Answers
1	What is biodiversity?	the number of different plant and animal species in an area
2	What is stratification?	the vertical layering of rainforest vegetation in competition for sunlight and nutrients
3	What are buttress roots?	the thick, shallow roots of rainforest trees which spread to support the weight of the tree above
4	What is leaching?	a process by which the nutrients in the soil are washed away, in solution, by heavy rains
5	What are drip tips?	a rainforest tree adaptation to drain water from the leaves
6	What are the ways in which animals adapt to survive in a tropical rainforest?	camouflage; mimicry; limiting diets; habitat adaptation; and bright colours and poisons
7	What is a drought?	a long period when there is much less precipitation than usual in an area
8	What is a carbon sink?	a natural store for carbon-containing compounds like CO_2 or methane
9	What is meant by indigenous people?	the original inhabitants of a region, some still living traditional lifestyles in tribes, and hunting and gathering their food
10	What is shifting cultivation (slash and burn farming)?	traditional, sustainable, clearance of small patches of forest to provide land and fertile ashes for a few years before moving on

Put paper here

Previous questions / Answers

	Previous questions	Answers
1	What are biotic features?	living components of an ecosystem or biome (e.g. plants, animals, and fish)
2	What is meant by nutrient cycling?	nutrients moving between biomass, litter, and soil as part of a continuous cycle which keeps both plants and soils healthy
3	What is evapotranspiration?	the loss of moisture from vegetation through evaporation and transpiration
4	What is interception?	vegetation leaves and branches capture rainfall – some evaporates, the rest drips onto the soil

Put paper here

Exam-style questions

▲ **Fig. 1** – *the stratified structure of a tropical rainforest*

1 **(a)** Study **Fig. 1**, the stratified structure of a tropical rainforest.

   (i) Identify layer A. [1]

   (ii) State **one** way in which trees in layer A are adapted to their environment. [1]

   (iii) Identify layer D. [1]

   (iv) Explain the vegetation in layer D. [2]

   (v) Suggest how leaves in layers A, B, and C, are adapted to the rainfall conditions. [2]

   (vi) Explain how the vegetation can support large numbers of animals. [2]

   (b) Describe the climate of tropical rainforests. [3]

> **EXAM TIP**
>
> **Describe** requires you to give the main characteristics of something. (No explanation is needed, but statistics in support will add value to your answer.)

   (c) Explain **two** ways in which **either** plants **or** animals are adapted to conditions in the tropical rainforest. [4]

   (d) Explain nutrient cycling in tropical rainforests. [4]

> **EXAM TIP**
>
> **Explain** requires you to give reasons why something happens. Given the number of marks (4), detail is essential. Use a diagram if it helps, and define specialist terms where it will help to make the explanation clearer.

2 **(a)** Identify which statement is false.

   A Plants and animals in the tropical rainforest biome are connected through complex food webs.

   B Food webs in the tropical rainforest biome represent a delicate balance between species.

   C Most animals in the tropical rainforest biome are not selective about what they eat.

   D If trees are cleared in the tropical rainforest biome, then primary consumers will suffer.

   Write the correct letter in the box. ☐ [1]

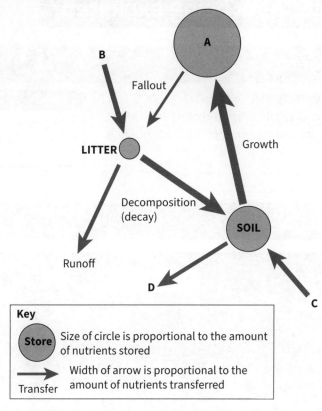

Key

Store Size of circle is proportional to the amount of nutrients stored

Transfer Width of arrow is proportional to the amount of nutrients transferred

▲ **Fig. 2** – *the nutrient cycle in a tropical rainforest*

(b) Study **Fig. 2**, the nutrient cycle in a tropical rainforest.

(i) State the collective name for the orange circles. **[1]**

(ii) State the collective name for the green arrows. **[1]**

(iii) Identify component **A**. **[1]**

(iv) Identify component **B**. **[1]**

(v) Identify component **C**. **[1]**

(vi) Identify component **D**. **[1]**

(c) Explain how animals adapt to conditions in the tropical rainforest. **[4]**

> **EXAM TIP**
>
> **Identify** requires you to name an example, sometimes from a map, photo, or graph.

Questions referring to previous content

3 (a) Define the term 'ecosystem'. **[2]**

(b) Outline the role of decomposers in an ecosystem. **[2]**

Knowledge

14 Why are tropical rainforests being exploited?

Human impacts in tropical rainforests

Human activities threaten all forest biomes – directly (e.g. deforestation) or indirectly (e.g. pollution or global warming). In 2019 the Tropics lost nearly 12 million ha of tree cover, one-third of which was primary rainforest – untouched and in its original condition!

LINK

To understand Geographical Information Systems (GIS), refer to page 191.

Using GIS to show deforestation

Figure 1 is a **Geographical Information System (GIS)** image. It shows:

- brown areas where the land has already been cleared for logging, commercial ranching, and subsistence farming
- dark green areas of tropical rainforest
- smoke plumes indicating fires burning in real time, their sources identified in red.

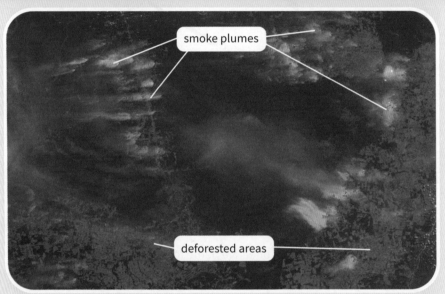
smoke plumes

deforested areas

▲ **Figure 1** GIS satellite image of the Amazon, September 2020

Direct threats to the tropical rainforest

Cause	Reasons for deforestation	Examples
Small-scale **subsistence agriculture**	• Indigenous people using traditional sustainable shifting cultivation • Shifting cultivation is done by less experienced locals who may have no other way of making a living • Slash and burn fires can accidentally grow out of control – destroying large areas of forest	This accounts for 5% of deforestation in the Amazon
Large-scale **commercial agriculture**	• Commercial crops such as palm oil and cocoa beans – much on **plantations** • Soybeans are grown for fodder for beef cattle ranching • Biofuels (e.g. sugar cane for ethanol, and palm oil for biodiesel)	• 80% of cleared land in the Amazon is for cattle ranching • Up to 10 million ha of Indonesian rainforest has been cleared for palm oil plantations

▲ **Figure 2** The causes of tropical rainforest deforestation

Direct threats to the tropical rainforest

Logging	• Destructive **clear-felling** of highly valued tropical hardwoods (e.g. mahogany and teak) • Selective logging of mature trees only is now encouraged	Malaysia is one of the world's largest exporters of tropical hardwoods
Infrastructure including mineral extraction and energy projects	• Economic development results in expanding cities, new settlements, roads, and energy projects • Mineral extraction, oil and gas drilling, and hydroelectric power (HEP) projects all need land and access – and HEP reservoirs require the drowning of valleys	Tucurui Dam in the Amazon, supplying power for iron ore and bauxite mining, has a reservoir covering 1750 km²

Indirect threats to tropical rainforest

Global warming increases climate and ecosystem stress, such as droughts in tropical rainforest areas. For example, severe droughts in the Amazon changed the rainforest from a carbon sink into a carbon emitter in 2005, 2010, and 2014. Fires broke out in the dry conditions, releasing vast amounts of CO_2.

• Drying leaf litter killed decomposer organisms and threatened the nutrient cycle.

• Canopy leaves died, reducing food supply and biodiversity.

In the long term, climate stress could turn tropical rainforests into tropical grasslands (savannah).

> **LINK**
>
> To understand the human causes and impacts of climate change, refer to page 32.

Sustainable tropical rainforest management

Rainforests need to be managed in a way that promotes **sustainability** to:

• ensure that they remain a lasting resource for future generations

• utilise valuable resources without causing long-term damage to the environment.

Selective logging: only mature fully-grown trees are cut down, while younger trees are left to grow

Agroforestry: crops are grown in carefully controlled cleared areas among living trees. Some trees may be harvested for building timber and fuelwood

Sustainable forest management strategies

Ecotourism: nature tourism, usually involving small groups with minimal impact on the environment, providing an incentive to safeguard rainforest trees and biodiversity

Reforestation: collecting seeds for nursery cultivation of saplings before replanting in deforested areas

There are three main benefits to this approach:

• economic – new sources of income from carefully controlled agroforestry and ecotourism

• social – providing or improving community facilities such as schools and health clinics

• environmental – protecting forest biodiversity and using renewable energy to limit pollution.

Knowledge

14 Why are tropical rainforests being exploited?

 ### Case study: Ecotourism in Costa Rica

Ecotourism in Costa Rica, Central America, introduces strictly controlled, limited numbers of people to the natural world (see **Figure 3**). Eco-lodges use solar power and drinking water from natural springs, and all the ecotourist activities are intended to have minimal impact on the environment. For example:

- walking and hiking
- river kayaking
- white-water rafting
- bird watching.

Ecotourism in Costa Rica is a vital part of its economy and is a type of sustainable development, providing:

- jobs and long-term income to local people
- (airport) taxation revenue for the government
- a positive incentive to retain and protect rainforest trees and biodiversity.

However, given that scenery, wildlife, remoteness, and local culture are the main attractions, ecotourism can only be low-impact if kept small scale – employing local people, using local produce, and with the profits staying in the local area.

SPECIFICATION TIP

You need a named example of an attempt to sustainably manage an area of tropical rainforest. A case study you may have studied is given here.

REVISION TIP

Just as the 5 'W's – What, Where, When, Why, and Who? – can help in structuring case study exam answers, they can also help you structure your learning too.

▲ *Figure 3 A rainforest eco-lodge in Costa Rica*

 Key terms | Make sure you can write a definition for these key terms

agroforestry   clear-felling   commercial agriculture
ecotourism   GIS   plantation
reforestation   selective logging
subsistence agriculture   sustainability

Learn the answers to the questions below, then cover the answers column with a piece of paper and write down as many answers as you can. Check and repeat.

Questions — Answers

#	Question	Answer
1	What is a geographical information system (GIS)?	a database of located geographical information based on maps, satellite images and aerial photographs layered with additional data
2	What is deforestation?	the deliberate clearance of forested land to exploit forest resources, or for conversion to another land use
3	What is clear-felling?	when all trees are chopped down, leading to complete destruction of forest habitats
4	What is selective logging?	when only mature fully-grown trees are cut down, and younger trees are left unharmed
5	What is subsistence agriculture?	when farmers grow crops and rear animals to feed their own families
6	What is commercial agriculture?	growing crops or raising livestock for profit
7	What is a plantation?	an estate specialising in a single cash crop
8	What is meant by sustainability?	actions that meet the needs of the present without reducing the ability of future generations to meet their needs
9	What is agroforestry?	where crops are grown in carefully controlled cleared areas amongst living trees, but allowing some to be harvested for building timber and fuelwood
10	What is reforestation?	collecting seeds for nursery cultivation of saplings before replanting in deforested areas
11	What is ecotourism?	nature tourism usually involving small groups of people with minimal impact on the environment

Put paper here

Previous questions — Answers

#	Question	Answer
1	What is meant by biodiversity?	the number of different plant and animal species in an area
2	What is meant by a carbon sink?	natural stores for carbon-containing compounds like CO_2 or methane
3	What is biomass?	collective scientific term for all organic material from living organisms, such as plants and animals

Put paper here

Practice

Exam-style questions

1   (a)   Explain the term 'ecotourism'.   [2]

(b)   Explain **one** advantage and **one** disadvantage of commercial exploitation of tropical rainforest resources.   [4]

(c)   Explain how tropical rainforests are being threatened by global warming.   [3]

(d)   Examine the causes of deforestation in tropical rainforests.   [8]

(e)   **CASE STUDY – sustainable rainforest management**

Name of chosen sustainable rainforest management strategy:

_____

Evaluate the success of **one** sustainable rainforest management strategy.   [6]

> **EXAM TIP** ⊙
>
> **Examine** requires you to investigate in detail. Given the high number of marks make sure you fully cover the causes and include located examples

> **EXAM TIP** ⊙
>
> **Evaluate** requires you weigh up the advantages and challenges of the strategy before making your judgement. Don't forget to include located examples from your case study.

Questions referring to previous content

Crops grown among stumps need regular weeding in the hot, humid conditions

Huts made of timber, branches, and leaves

Surrounding trees give shelter from the driving rain

Ashes spread to add nutrients to the soil

Living roots hold soil together – and allow the trees to regrow

Trees cut to shoulder height (easier to chop)

Clearing abandoned after 5–6 years to allow the vegetation and soils to recover

▲ *Fig. 1 – A traditional system of agriculture in tropical rainforests*

2   (a)   Study **Fig. 1**, a traditional system of agriculture still found in the tropical rainforests of South America and Africa.

(i)   State the name of this system of farming.   [1]

(ii)   Explain why this system of farming is sustainable.   [4]

(iii)   Suggest **two** reasons why this system of farming is under threat.   [2]

15 What will you find in polar environments?

Characteristics of polar climates

At opposite ends of the Earth, the Arctic and Antarctica have extreme, but not identical polar climates of:

- long cold, dry winters with several months of well below freezing temperatures, because the Sun barely rises above the horizon at such high latitudes

- short summers (in the Arctic) when temperatures can rise to 10°C

- desert-like conditions – the low temperatures mean little evaporation and cloud formation

- very strong winds.

The Arctic is mainly ocean, covered by **sea ice** in winter. It is surrounded by the tundra biome, characterised by **permafrost** and a short growing season.

> **LINK**
>
> To understand the distribution and key characteristics of high latitude tundra biomes, refer to page 71.

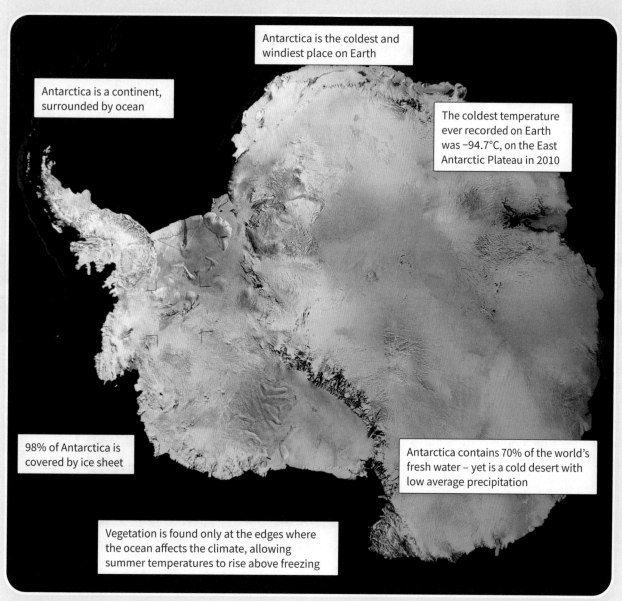

Antarctica is the coldest and windiest place on Earth

Antarctica is a continent, surrounded by ocean

The coldest temperature ever recorded on Earth was −94.7°C, on the East Antarctic Plateau in 2010

98% of Antarctica is covered by ice sheet

Antarctica contains 70% of the world's fresh water – yet is a cold desert with low average precipitation

Vegetation is found only at the edges where the ocean affects the climate, allowing summer temperatures to rise above freezing

▲ **Figure 1** Antarctica from space

⚙ Knowledge

15 What will you find in polar environments?

Polar flora and fauna

The Arctic and Antarctica support marine and land ecosystems. Both demonstrate the interdependence of all ecosystems – they are fragile and easily damaged by environmental changes such as global warming. Biodiversity is very low because plants and animals can only survive with special adaptations to the harsh climate, so food webs are simple.

	Flora	Fauna
Arctic	• Mosses and lichens on the edges of the ice. • Low-growing, flowering vegetation and shrubs in the tundra. • Plant adaptations include small waxy leaves to retain moisture and stunted growth to shelter from winds.	• Polar bears on the coast. • Marine ecosystems support seals, whales, and walruses. • The tundra is richer in wildlife – particularly insects and large animals with thick, insulating fur (e.g. Arctic fox, bison, and reindeer).
Antarctica	• Algae, lichens, moss, and grass – few other plants could survive the extreme cold, dryness, strong winds, and lack of soil.	• Cold ocean waters support a rich variety of fish, seals, whales, and marine birds (e.g. petrels and penguins). • Penguins nest on ice shelves.

▲ **Figure 1** Flora and fauna in the Arctic and Antarctica

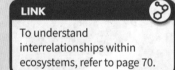

LINK

To understand interrelationships within ecosystems, refer to page 70.

Human activity in polar environments

Indigenous people

Inuits in North America and the Sami in northern Europe have inhabited parts of the Arctic for thousands of years (**Figure 2**). The traditional hunting, fishing, and animal herding lifestyles of these and other indigenous communities are sustainable.

▲ **Figure 2** A reindeer breeder in the Siberian tundra

Commercial exploitation

Polar resources are rich, but not necessarily sustainable (**Figure 2**).

Type of exploitation	Impact of exploitation
Mineral exploitation in the Arctic, particularly of oil and gas	Tanker accidents and oil spills from sometimes poorly maintained pipelines (**Figure 4**) cause huge damage to marine, mammal and bird life.
Overfishing and illegal fishing in the Arctic's waters	Fish stocks collapse – e.g. overfishing by Canada's provinces of Newfoundland and Labrador resulted in northern cod stocks collapsing in the 1990s.
Commercial whaling in the Arctic and Antarctica	Many whale species hunted almost to extinction. The need for conservation is now internationally agreed – modern whaling is mostly restricted to 'scientific research' only.
Cruise liner tourism in the Arctic and Antarctica	Threatens sensitive ecosystems with: • erosion and wildlife disturbance at landing sites • marine pollution from waste discharges. But this is not mass tourism – numbers are limited to only the most wealthy for cruise liners and **adventure tourism**. Regulation and controls on cruise liner visits are tight.
Scientific research in Antarctica	Thirty nations run scientific research stations in over 50 widely scattered interior and coastal locations. Their investigations include atmospheric, terrestrial, and oceanic systems – with particular emphasis on deep ice core drilling, through layers of hundreds of thousands of years of snowfall, to understand past climatic conditions.

▲ **Figure 3** *Commercial exploitation in the Arctic and Antarctica*

▲ **Figure 4** *Fragile river ecosystems polluted and destroyed by broken oil pipeline in Siberia, Russia*

LINK

The significance of Antarctic and Arctic ice core data is covered on page 31.

REVISION TIP

Set yourself a fixed word count (50 or 100) and write a topic summary. Writing to an exact word count forces you to identify the key information. And writing out the finished summary helps fix knowledge into your long-term memory!

Knowledge

📖 Case study: Sustainable management of polar environments

Small-scale sustainable management

The Arctic

Clyde River, Baffin Island, northern Canada:

- Canada's first Marine Wildlife Area
- sanctuary for the conservation of bowhead whales
- other species including polar bears, seals, geese, and ducks benefit from protection

Antarctica

Union Glacier, Ellsworth Range

- logistics hub for research, expeditions, and tourism operated by Antarctic Logistics and Expeditions (ALE)
- natural blue-ice runway for cargo planes
- summer (November–January) camp for walkers, cross-country skiers, bird watchers, and climbers
- strict **biosecurity** measures and waste disposal **protocols** followed

Global sustainable management

The Arctic Council:

- formed in 1996 by eight countries and six indigenous communities
- promotes environmental protection but has no legal powers
- the global environmental campaigning group Greenpeace is proposing an Arctic Sanctuary covering the central Arctic Ocean with similar protections to those agreed in the Antarctic Treaty (see below)

The Antarctic Treaty (including additional environmental protection protocols):

- 52 nations signed up to this highly successful international agreement
- guarantees free access and research rights to all countries
- prohibits military activity, such as nuclear bomb tests
- bans dumping of nuclear waste and all mineral resource activity including exploration of the continental shelf
- controls fishing in the Southern Ocean
- promotes comprehensive monitoring and assessment to minimise human impacts on Antarctica's fragile ecosystems

▶ **Figure 5** *Arctic adventure tourists in Norway's Svalbard – the world's most northerly inhabited territory*

 Key terms Make sure you can write a definition for these key terms

adventure tourism
biosecurity
overfishing   permafrost
protocol   sea ice

Learn the answers to the questions below, then cover the answers column with a piece of paper and write down as many answers as you can. Check and repeat.

Questions / Answers

	Questions	Answers
1	What is meant by Arctic sea ice?	floating pack-ice that extends in winter and retreats in summer
2	What is meant by Antarctic sea ice?	ice shelves extending from the continental ice sheets
3	What is tundra?	a major zone of treeless, level, or rolling ground found in cold regions, mostly north of the Arctic Circle
4	What is permafrost?	permanently frozen ground consisting of soil and rock
5	What is overfishing?	when more fish of a particular species are caught than can be replaced through natural reproduction
6	What is meant by conservation?	the careful maintenance and upkeep of a natural resource to prevent it from disappearing
7	What is adventure tourism?	tourism involving travel to remote or exotic locations in order to take part in physically challenging outdoor activities
8	What is meant by biosecurity?	measures aimed at preventing the introduction and/or spread of harmful organisms to animals and plants in order to minimise the risk of transmission of infectious disease
9	What is a protocol?	a system of rules that explain the correct conduct and procedures to be followed

Put paper here

Previous questions / Answers

	Previous questions	Answers
1	What is meant by deforestation?	the deliberate clearance of forested land to exploit forest resources, or for conversion to another land use
2	What is clear-felling?	all trees are chopped down – leading to complete destruction of forest habitats
3	What is selective logging?	only mature fully-grown trees are cut down, and younger trees left unharmed
4	What are biotic features?	the living components of an ecosystem (e.g. plants, animals, and fish)
5	What are abiotic features?	the non-living environmental factors affecting an ecosystem or biome (e.g. the atmosphere, water, climate, rock, soil, and light)

Put paper here

Practice

Exam-style questions

1 (a) Select the correct definition for sustainable management.

   A Managing an environment to ensure it will benefit both current and future generations

   B Managing an environment for the use of the current generation

   C Managing an environment at the expense of future generations

   D Managing an environment to provide essential resources

   Write the correct letter in the box. ☐   **[1]**

EXAM TIP

As an absolute last resort with multiple choice questions, you can always guess! Remember, narrowing down possible answers improves your chances of guessing correctly. Whatever you do, don't leave a blank answer.

(b) Describe similarities in the climate of polar regions.   **[3]**

(c) Suggest reasons why food webs in polar regions are fairly simple.   **[3]**

EXAM TIP

Suggest requires you to give an explanation for something when you can't be sure.

(d) Explain **two** ways in which **either** plants **or** animals are adapted to conditions in polar regions.   **[4]**

▲ *Fig. 1* – *Heated, insulated, overground water, sanitation, and electricity pipes in Svalbard*

(e) Study **Fig. 1**, which shows heated, insulated, overground water, sanitation, and electricity pipes in Svalbard, 78°N. Explain why these services are above ground.   **[2]**

(f) Describe the impacts of human activity on **either** the Arctic **or** Antarctic ecosystem.   **[6]**

(g) Evaluate the success of one global scale sustainable management solution in **either** the Arctic **or** the Antarctic.   **[8]**

EXAM TIP

Evaluate as a command word requires you weigh up the good and bad points to make a judgement. Make sure that you include specific, located facts from your case study. Only with these details can you access the highest level in the mark scheme.

(h) **CASE STUDY: A small-scale example of sustainable management in either the Arctic or Antarctic.**

Name of chosen small-scale example of sustainable management:

_____

Evaluate the success of one small-scale example of sustainable management in **either** the Arctic **or** Antarctic. [6]

Questions referring to previous content

2 (a) Define the term 'clear-felling'. [2]

(b) Explain why selective logging represents a more sustainable approach to forest management. [2]

What is urbanisation?

Urbanisation is the increase in the proportion of people living in built-up, urban areas (towns and cities). **Urban growth** is the physical expansion of built-up areas.

- Rates of urbanisation differ globally, and always have (**Figure 1**).

- Nowadays, urban populations are growing more quickly in less developed regions than in more developed regions.

- The greatest rates of urbanisation are found in African low-income developing countries (LIDCs) and Asian emerging and developing countries (EDCs).

- In European, North American, and Oceanian advanced countries (ACs), rates have slowed, with **counter-urbanisation** – people moving out of urban areas – happening.

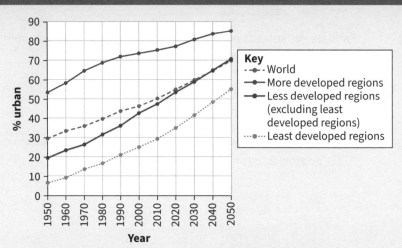

Key
- World
- More developed regions
- Less developed regions (excluding least developed regions)
- Least developed regions

▲ **Figure 1** Urban population, 1950–2050: the data for 2030, 2040, and 2050 are projections

WATCH OUT ❗

Urban growth is not the same as urbanisation, but usually comes with it. Make sure you understand the difference and use each term appropriately.

What are megacities?

The recent growth of **megacities** (with a population of over 10 million) is associated with urbanisation. In 1950, there were only two megacities – New York and Tokyo. Now there are over 30 – most in less developed regions – and by 2050 there may be 50! There are three main types of megacity (**Figure 2**).

Type	Features	Examples
Slow-growing	No squatter settlements	Often in ACs (e.g. Tokyo, Japan)
Growing	Under 20% of population in squatter settlements	Often in EDCs (e.g. Beijing, China)
Rapid-growing	Over 20% of population in squatter settlements	Often in EDCs or LIDCs (e.g. Manilla, Philippines)

▲ **Figure 2** Types of megacity

Natural population increase: better urban healthcare, so death rates fall and life expectancy increases

Coastal location: port cities enable trade

Why do some cities grow into megacities?

Migration: people migrate from rural areas, and other countries, in search of employment and a better life

Economic development: trade promotes business, resulting in more jobs and attracting more people

What are world cities?

World cities are the most important cities in the global economy – they may be:

- **economic hubs** of international trade – and often major ports
- the headquarters of **trans-national companies (TNCs)**
- centres for international banking and finance
- centres of world-class higher education, research, and innovation
- centres for global media, communications, and culture.

> **WATCH OUT**
>
> Some world cities are also megacities (e.g. New York and Tokyo). With a population of less than 9 million, London is not a megacity, but ranks (with New York) as one of the top two world cities.

Causes of rapid urbanisation in LIDCs

More than half the world's population live in urban areas, and this is expected to increase to around 70% by 2050. The main reasons for this are:

- Natural increase is higher in LIDCs (and some EDCs) – there are higher proportions of (fertile) young adults aged 18–35 and improvements in healthcare have significantly lowered death rates.

- **Rural–urban migration** – the movement of people from the countryside into towns and cities. This is caused by push and pull factors:

Push factors (drive people out of the countryside)	Pull factors (attract people to towns and cities)
• Farming is hard, prone to hazards and poorly paid • Poverty is widespread • Rural areas are isolated, often with limited services (electricity, water, schools, healthcare)	• Employment opportunities mean a higher standard of living is possible • Better services, including shops, entertainments, and transport infrastructure • Friends and family already living there

Informal housing in LIDCs

Informal housing is homes built by migrants close to cities on any available land that is often unsuitable for formal building. For example:

- close to industrial activity or railway tracks
- on steep and unstable slopes prone to landslides
- on marshy land.

These often-illegal slum squatter settlements or shanty towns are known differently depending on their location. For example, bustees in India, or favelas in Brazil (**Figure 3**). They are characterised by:

- a lack of basic services – clean water, sanitation (sewage system), reliable electricity or street lighting
- high population densities and vulnerability to hazards (e.g. fire), disease, and crime
- potential for improvement through self-help (e.g. site and service schemes).

▲ *Figure 3* Rocinha favela, Brazil

Knowledge

16 Why do people live in urban areas?

Informal economy in LIDCs

Rapid urban growth has resulted in the growth of an informal economy. Migrants often have limited education and skills, so are forced to find their own employment such as:

- waste picking – sorting rubbish for recycling
- car washing and shoe shining
- casual labour on building sites.

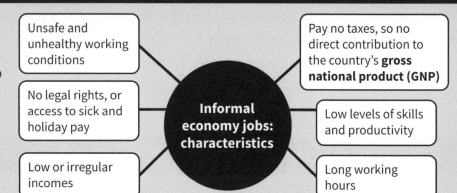

Unsafe and unhealthy working conditions

No legal rights, or access to sick and holiday pay

Low or irregular incomes

Informal economy jobs: characteristics

Pay no taxes, so no direct contribution to the country's **gross national product (GNP)**

Low levels of skills and productivity

Long working hours

Urban trends in advanced countries

Over 80% of the UK's population live in cities. As in other ACs, urbanisation is less of a factor than suburbanisation, **counter-urbanisation**, and re-urbanisation (**Figure 4**).

Trends	Causes	Consequences
Suburbanisation (people moving from inner city areas to the suburbs)	• 20th century public transport and private car ownership allowed commuting to the city centre • Late 20th century increasing home ownership, and demand for gardens and public open spaces	• Increased demand for suburban public services – shops, schools, etc. • Increased traffic congestion and pollution • Inner city areas end up derelict • Urban sprawl • Pressure to restrict further development (**green belts**)
Counter-urbanisation (people moving to rural areas from cities)	• Late 20th century increasing urban–rural migration of older people and young families seeking a better quality of life • Businesses and offices looking for space to expand on cheaper land, with better quality of life for their workers	• Creation of dormitory villages with breakdown of community spirit • **Gentrification** and house price inflation prices out locals • Further neglect and deterioration of urban (especially inner city) areas
Re-urbanisation (people moving back into inner city areas as decline is reversed)	• Government initiatives encourage people and businesses back into inner city areas • Urban regeneration brings derelict land and buildings back into use • Young people move for higher education and job opportunities close to leisure and entertainment amenities	• Inner city redevelopment creates new homes and jobs, attracting people • Increased traffic congestion and pollution • Gentrification and house price inflation prices out lower income workers

▲ **Figure 4** *Causes and consequences of suburbanisation, counter-urbanisation and re-urbanisation*

Key terms

Make sure you can write a definition for these key terms

counter-urbanisation   economic hub   gentrification   green belt   GNP   megacity   TNCs   rural–urban migration   urban growth   urbanisation

Learn the answers to the questions below, then cover the answers column with
a piece of paper and write down as many answers as you can. Check and repeat.

Questions

Answers

	Questions	Answers
1	What is urbanisation?	the proportional increase in numbers of people living in towns and cities
2	What is urban growth?	the physical expansion of urban areas
3	What are push and pull factors?	migrants either driven to cities from hardships in the countryside (push) or attracted to cities by social and economic opportunities (pull)
4	What is a megacity?	city with a population of over 10 million
5	What is a squatter settlement?	unplanned, often illegal area of poor-quality housing, lacking in services such as water supply, sanitation, and electricity
6	What is an economic hub?	the focal point for the economy of a country or region
7	What is infrastructure?	the basic services needed for a country to operate (including transport, power and water supplies, and waste disposal)
8	What is the informal economy?	employment outside the official knowledge of the government (unregulated and contributing no tax revenue)
9	What is dereliction?	abandoned buildings and wasteland
10	What is urban sprawl	unplanned growth of urban areas into the surrounding rural or rural-urban fringe areas
11	What is a green belt?	land around a city that is protected from new development by strict planning regulations
12	What is gentrification?	the improvement of built-up areas by individual property owners
13	What is re-urbanisation ?	people moving back into inner city areas as their decline is addressed
14	What is urban regeneration?	an attempt to reverse the decline and decay of an urban area by improving its physical structure

Put paper here

Exam-style questions

1 **(a)** Select the correct definition for urbanisation.

     A a built-up area

     B growth of an urban area

     C growth in urban population

     D growth in the proportion of urban population

    Write the correct letter in the box. ☐ **[1]**

(b) **(i)** Use the data in **Table 1** to complete the graph. **[1]**

> **LINK** 🔗
>
> To understand the skill of constructing and reading a bar graph, refer to the Geographical Skills section page 189.

> **EXAM TIP** 🎯
>
> Accuracy is essential. Plot graphs in pencil so you can correct any mistakes when you check your answers.

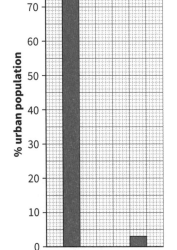

Table 1

Country	% urban population (1950)
UK	79
Nigeria	10
Botswana	3

    (ii) Suggest how this graph might look today. **[2]**

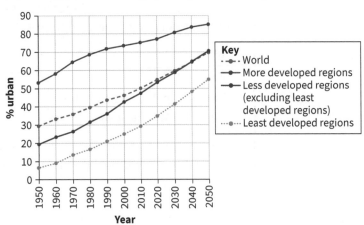

▲ *Fig. 1 – Percentage of urban population, 1950–2050: the data for 2030, 2040, and 2050 are projections*

(c) **(i)** Look at **Fig. 1,** the percentage of urban population, 1950–2050. Describe the trend of more developed regions. **[2]**

    (ii) Outline how trends in the world's population living in urban areas differ between advanced countries (ACs) and low-income developing countries (LIDCs). **[3]**

> **EXAM TIP** 🎯
>
> **Outline** requires you to summarise the key points – so keep the answer to the point.

(d) (i) Explain why some cities grow to become megacities. [3]

(ii) Explain the difference between a 'megacity' and a 'world city'. [4]

(e) Suggest **two** push factors that drive people to move to cities. [2]

(f) Outline what a squatter settlement is. [2]

Kershar's story

My name is Kershar. Last year my parents, sister Sundra and I moved from our village to live in Belgachia. This is a district in Kolkata, West Bengal, India. Our house has two rooms, and electricity. My father works as a labourer, but his work is not regular. Kolkata is crowded, noisy and very, very busy! Outside our house people wash laundry, mend clothes, and flatten tin cans to sell and recycle. There are thousands of small workshops here—our district is very smelly, with open sewers. Sundra and I like to walk to Eden Gardens Park where it is beautiful, but we haven't been inside the nearby cricket ground. We go to school every morning and learn maths and literacy. In the afternoon we scavenge for useful scrap which my father can sell. We also help my mother in the house whenever she asks.

(g) Study Kershar's story. What evidence suggests that Kershar's family is poor? [3]

◀ *Fig. 2 – Workers in New Delhi, India, dismantle old computers to extract valuable metals*

2 (a) Study **Fig. 2,** workers in New Delhi, India, dismantling old computers to extract valuable materials such as copper and nickel.

(i) Define the term 'informal economy'. [2]

(ii) Which of the following is **not** likely to be faced by a worker in the informal sector?

A working long hours

B paying into a pension fund

C having little job security

D irregular earnings

Write the correct letter in the box. ☐ [1]

(iii) Describe the characteristics of jobs in the informal economy of low-income developing countries (LIDCs) and emerging and developing countries (EDCs). [4]

(b) (i) Define the term 're-urbanisation'. [2]

(ii) Describe the causes of re-urbanisation in advanced countries (ACs). [3]

(c) Explain the causes **and** consequences of suburbanisation **and** counter-urbanisation in advanced countries (ACs). [6]

# Knowledge

17 A city in an advanced country

 Case study: Bristol, UK

What makes Bristol important?

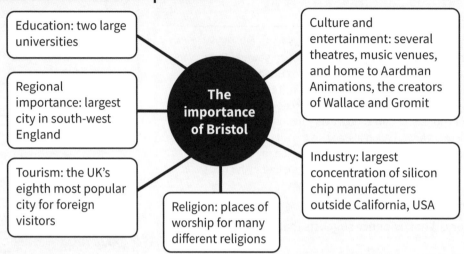

Education: two large universities

Regional importance: largest city in south-west England

Tourism: the UK's eighth most popular city for foreign visitors

The importance of Bristol

Culture and entertainment: several theatres, music venues, and home to Aardman Animations, the creators of Wallace and Gromit

Religion: places of worship for many different religions

Industry: largest concentration of silicon chip manufacturers outside California, USA

Bristol's importance in industry, education, and transport is international. Global industries (including aerospace, finance, high-tech businesses, and media) attract inward investment from abroad, and its universities attract international students. Bristol also has:

- good road and rail links
- two major docks including ferry services to Europe
- an airport with links to Europe and the USA.

What is the impact of migration on Bristol?

Until 2015, migration from abroad accounted for about half of Bristol's population growth, including large numbers from European Union (EU) countries. Migration has brought both opportunities and challenges:

Opportunities	Challenges
• A workforce which can be hard-working • Enriching the city's cultural life by bringing a variety of different cultural experiences • Mainly young migrants help to balance the ageing population	• Extra people can put pressure on housing and employment • Education has to adapt to cater for children whose first language is not English • Some migrants may find it harder than others to integrate into the wider community

Ways of life

Bristol's population is growing rapidly. High levels of migration have resulted in an ethnically diverse and young population. Good transport links (including motorways and a second River Severn crossing) have increased the city's **connectivity** – making it good for commuters. Over 2 million people live within 50 km of the city (**Figure 1**).

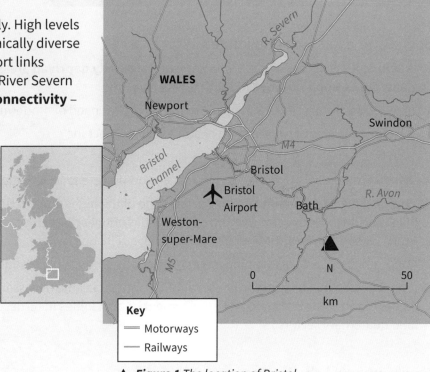

Key
— Motorways
— Railways

▲ *Figure 1 The location of Bristol*

Opportunities

Type of opportunity	What Bristol offers

Economic	• Following closure of Bristol's city centre port, **de-industrialisation** has given way to major developments in tertiary services and the high-tech **quaternary sector**. High-tech industries have been attracted by:
	  ○ superfast broadband connectivity
	  ○ collaboration with local universities
	  ○ a cleaner and less-polluted environment
	• Major industries now include financial services employing 35 000 people

Social (cultural)	• Wide variety of recreation and entertainment, ranging from shopping and sport to theatre and music • Cabot Circus, constructed in 2008 at a cost of £500 million, provides shops and entertainment facilities including a cinema • Sports include City and Rovers football teams, Bears rugby union and the headquarters for Gloucestershire County Cricket • Bristol's Harbourside has seen workshops and warehouses converted into bars and nightclubs, supporting a lively underground music scene. Theatres include the Bristol Hippodrome and The Tobacco Factory
Environmental	• In 2015 Bristol became the UK's first ever European Green Capital and plans to be carbon neutral by 2030 • It has developed an **integrated transport system** (including Metrobus, cycle routeways and electrified railway), connecting suburban housing areas with retail parks, motorway junctions, railway stations and universities • Bristol has also increased open space, for recreation and health, through **urban greening**. More than one-third of the city is now open space, including eight nature reserves and 400 parks and gardens

Knowledge

17 A city in an advanced country

Social and economic challenges

15% of Bristol's residents live in some of the most **socially deprived** areas in England. For example, Filwood in south Bristol has:

- many council-run estates and high-rise flats in urgent need of modernisation
- lower than average levels of good health and life expectancy
- high levels of obesity and smoking
- Bristol's lowest participation rates in active sport and creative activities.

By contrast, the employment rate for Bristol is one of the highest in UK cities, highlighting major social and economic inequalities between wealthy suburbs such as Stoke Bishop to the north-west and areas, such as Filwood, where:

- there are high levels of unemployment – especially among young adults
- only 34% of students gain top grades at GCSE and so lack the necessary skills to benefit from Bristol's developing employment opportunities in tertiary services and quaternary sectors.

Environmental challenges

Type of challenge	Where the challenge is
Urban dereliction	De-industrialisation including the decline of city centre port and railway industries has left many warehouses and other historic buildings derelict (**Figure 3**)
Building on brownfield and greenfield land	• **Brownfield sites** can be costly to clear and decontaminate • Greenfield sites require less groundwork before developing, but local people and environmentalists often object to development of greenfield land
Urban sprawl	Urban sprawl, extending Bristol to the north and south, has been controversial owing to: • loss of countryside • impacts on wildlife biodiversity • increased traffic congestion, noise, and air pollution Strict green belt planning restrictions cover wide areas
Waste disposal	Waste reduction initiatives have reduced Bristol's rubbish to 140 000 tonnes annually – 61% is recycled leaving 39% for mechanical and biological treatment (including biogas electricity generation)

▲ **Figure 3** Urban dereliction can be hazardous and an eyesore

Urban sustainability

Urban sustainability involves creating an environment that meets the social, economic, and environmental needs of existing residents without compromising the same for future generations. Urban initiatives include:

Water conservation:
- **green roofs** collect rainwater to use indoors
- permeable pavements allow rainwater to soak through.

Create green spaces: parks and gardens act as the 'lungs' of the city – helping keep the air clean, providing natural habitats for wildlife, and much-needed recreational and social space.

Urban sustainability initiatives

Energy conservation:
- renewable energy sources, such as solar panels on roofs or burning biomass
- combined heat and power systems
- increasing efficiency of domestic services and appliances
- energy saving through building insulation and double glazing.

Reduce traffic congestion:
- develop an integrated transport system (e.g. Bristol's MetroWest railway, MetroBus, and park and ride schemes)
- make public transport more widespread and affordable
- reduce car parking spaces
- encourage people to cycle (e.g. Bristol's network of cycle routes).

Waste recycling: recover and reprocess urban waste. For example:
- reduced packaging using recyclable materials
- food waste used to create energy (biogas).

▲ **Figure 4** *This Bristol cycle route follows an old railway line*

 Key terms **Make sure you can write a definition for these key terms**

brownfield site   connectivity   de-industrialisation   green roof
integrated transport system   quaternary sector   socially deprived
urban greening   urban sustainability

Retrieval

Learn the answers to the questions below, then cover the answers column with a piece of paper and write down as many answers as you can. Check and repeat.

Questions | Answers

#	Question	Answer
1	What are the positive impacts of migration on Bristol?	opportunities such as a hard-working workforce helping to balance the ageing population, and enriching the city's cultural life
2	What are the negative impacts of migration on Bristol?	challenges such as pressures on housing and employment, language barriers in schools, and possible difficulties with integration into the wider community
3	What has attracted high-tech industries to Bristol?	superfast broadband connectivity, collaboration with local universities, and a cleaner and less-polluted environment
4	What is de-industrialisation?	the decline of a country's traditional manufacturing industry due to exhaustion of raw materials, loss of markets and competition from EDCs
5	What is an integrated transport system?	different forms of transport linked together to make it easy to transfer from one to another
6	What is urban greening?	process of increasing and preserving open space in urban areas (e.g. public parks)
7	What is meant by socially deprived?	the extent to which an individual or a community is deprived of services and amenities
8	What are examples of deprivation?	living at high density; suffering from high rates of crime and unemployment; poor quality housing; low incomes or relying on benefits
9	What is inequality in a society?	unequal or unjust distribution of resources and opportunities among people
10	What is a brownfield site?	land that has been used, abandoned, and now awaits reuse – often found in urban areas

Put paper here

Previous questions | Answers

#	Question	Answer
1	What is urbanisation?	the proportional increase in numbers of people living in towns and cities
2	What are push and pull factors?	migrants either driven to cities from hardships in the countryside (push) or attracted to cities by social and economic opportunities (pull)
3	What is infrastructure?	the basic services needed for a country to operate (including transport, power and water supplies, and waste disposal)
4	What is re-urbanisation ?	people moving back into inner city areas as their decline is addressed

Put paper here

Exam-style questions

1 (a) (i) Complete the table with facts about a city in an advanced
            country you have studied.   [2]

Name of city	
Location in the country	
Importance in the country	

   (ii) State **one** example of a service industry in which this city is
         internationally important.   [1]

   (iii) Outline **two** challenges associated with migration into this city. [2]

   (iv) Describe ways in which migration into this city has affected
         its character, by creating both opportunities and challenges.   [4]

   (v)   Explain what makes this city important.   [4]

   (b) Explain how the sustainability of urban areas can be improved
        through traffic management strategies.   [4]

   (c) Explain how the sustainability of urban areas can be improved
        through water and energy conservation schemes.   [4]

   Stoke Bishop and Filwood are two contrasting areas in Bristol. Stoke
   Bishop is a wealthy suburb to the north-west of the city. Filwood is one
   of the most socially deprived areas in south Bristol.

Housing tenure	Stoke Bishop (%)	Filwood (%)
Owner-occupied	75	46
Social rented	12	41
Private and other rented	13	13

▲ *Table 1*

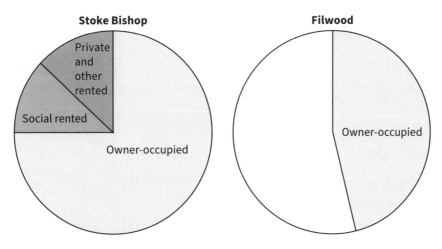

2 (a) (i) Complete the pie chart for Filwood to compare the data
            in **Table 1**.   [2]

   (ii) Compare the graphs, suggesting reasons for your
         observations.   [3]

EXAM TIP

Outline requires you to
summarise the key points.
Think of each as a one-
mark question.

EXAM TIP

Explain requires you
to give reasons why
something happens. Use
examples to reinforce your
points.

LINK

To understand pie charts,
refer to page 192.

EXAM TIP

Compare requires you to
describe similarities and
differences between two or
more things.

It's often helpful to quote
percentages in your answer.
Sometimes it may be of
more value to manipulate
the data by highlighting
proportional differences
(e.g. 'twice as much' or
'double'). This will show
better understanding.

(b) Describe **two** benefits of urban greening. [2]

(c) Outline what a brownfield site is. [2]

(d) To what extent has urban change created social, economic, and environmental opportunities in a city in an advanced country you have studied? [8]

(e) **Case study – a city in an advanced country (AC)**

Name of chosen city: _____

Describe the environmental challenges of urban change. [6]

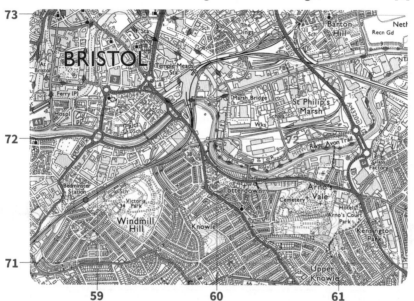

▲ **Fig. 1** – *1:25 000 Ordnance Survey map of part of Bristol, a city in the UK*

3 **(a)** Study **Fig. 1**, a 1:25 000 Ordnance Survey map showing part of Bristol.

    (i) What is the approximate area covered by the map extract?

        A 2 km²

        B 4 km²

        C 6 km²

        D 8 km²

    Write the correct letter in the box. ☐ [1]

    (ii) State the four-figure grid reference for Victoria Park. [1]

    (iii) Identify the river that flows roughly from east to west across the map. [1]

    (iv) State the six-figure grid reference of Marsh Bridge. [1]

    (v) Describe the location of Temple Meads Station. [2]

(b) Explain how the sustainability of urban areas can be improved through creating urban green space. [3]

 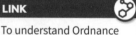

▲ **Fig. 2** – *Broadway in Filwood – one of the most socially deprived areas in south Bristol*

▲ **Fig. 3** – *The centre of Stoke Bishop – a wealthy suburb in north-west of Bristol*

Measure	Filwood	Stoke Bishop	Bristol (average)
Health – % with health conditions	31	25	26
Free school meals (%)	40	16	23
School absence rate (%)	10	7	7

▲ **Table 2** – *Measures of health and education in Filwood and Stoke Bishop (2020)*

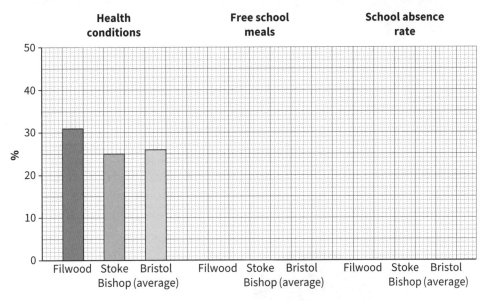

4 **(a)** Study **Figs. 2, 3, and Table 2.**

   (i) Complete the bar graph for the data in **Table 2**. [2]

   (ii) State in which of the two areas people are healthier. [1]

   (iii) Explain your answer to **(ii)** above. [3]

   (iv) Suggest how school absence rates may contribute to Filwood's fairly low GCSE attainment score (34%) compared with Stoke Bishop (48.8%) and the Bristol average (44.2%). [2]

   (v) In addition to **Figs. 2**, **3,** and **Table 2**, suggest what other data would enable you to make a more accurate comparison of social inequalities between Filwood and Stoke Bishop. [2]

LINK

To understand bar graphs, refer to page 189.

Questions referring to previous content

5 **(a)** State the key characteristic of a rapidly growing megacity. [1]

   (b) Suggest **two** pull factors that attract people to megacities. [2]

18 A city in an emerging developing country

Case study: Rio de Janeiro, Brazil

The location and importance of Rio de Janeiro

Rio de Janeiro (Rio) is located on the south-east Atlantic coast of Brazil (**Figure 1**). It has regional, national, and international importance.

SPECIFICATION TIP

You need a case study of one city in an LIDC or EDC to show challenges and opportunities in that city. A case study you may have studied is given here.

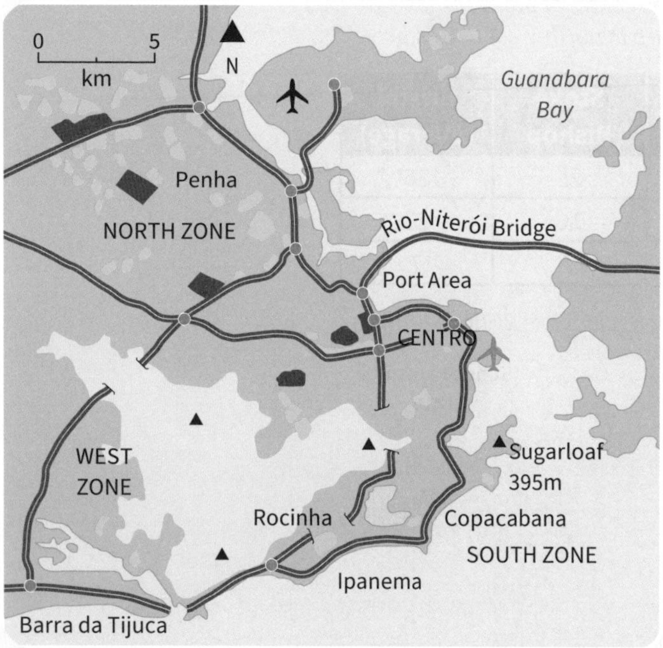

Guanabara Bay

Penha
NORTH ZONE
Rio-Niterói Bridge
Port Area
CENTRO
WEST ZONE
Rocinha
Ipanema
Barra da Tijuca
Sugarloaf 395m
Copacabana
SOUTH ZONE

Brazil
● Rio de Janeiro

Key
- Tijuca National Forest Park
- Squatter settlements (favelas)
- Industrial areas
- Motorways/expressways
- Junctions
- International airport
- Granite mountains

▲ **Figure 1** *Location map of Rio de Janeiro*

Regional:
- Major manufacturing centre (chemicals, pharmaceuticals, and clothing)
- Major service centre (company HQs, finance, education, tourism, and retail)
- Stunning natural surroundings (such as Sugarloaf Mountain)

The importance of Rio

National:
- Brazil's arts and cultural capital (including world-famous annual carnival)
- Major port (exporting coffee, sugar, and iron ore) and transport hub (international airport)

International:
- A UNESCO World Heritage Site (including iconic Christ the Redeemer statue)
- 2016 Olympic/Paralympic Games and 2014 World Cup host

What is the impact of migration on Rio?

Rio has a rapidly growing population, mainly owing to its regional, national, and international migration and also its young population. It has trebled since 1950 to 6.7 million people in the city itself and 13.5 million including the surrounding area (2020). Pull factors include:

- employment, economic development, and business opportunities
- access to services (healthcare and education)
- access to resources (water supply and energy).

Ways of life in Rio

Rio's employment opportunities:

- represent one of the most diverse ranges of industries in any Brazilian city
- support one of the highest levels of income per head in the country
- improve quality of life indicators, such as **life expectancy**, **literacy**, and **infant mortality** – all better in Rio than in Brazil as a whole
- promote Rio's rich cultural heritage, attractive beaches, tropical climate, and magnificent landforms as a thriving tourist destination.

Rio's social and economic challenges and solutions

The city's rapid growth presents both social and economic challenges (see **Figure 2**):

	Challenges	Solutions
Healthcare	Healthcare and hospital access is better in the wealthier south and west zones.	Community-based 'family health teams' have improved vaccination programmes and health cover from 4% to 70% in some **favelas** (such as Santa Marta).
Education	Only about half of children continue their education beyond age 14 due to: • insufficient schools and teachers • the distance needed to travel to school • a need for teenagers to work to support their families.	In the poorer favelas, where school attendance has traditionally been poor: • NGOs such as *Schools for Tomorrow* work with communities to improve education provision • local government grants are provided to help children stay in school • Rocinha favela has opened a university.
Water supply	Water supply and sanitation provision for all is essential – particularly in the densely populated favelas.	Since 1998, seven new treatment plants and 300 km of new water pipes have been built. 96% of the city now has safe piped water.
Energy provision	Electricity supplies get overloaded, leading to frequent power cuts. Many poorer people illegally tap dangerously into the main supply.	New power lines have been installed and a **hydro-electric power (HEP) station**. A third nuclear power plant is due to open in 2023.
Unemployment	Difficult to measure because of the estimated 3.5 million workers employed in the informal economy. Female (18% in 2019) and youth unemployment rates are particularly high.	Solutions centre on education initiatives (see above).
Crime	Murder, drug trafficking, kidnapping, and armed assaults occur regularly in Rio.	In 2013 Pacifying Police Units (PPUs) were set up to take greater control of the favelas from criminals.

▲ *Figure 2* *Rio's social and economic challenges*

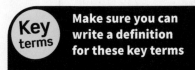 **Make sure you can write a definition for these key terms**

favela   HEP station   infant mortality
life expectancy   literacy   smog

18 A city in an emerging developing country

Housing – the Favela Bairro Project

With over 100 000 migrants arriving each year, Rio faces major housing problems. Many people rent multiple-occupancy housing or occupy land as squatters, often in hazardous environments (e.g. steep hillsides).

Since the mid-1980s, city planners have upgraded the infrastructure (e.g. a cable car system) of some favelas and provided essential services such as new water pipes, improving the lives of over 250 000 residents in 73 communities. The Favela Bairro Project ran from 1994 to 2008 and was part of this improvement.

Figure 3 shows Rocinha, a favela that has benefitted. It overlooks the South Zone's main beaches, tourist hotels and high-rise luxury apartments.

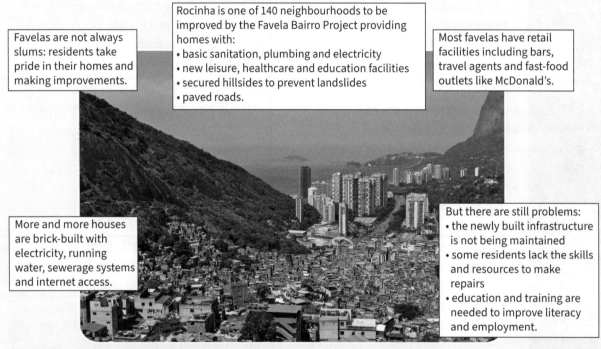

Favelas are not always slums: residents take pride in their homes and making improvements.

Rocinha is one of 140 neighbourhoods to be improved by the Favela Bairro Project providing homes with:
• basic sanitation, plumbing and electricity
• new leisure, healthcare and education facilities
• secured hillsides to prevent landslides
• paved roads.

Most favelas have retail facilities including bars, travel agents and fast-food outlets like McDonald's.

More and more houses are brick-built with electricity, running water, sewerage systems and internet access.

But there are still problems:
• the newly built infrastructure is not being maintained
• some residents lack the skills and resources to make repairs
• education and training are needed to improve literacy and employment.

▲ *Figure 3* Rocinha – Rio's largest and oldest favela

Pollution and its sustainable solutions

The main environmental challenges in Rio relate to air, water, and land pollution:

	Issues	Sustainable solutions
Air	High crime levels mean people prefer to travel in their own cars. This increases traffic congestion and **smog**.	• Expansion of the metro system (cutting car use) • New toll roads • Making coast roads one-way during rush hours
Water	Guanabara Bay is polluted by sewage, industrial waste, and oil spills and ship ballast.	• New sewage works and pipes have been installed • Ship owners are fined for illegal discharges
Land	Waste collection varies hugely across Rio and is infrequent in favelas – encouraging rats and causing diseases.	• Every year, 3.5 million tonnes of waste go to landfill • A power plant converts landfill biogas (LFG) to generate electricity

Learn the answers to the questions below, then cover the answers column with a piece of paper and write down as many answers as you can. Check and repeat.

Questions | Answers

	Questions	Answers
1	What is Rio de Janeiro's regional importance?	a major manufacturing and service centre, with stunning natural surroundings
2	What is Rio de Janeiro's national importance?	it is Brazil's arts and cultural capital (including annual carnival); a major port; and transport hub with international airport
3	What is Rio de Janeiro's international importance?	a UNESCO World Heritage Site; and the 2016 Olympic/Paralympic Games and 2014 World Cup host
4	Why has Rio's population more than trebled since 1950?	natural increase and especially migration – pull factors including employment, economic development, and business opportunities, and access to services and resources
5	What is infant mortality rate?	the number of babies that die under one year of age, per 1000 live births
6	What is a favela?	a Brazilian shanty town (squatter settlement)
7	What is an NGO?	non-governmental organisation – organisations independent from governments, which work for humanitarian causes
8	What are the social challenges facing Rio?	access to services (e.g. healthcare and education); access to resources (e.g. water supply, sanitation, and energy); high crime rate
9	What are the economic challenges facing Rio?	high unemployment; around one-third of the workforce working in the informal economy; traffic congestion increasing journey times
10	What are the three main environmental challenges facing Rio?	air pollution (smog), water pollution, and waste disposal

Put paper here

Previous questions | Answers

	Previous questions	Answers
1	What is meant by socially deprived?	the extent to which an individual or a community is deprived of services and amenities
2	What are examples of deprivation?	living at high density; suffering from high rates of crime and unemployment; poor quality housing; low incomes or relying on benefits
3	What sorts of countries demonstrate the greatest rates of urbanisation?	African low-income developing countries (LIDCs) and Asian emerging and developing countries (EDCs)
4	What proportion of the world's population already live in urban areas?	more than half (56% in 2021)

Put paper here

Exam-style questions

1 **(a)** State **one** example of a service industry in which a city in an LIDC or EDC is internationally important. **[1]**

(b) Describe the causes of migration affecting the growth of a city in an LIDC or EDC. **[3]**

 EXAM TIP

Describe requires you to give the main characteristics of something. (No explanation is needed.)

 LINK

To understand line graphs, refer to page 190.

Date	Population (millions)
1950	3
1960	4.5
1970	6.8
1980	8.8
1990	9.7
2000	11.3
2010	12.4
2020	13.5

▲ **Table 1** Population of Rio de Janeiro (1950–2020)

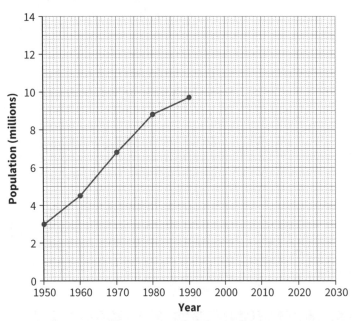

▲ **Fig. 1**

(c) Study **Fig. 1**. Use **Table 1** to plot population totals for 2000, 2010 and 2020 on **Fig. 1**. **[2]**

(i) Calculate the percentage change of population between 2010 and 2020. **[1]**

(ii) Assuming the rate of change stays the same, calculate the expected population in 2030. **[1]**

(iii) Plot this new value on the graph. **[1]**

(iv) Analyse the trend of population growth (1950–2030). **[3]**

 LINK

To understand how to calculate a percentage, refer to page 195.

EXAM TIP

Analyse requires you to identify and describe patterns and trends, make links, identify anomalies, and explain reasons. Make sure you refer to data from the graph.

▲ *Fig. 2 – Slum housing in Rio de Janeiro*

2   (a)   Study **Fig. 2,** slum housing in Rio de Janeiro, Brazil. Using the evidence shown in **Fig. 2** and your own understanding, describe the housing challenges faced by many cities in LIDCs and EDCs.   [3]

     (b)   **Case study – a city in a low-income developing country (LIDC) or emerging and developing country (EDC).**

            Name of chosen city: _____

Explain how urban growth has created challenges.   [6]

> **EXAM TIP**
>
> **Explain** requires you to give reasons why something happens.

     (c)   **Case study – a city in a low-income developing country (LIDC) or emerging and developing country (EDC).**

            Name of chosen city: _____

Suggest the main challenges facing the management of squatter settlements.   [6]

> **EXAM TIP**
>
> **Suggest** requires you to give an explanation for something when you can't be sure.

     (d)   **Case study – a city in a low-income developing country (LIDC) or emerging and developing country (EDC).**

            Name of chosen city: _____

Evaluate **one** sustainable management issue faced by the city authorities.   [6]

Questions referring to previous content

3   (a)   Define the term 'socially deprived'.   [1]

     (b)   State **two** examples of social deprivation.   [2]

> **EXAM TIP**
>
> **Evaluate** requires you to make judgements about which management issues are most or least effective. Make sure you refer to actual facts and located examples throughout your answer.

Knowledge

19 Why are some countries wealthier than others?

What is development?

Development is the progress a country has made in terms of economic growth, use of technology, and human welfare. Development usually improves living standards and **quality of life**. But there are wide-ranging differences in these standards between the world's advanced countries (ACs), emerging and developing countries (EDCs) and low-income developing countries (LIDCs).

In 2001, a small group of countries with rapidly growing economies were identified: Brazil, Russia, India, and China. South Africa was added in 2010 to make the BRICS. In 2014, another group of EDCs were identified: the MINTs (Mexico, Indonesia, Nigeria, and Turkey).

REVISION TIP

Make sure you know the difference between ACs, EDCs, and LIDCs. Learn a couple of examples for each category.

Economic and social measures of development

Gross National Income (GNI) per capita is an economic measure of development. It is the total income of a country, including earnings abroad, divided by its population total. There are huge global differences between ACs, EDCs and LIDCs.

The **Human Development Index (HDI)**, a social measure of development compiled by the UN and the most widely used, covers income, life expectancy, and years in education. Values range from 0–1 (**Figure 1**), with 0 being the least and 1 being the most developed.

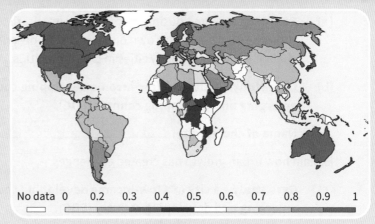

No data 0   0.2   0.3   0.4   0.5   0.6   0.7   0.8   0.9   1

▲ **Figure 1** The Human Development Index (2019)

Other measures of development

Birth rate: In poorer LIDCs, large families help ensure income and support for ageing relatives, but development sees more education of women – with careers, later marriages, and fewer children

Death rate: Often low in LIDCs and EDCs as healthcare improves. But it is high in ACs with ageing populations, and in the poorest LIDCs too (with high infant mortality), which makes it a poor measure of development

Other measures of development

Infant mortality: A good measure of development reflecting a country's healthcare system

Literacy rate: Another good indicator of development, but only easy to measure in ACs

Access to clean water: High in ACs, but lower in LIDCs where modern infrastructure (e.g. dams, reservoirs, and treatment plants) may be less widespread

Figure 2 shows measures of development for an AC, EDC and LIDC. They may give a false picture of development because they:

- average everyone throughout the whole country
- include hard to measure, unreliable, and out of date data.

Country	GNI per capita (US$)	HDI	Birth rate (per 1000 per year)	Death rate (per 1000 per year)	Infant mortality (per 1000 live births per year)	Literacy rate (%)	Access to safe water (%)
UK (AC)	42 370	0.932	11.87	9.40	4.8	99	100
Nigeria (EDC)	2 030	0.539	34.39	12.40	94.3	62	85
Zimbabwe (LIDC)	1 390	0.571	33.57	10.20	32.3	89	81

Figure 2 Measures of development for three countries, 2020

Causes of uneven development

	Causes of uneven development
Physical	• Extreme climate and weather conditions can create hostile environments to live and work in, e.g. climate-related pests and diseases, clean water shortages, and tropical storms, floods, and droughts (**Figure 3**). • Landlocked countries (e.g. Niger in Africa and Afghanistan in Asia) are unable to access sea trade which is so important for economic development. • Harsh relief, e.g. remote, mountainous regions, makes it difficult to develop infrastructure.
Economic	• Poverty prevents improvements to education, infrastructure, and living conditions. • **Trade** benefits wealthier countries, e.g. prices of raw materials (**commodities**) from LIDCs vary widely and are worth far less than the products made from them. • Many of the world's poorest countries built up debt in the 1970s and 1980s leading to a **debt crisis** (unable to repay). Since 2000, 30 of the poorest have benefited from international debt relief.
Historical	• Many ACs, especially in Europe, have a long history of industrial and economic development based on colonial exploitation of what are now LIDCs (**colonialism**). • From the mid-twentieth century, former colonies gained independence. However, problems such as ethnic rivalries, power struggles, civil wars, and **corruption** have continued to hold back development in many countries.

▲ *Figure 3 Extreme impacts of drought*

 WATCH OUT

The wide-ranging differences in development between ACs, EDCs, and LIDCs is often referred to as the **development gap**. Make sure you can define this term.

19 Why are some countries wealthier than others?

Consequences of uneven development

Uneven development exists both between countries and within them. Consequently, poverty, wealth, and health inequalities exist everywhere.

Differences in wealth

- The highest levels of wealth are found in the most developed regions, e.g. 34% of global wealth is found in North America (**Figure 3**).
- Of the EDCs, growth since 2000 has been highest in China, and personal wealth in India and China has quadrupled.
- The continent with the smallest share of global wealth is Africa (with about 1%).

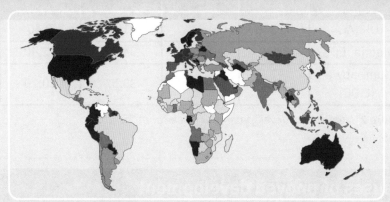

GNI per capita in 2018 (US$)
- ■ >50 000
- ■ 30 000–50 000
- ■ 20 000–30 000
- ■ 10 000–20 000
- □ 7 500–10 000
- ■ 5 000–7 500
- ■ 3 500–5 000
- ■ 2 000–3 500
- ■ 1 000–2 000
- □ <1 000
- □ Data unavailable

▲ **Figure 3** *Gross National Incomes per capita (2018)*

Differences in health

Countries with a low level of development tend to have poorer healthcare – with uneven access to doctors, clinics, and hospitals (see **Figure 4**). Infectious diseases such as cholera are more commonly found in LIDCs while people in ACs tend to have diseases associated with higher standards of living such as diabetes.

	LIDCs	ACs
Infants	High infant mortality	Low infant mortality
Children	4 in every 10 deaths	1 in every 100 deaths
Elderly	2 in every 10 deaths	7 in every 10 deaths
Main causes of death	Infectious diseases (e.g. HIV/AIDS, diarrhoea, and tuberculosis) as well as malaria	Chronic diseases (e.g. cancer, heart disease, diabetes, and dementia)

▲ **Figure 4** *Differences in health between LIDCs and ACs*

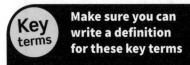 **Make sure you can write a definition for these key terms**

commodity   corruption   debt crisis
development   development gap   GNI
HDI   quality of life   trade

Learn the answers to the questions below, then cover the answers column with a piece of paper and write down as many answers as you can. Check and repeat.

Questions / Answers

#	Questions	Answers
1	What is development?	the progress a country has made in terms of economic growth, use of technology, and human welfare
2	What is quality of life?	variables contributing to human welfare – including happiness, wealth, safety, security, freedom, voting rights, and good health
3	What is the development gap?	the difference in standards of living between the world's richest and poorest countries
4	What is the Human Development Index (HDI)?	a UN social measure of development covering income, life expectancy, and years in education
5	What is the debt crisis?	when many poor countries borrowed money to develop their economies but couldn't repay their debts or the high interest levels
6	What is colonialism?	full or partial political control over another country, occupying it with settlers, and exploiting it economically (e.g. the British Empire)
7	What are the physical causes of uneven development?	extreme climatic and weather conditions; lack of clean water sources; landlocked countries cut off from sea trade; and harsh relief
8	What are the economic causes of uneven development?	poverty preventing improvements to education, infrastructure, and living conditions; trade stacked in favour of richer countries
9	What are the historical causes of uneven development?	since gaining independence, many former colonies (often LIDCs) have suffered from ethnic rivalries, power struggles, civil wars, and corruption
10	What is corruption?	dishonest or illegal behaviour – especially by powerful people (such as government officials)

Put paper here

Previous questions / Answers

#	Previous questions	Answers
1	What is literacy?	the ability to read and write
2	What is infant mortality rate?	the number of babies that die under one year of age, per 1000 live births
3	What are push and pull factors?	migrants either driven to cities from hardships in the countryside (push) or attracted to cities by social and economic opportunities (pull)
4	What is a squatter settlement?	unplanned, often illegal poor-quality housing, lacking in services such as water supply, sanitation, and electricity

Put paper here

Practice

Exam-style questions

Country	GNI (US$ per person per year)	Birth rate (per 1000 per year)	HDI
Japan	41 690	7.32	0.919
China	10 410	11.62	0.761
Bangladesh	1 940	18.13	0.632

▲ **Table 1** *Selected measures of development in three countries, 2020*

1 **(a)** Study **Table 1,** selected measures of development in contrasting countries.

    (i) State which country would be best described as an emerging and developing country (EDC). [1]

    (ii) Outline any relationships in the data. [2]

    (iii) State **two** reasons for the differences in birth rates shown. [2]

  (b) Explain why birth rate is a better measure of development than death rate. [4]

  (c) What is meant by 'quality of life'? [2]

  (d) Why is the Human Development Index (HDI) the most widely used measure of development? [2]

  (e) Define the term 'infant mortality rate'. [2]

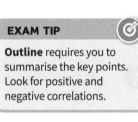

EXAM TIP

Outline requires you to summarise the key points. Look for positive and negative correlations.

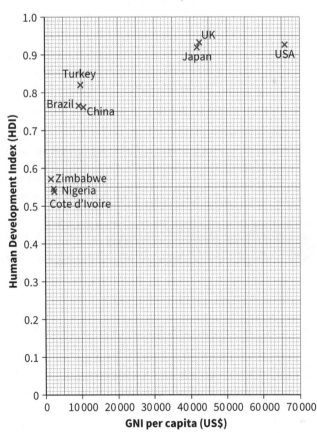

▲ **Fig. 1** *Scattergraph showing GNI and HDI for selected countries, 2020*

2   **(a)**   Study **Fig. 1**, a scattergraph showing Gross National Income (GNI) and the Human Development Index (HDI) for selected countries in 2020.

(i)   Use a cross to plot the following data on to **Fig. 1**.   [1]

Country	GNI (US$ per person per year)	Human Development Index
Bangladesh	1940	0.632

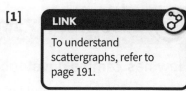
LINK

To understand scattergraphs, refer to page 191.

(ii)   Draw a best fit line on **Fig. 1**.   [1]

(iii)   Outline any relationships in the data.   [2]

(b)   Compare the main causes of death in LIDCs with those in ACs.   [3]

(c)   Outline physical causes of uneven development.   [4]

(d)   State **two** ways in which climate and weather can affect economic development.   [2]

(e)   Explain how physical and historical factors can cause uneven development.   [6]

EXAM TIP

Compare requires you to describe similarities and differences between two or more things. Use data to support your answer.

Questions referring to previous content

3   **(a)**   Outline what a squatter settlement is.   [2]

(b)   Explain what is meant by site and service provision in squatter settlements.   [3]

Knowledge

20 How has an LIDC developed so far?

Case study: Zambia - part 1

How has Zambia developed?

Zambia is an LIDC in central Southern Africa (**Figure 1**). Before it was colonised by Britain in 1888, Zambia was inhabited by different groups of African people. Many of them were farmers. Each group had different languages and cultures.

SPECIFICATION TIP

You need one case study of an LIDC to show how it has developed. A case study you may have studied is given here.

- Landlocked
- Low life expectancy
- Around 50% of the population live in poverty

Key facts about Zambia

- Gained independence from Britain in 1964
- Rich in copper
- GNI per capita $3 360 (2020)

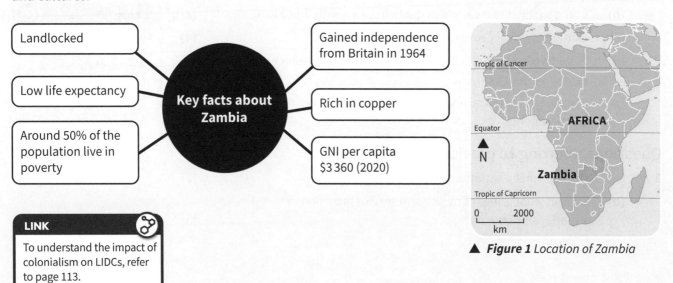
▲ **Figure 1** Location of Zambia

LINK

To understand the impact of colonialism on LIDCs, refer to page 113.

Rostow's model of economic development

Models show a simplification of something that can be seen in the real world. **Rostow's model** of economic development outlines five stages that countries should go through as they develop (**Figure 2**). The model was based on ACs, like the USA.

Stage	Explanation
1 Traditional society	Limited technology, agriculture is the main industry
2 Pre-conditions for economic take-off	Agriculture, trade, and communications improve, natural resources are extracted
3 Economic take-off	The manufacturing sector develops
4 Drive to maturity	Different industries develop; lots of investment
5 Age of high mass consumption	Lots of jobs in the service sector and infrastructure improves

▲ **Figure 2** Rostow's model of economic development

REVISION TIP

Examiners will be looking for answers that demonstrate your knowledge of the development stages that countries go through – so, make sure you learn what happens at each stage and how the sequence progresses.

Zambia's economic development

Zambia has struggled to develop economically. Its development has not been as straightforward as Rostow's model suggests. There have been obstacles that have held back development, as well as many opportunities for Zambia:

LINK

To understand what debt relief is, refer to page 113.

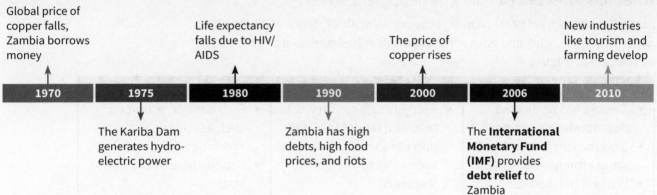

Global price of copper falls, Zambia borrows money

Life expectancy falls due to HIV/AIDS

The price of copper rises

New industries like tourism and farming develop

| 1970 | 1975 | 1980 | 1990 | 2000 | 2006 | 2010 |

The Kariba Dam generates hydro-electric power

Zambia has high debts, high food prices, and riots

The **International Monetary Fund (IMF)** provides **debt relief** to Zambia

Zambia's Millennium Development Goals

In 2000, the governments of 189 countries agreed eight Millennium Development Goals (**MDGs**), which were outlined by the United Nations (UN). They aimed to halve world poverty by 2015. Zambia had mixed progress towards the MDGs (**Figure 3**).

Millenium Development Goal	What was achieved?
1 Eradicate extreme hunger and poverty	• Access to safe drinking water improved • Poverty reduced in urban areas more than in rural areas • Many people did not have improved sanitation
2 Achieve universal primary education	• The number of children in primary school increased
3 Promote gender equality and empower women	• There was equal gender enrolment in primary school • Equal gender enrolment needed to be improved in secondary schools and universities
4 Reduce child mortality	• **Child mortality** fell but was still high
5 Improve maternal health	• The number of women dying in childbirth fell but was still high
6 Combat HIV/Aids, malaria, and other diseases	• The number of HIV/AIDS infections fell
7 Ensure environmental sustainability	• Deforestation increased, although use of hydro-electric power projects has increased
8 Develop a global partnership for development	• **Foreign investment** was attracted

Figure 3 *Zambia's progress towards MDGs*

⚙ Knowledge

20 How has an LIDC developed so far?

 Case study: Zambia - part 1

What has affected Zambia's development so far?

Zambia is one of the fastest growing economies in Africa. Since 2000, Zambia's wider political, social, and environmental context has contributed to the country's development (**Figure 4**).

Political	Social	Environmental
• Zambia has an elected, **democratic** government • Government is able to attract foreign investment • Well-established banks, and law and insurance companies	• A largely safe country, with beautiful landscapes and popular tourist attractions such as Victoria Falls (**Figure 5**)	• Rich natural resources, such as copper and semi-precious gemstones • Four hydro-electric power stations

▲ *Figure 4 Zambia – political, social, and environmental context*

LINK

To understand the advantages and disadvantages of foreign investment, refer to page 125.

Key terms **Make sure you can write a definition for these key terms**

child mortality   debt relief   democratic
foreign investment   IMF   MDGs   Rostow's model

▲ *Figure 5 Victoria Falls, Zambia*

Learn the answers to the questions below, then cover the answers column with a piece of paper and write down as many answers as you can. Check and repeat.

Questions | Answers

	Questions	Answers
1	What does Rostow's model show?	five development stages that countries go through
2	What are the five stages in Rostow's model?	traditional society; pre-conditions for economic take-off; economic take-off; drive to maturity; and age of high mass consumption
3	What is Zambia's GNI per capita?	3 360 US$ (in 2020)
4	What percentage of Zambia's population live in poverty?	50%
5	What problems held back development in Zambia in 1990?	high debts, high food prices, and riots
6	What is debt relief?	the total or partial cancellation of the debts of the least developed countries in the world by the International Monetary Fund (IMF)
7	What new industries are helping Zambia to develop?	tourism, farming, and HEP
8	How many MDGs were there?	eight
9	What was the main aim of the MDGs?	to halve world poverty by 2015
10	Which aspects of the MDGs did Zambia make good progress in?	increasing the number of children in primary school; achieving equal gender enrolment in primary school; reducing HIV/AIDS infections; improving access to safe drinking water
11	Which aspects of the MDGs did Zambia make less progress in?	improving: gender enrolment at secondary school and universities and sanitation; reducing: child mortality; women dying in childbirth; poverty in rural areas

Put paper here

Previous questions | Answers

	Previous questions	Answers
1	What is development?	the progress a country has made in terms of economic growth, use of technology, and human welfare
2	What is the debt crisis?	when many poor countries borrowed money to develop their economies but couldn't repay their debts or the high interest levels
3	What is inequality in a society?	unequal or unjust distribution of resources and opportunities among people

Put paper here

Practice

Exam-style questions

Measure	2010	2015
GNI per capita (US$ per person per year)	1 489	1 314
Fertility rate	5.6	5.2
HDI	0.529	0.562
Urban population (%)	39.4	41.9
Life expectancy (males)	49.6	57
Life expectancy (females)	54	61
Individuals using the internet (per 100 inhabitants)	10	21

▲ *Table 1*

1   Study **Table 1**, which shows selected measures of development for Zambia in 2010 and 2015.

   (a) **(i)**   Calculate the percentage increase in the number of individuals using the internet. Show your working.   **[2]**

LINK

To understand how to calculate percentage increase, refer to page 195.

   (ii)   Which one of the following is the correct meaning of GNI?

   A   Gross National Import

   B   Gross National Input

   C   Gross National Income

   D   Gross National Investment

   Write the correct letter in the box.   ☐   **[1]**

   (iii)   State **two** reasons for Zambia's increase in GNI per capita between 2010 and 2015.   **[2]**

   State as a command word requires you to give a simple word or statement.

EXAM TIP

State requires you to give a simple word or statement.

   (iv)   State **one** piece of evidence which suggests that quality of life for people in Zambia has improved.   **[1]**

2   **(a)**   Describe the economic development of **one** LIDC that you have studied.   **[4]**

   (b)   State **two** influences on the economic development of one LIDC that you have studied.   **[2]**

EXAM TIP

Describe requires you to give the main characteristics of something. (No explanation is needed)

3   Outline what Rostow's model of economic development shows.   **[2]**

4   **(a)**   Explain how **two** of the Millennium Development Goals have been achieved by **one** named LIDC you have studied.   **[4]**

EXAM TIP

Outline requires you to summarise the key points.

   (b)   Explain how **two** of the Millennium Development Goals have not been achieved by **one** named LIDC you have studied.   **[4]**

   (c)   Explain **one** reason why an LIDC you have studied has struggled to develop.   **[2]**

Country	GNI per capita (US$)	Employment in agriculture (%)
Nigeria	5 710	37
South Africa	3 250	6
Tanzania	3 160	67

▲ *Table 2*

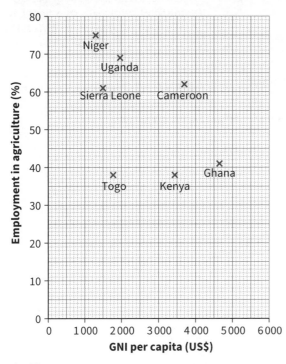

▲ *Fig. 1*

LINK

To understand scattergraphs, refer to page 191.

5   Study **Table 2** and **Fig.1**, which show GNI per capita and employment in agriculture for selected African countries in 2019.

   (a)   Use a cross to plot Nigeria, South Africa, and Tanzania onto **Figure 3**. **[1]**

   (b)   Draw a best-fit line. **[1]**

   (c)   Draw a circle around each of the residuals (anomalies). **[1]**

   (d)   Describe the relationship between GNI and employment in agriculture. **[2]**

6   **CASE STUDY – Development in an LIDC**

   Name of LIDC: _____

   For an LIDC you have studied, to what extent can the country's development be explained by Rostow's model of economic development? **[8]**

EXAM TIP

To what extent requires you to judge the importance of something. In such a high-mark question, making judgements based on evidence from your understanding of Rostow's model is the key to success. Your spelling, punctuation and grammar will also be assessed in this question.

Questions referring to previous content

7   **(a)**   Define the term 'colonialism'. **[2]**

   (b)   Outline the historical consequences of colonialism for many LIDCs. **[3]**

Knowledge

21 Global connections influencing the LIDC's development

Case study: Zambia - part 2

Copper

Copper is Zambia's most important commodity for international trade. In 2020:

- 73% of Zambia's **exports** were copper
- copper exports totaled US$5.74 billion
- Switzerland and China were the main two importers of copper from Zambia.

The main area for mining copper is the Copperbelt Province. As the economy relies on exporting copper, Zambia is vulnerable to changes in copper's global price. When the global price fell in the 1970s, Zambia's GDP per capita fell. In 2000, there was a rise in copper prices, and Zambia's income rose.

▲ **Figure 1** Zambia's GDP per capita, 1950–2018

China's investment

China is the world's largest importer of copper, so Zambia is very attractive for Chinese foreign investment in mines. In 2020, over 600 Chinese companies operated in Zambia. China has also invested in:

- hydro-electric dams for power
- railways to improve accessibility for landlocked Zambia
- farms to improve rural areas
- tourism to help **diversify** the economy.

▲ **Figure 2** The Chinese-funded TAZARA railway line runs between Zambia and Tanzania

Transnational companies

Associated British Foods (ABF), a trans-national company (TNC) based in the UK, bought Zambia Sugar, which produces and exports most of Zambia's sugar from its cane plantations. Investing in Zambia is attractive to a TNC like ABF because the TNCs don't have to pay much tax. There are benefits and problems of TNCs operating in Zambia (**Figure 3**).

 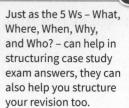

Benefits	Problems
• TNCs provide jobs for the local population • Workers pay tax to the government so the government can fund services such as healthcare and education • The local economy improves • Companies provide healthcare and education for the workers • Investment enables exploitation of natural resources	• Work may be seasonal (e.g. sugar cane harvesting) • Low wages • The company doesn't pay much tax • Profits may be transferred to another country so the local economy does not benefit • TNCs can prioritise profit over people • Local companies often find it hard to compete with TNCs • Exploiting natural resources can damage the environment

▲ **Figure 3** Benefits and problems of TNCs investing in LIDCs

International aid

There are different types of international aid:

• **Official Development Assistance (ODA)** – given by governments

• voluntary aid – given by individuals, companies, and NGOs (charities)

• tied aid – aid with conditions attached

• multi-lateral aid – given through international organisations, such as the IMF

• bi-lateral aid – given from one country's government to another

• short-term emergency aid – given during natural disasters or conflicts.

Advantages	Disadvantages
• Aid can help to address global inequalities and improves standards of living • ACs, who benefited from colonialism, can help LIDCs • Emergency aid saves lives during crises	• Countries may become dependent on aid • Aid may have conditions attached which benefit the donor • Corrupt governments may not spend the aid money in the right way • Giving money doesn't necessarily help countries to develop their own sources of income

▲ **Figure 3** Benefits and problems of TNCs investing in LIDCs

Debt relief

Many LIDCs have high levels of debt. In 2006, the IMF gave Zambia $6.5 billion as part of its **Heavily Indebted Poor Country (HIPC)** initiative. There are 39 countries which qualify for this assistance. This has allowed Zambia's government to spend money on improving healthcare and education, instead of repaying debts.

LINK

To understand what debt relief is, refer to page 113.

What development strategy is most appropriate for Zambia?

Top-down development strategies are often:	**Bottom-up development** strategies are often:
• large national projects • government-led • funded by the government or an international organisation like the IMF.	• smaller in scale • local projects • run and funded by NGOs working with local communities.

Knowledge

 ## Case study: Zambia – part 2

Top-down and bottom-up development projects

Project	Advantages	Disadvantages
Top-down: Kariba Dam – built in the 1950s, produces hydro-electric power (HEP) for Zambia and Zimbabwe. It is run jointly by the governments of Zambia and Zimbabwe.	• Large amounts of HEP can power Zambia's copper industry • HEP is a renewable energy source and so environmentally sustainable • Tourism and fishing have developed around Lake Kariba • The dam has led to development, which should help improve quality of life for Zambians • It has helped the capital city, Lusaka, to develop	• People living near the dam were moved from the valley and resettled far away • Many farmers were resettled on infertile land • Natural processes have been disrupted • Ecosystems and farmland have been lost • Many local communities have not benefited from energy production, as they are still without electricity • Local people were not consulted • The dam is likely to collapse due to erosion • It puts more people at risk from flooding
Bottom-up: Room to Read – run by the NGO 'Room to Read' since 2007. Its aim is to improve Zambia's literacy rates and reduce **gender inequality** in schools.	• Improves the literacy rate in local communities • Helps reduce the drop-out rate of girls from school • Raises awareness of the issues around girls' education, such as expectations to do domestic chores or early marriage • Improves the educational performance of Zambia's children • Teachers receive better training • Responds to the needs of local communities	• Operates on a smaller scale so helps a smaller number of people • Limited by the funding of the NGO – may rely on volunteers or donations • Projects can suddenly stop if funding is withdrawn • Projects may be less well-run • Projects may not be planned systematically, so some areas benefit while others do not

▲ *Figure 5 Two development projects in Zambia*

 Key terms | **Make sure you can write a definition for these key terms**

bottom-up development   diversify   export
gender inequality   HIPC   ODA   top-down development

REVISION TIP

Examiners will be looking for answers that demonstrate you can evaluate the success of different types of aid projects. So, make sure you learn the advantages and disadvantages of one top-down and one bottom-up strategy in the LIDC you have studied.

Learn the answers to the questions below, then cover the answers column with a piece of paper and write down as many answers as you can. Check and repeat.

Questions | Answers

	Questions	Answers
1	What is Zambia's most important commodity?	copper
2	What Zambian industries does China invest in?	copper, hydro-electric power (HEP), railways, agriculture, and tourism
3	Why is investing in Zambia attractive?	because companies don't have to pay much tax
4	What are the benefits of trans-national companies (TNCs) operating in Zambia?	jobs for the local population; workers increase tax revenue for the government; they provide healthcare and education for the workers
5	What are the problems of TNCs operating in Zambia?	they don't pay much tax; they prioritise profit; wages are low; and exploiting natural resources damages the environment
6	What is the difference between Official Development Assistance (ODA) and voluntary aid?	ODA is given by governments, and voluntary aid is given by individuals, companies, and NGOs
7	What are the advantages of aid?	it can help to address global inequalities; ACs can help LIDCs; emergency aid saves lives during crises
8	What are the disadvantages of aid?	countries may become dependent on aid; aid may have conditions attached which benefit the donor; corrupt governments may not spend the aid money in the right way; giving money doesn't necessarily help countries to develop their own sources of income
9	What are top-down development strategies?	large national projects – government-led, funded by the government or an international organisation
10	What are bottom-up development strategies?	smaller in scale – local projects, run and funded by NGOs working with local communities

Put paper here

Previous questions | Answers

	Previous questions	Answers
1	What is debt relief?	the total or partial cancellation of the debts of the least developed countries in the world by the International Monetary Fund (IMF)
2	What was the main aim of the Millennium Development Goals (MDGs)?	to halve world poverty by 2015
3	What is trade?	the buying and selling of goods and services
4	What are commodities?	basic or economic goods such as agricultural or mining products

Put paper here

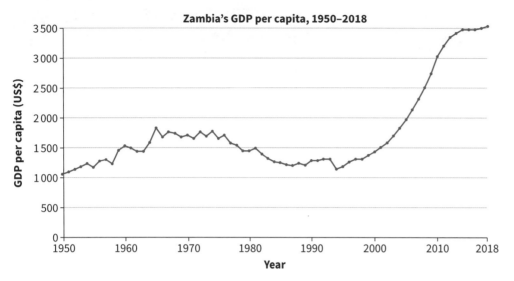

Practice

Exam-style questions

▲ *Fig. 1* – *GDP per capita for Zambia, 1950–2018*

1   Study **Fig. 1**, which shows GDP per capita for Zambia between 1950 and 2018.

   (a)   **(i)**   Calculate the difference between Zambia's GDP per capita
              in 1960 and 2015. Show your working.   **[2]**

       (ii)   Which **one** of the following best describes the trend in
              Zambia's GDP per capita between 1950 and 2018?

            A   Zambia's GDP per capita has fallen since 2000.

            B   Zambia's GDP per capita has been continuously rising
                 since 1950.

            C   Zambia's GDP per capita fell in 1970 but has since
                 been rising.

            D   Zambia's GDP per capita rose in 1970 but has since fallen.

            Write the correct letter in the box. ☐   **[1]**

      (iii)   State **one** reason for Zambia's change in GDP per capita
              between 1970 and 2000.   **[2]**

   (b)   Explain **two** ways in which international trade has influenced
         development in Zambia.   **[4]**

2   **(a)**   What is the definition of a TNC?

        A   trans-national commodity

        B   trans-national community

        C   trans-national colony

        D   trans-national company

      Write the correct letter in the box. ☐   **[1]**

   (b)   Explain **one** reason that TNCs find investment in LIDCs attractive.   **[2]**

   (c)   Explain the benefits of TNCs operating in LIDCs.   **[4]**

   (d)   Explain the problems of TNCs operating in LIDCs.   **[4]**

> **EXAM TIP** ⊙
>
> **Explain** requires you to give reasons why something happens. Make sure that you refer to specific examples.

3   **(a)**   Which **one** of the following best describes tied aid?

         A   Aid that has conditions attached

         B   Aid that is given by an NGO

         C   Aid that is given during a natural disaster

         D   Aid that is given though international organisations

         Write the correct letter in the box. ☐   **[1]**

    (b)   Identify **two** other types of aid.   **[2]**

    (c)   Explain how aid may **not** help a country to develop.   **[3]**

    (d)   Explain **two** advantages of aid to help countries develop.   **[4]**

    (e)   Outline how debt relief can help a country to develop.   **[3]**

> **EXAM TIP**
>
> **Identify** requires you to name an example of something.

4   **(a)**   Which **one** of the following best describes a top-down development strategy?

         A   A solar water pump installed in three villages

         B   A new railway connecting two coastlines of a country

         C   A school education programme on hygiene practices in one region

         D   A sustainable fertiliser scheme for rural farmers

         Write the correct letter in the box. ☐   **[1]**

    (b)   State **two** features of a bottom-up development strategy.   **[2]**

    (c)   Explain the advantages of bottom-up development strategies.   **[4]**

    (d)   Explain **two** disadvantages of bottom-up development strategies.   **[4]**

    (e)   Explain **one** disadvantage of a top-down development strategy.   **[3]**

    (f)   Explain how a top-down development strategy in an LIDC you have studied has helped it to develop.   **[4]**

5   **CASE STUDY – Development in an LIDC**

    Name of LIDC: _____

    For an LIDC you have studied, to what extent do the benefits of TNCs operating there outweigh the problems?   **[8]**

6   **CASE STUDY – Development in an LIDC**

    Name of LIDC: _____

    For an LIDC you have studied, to what extent do the advantages of a top-down development strategy in that country outweigh the disadvantages?   **[6]**

7   **CASE STUDY – Development in an LIDC**

    Name of LIDC: _____

    For an LIDC you have studied, to what extent do the advantages of a bottom-up development strategy in that country outweigh the disadvantages?   **[6]**

Questions referring to previous content

8   **(a)**   What is the development gap?   **[1]**

    (b)   Outline **two** economic causes of unequal development.   **[4]**

Knowledge

22 What does the UK look like in the 21st century?

What are the UK's human characteristics?

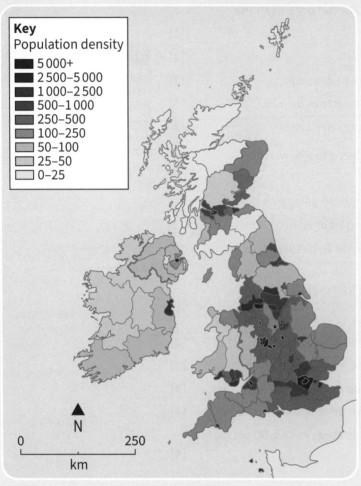

▲ **Figure 1** Population density in the UK

- The UK's population is nearly 68 million (2022).
- The **population density** is 281 per km², with England being the most **densely populated** country, and Scotland being the most **sparsely populated** (**Figure 1**).
- London has the highest number of people per square kilometre.
- Around 84% of people in the UK live in **urban** areas.
- More than half of the land in the UK is used for agriculture.
- Less than 6% of the UK is built on (**Figure 2**).

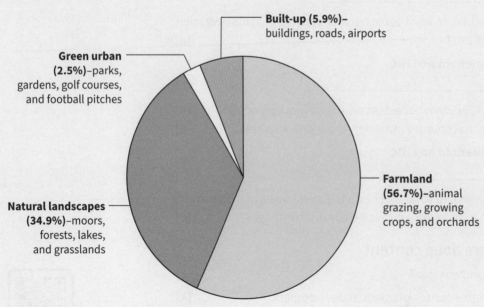

▲ **Figure 2** How land is used in the UK

What are the UK's physical characteristics?

- The UK has many varied landscapes and the **relief** of the land changes across the country (**Figure 3**).
- The UK's main mountainous areas are found in Scotland, North West England, and Central Wales.
- Many mountainous areas were shaped by ice travelling over the land during the last Ice Age.
- The land is flatter in South East England.
- There are areas of rolling hills in the south of England.
- The UK has a **temperate climate**.
- The UK's prevailing wind is from the south-west, which carries moist air from the ocean over the UK.
- The average annual rainfall varies from over 3 000 mm in Scotland to 553 mm in the East of England.
- Rainfall is highest in mountainous areas due to **relief rainfall (Figure 4)**.

LINK

To understand upland and lowland landscapes in the UK, refer to page 40.

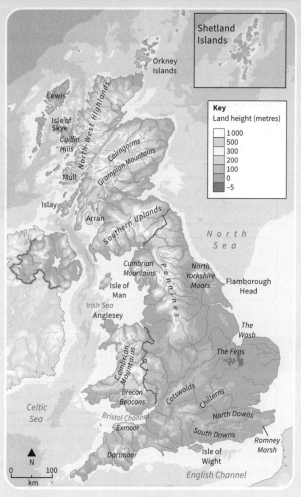

▲ *Figure 3 Relief map of the UK*

Warm air containing evaporated moisture from the ocean rises up over the mountains

The air cools, water vapour condenses and thick clouds form

REVISION TIP

If your Human Geography Fieldwork was an urban or rural geographical investigation, this would be a good time to revise it. Pages 178–181 will help.

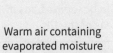

Atlantic Ocean

Air sinks on the leeward side of the mountain, and there is no rain, creating a rain shadow

Relief rain falls over the mountains

▲ *Figure 4 Relief rainfall in the mountainous areas of the UK*

⚙ Knowledge

How the UK's characteristics impact on housing

The UK's growing population needs more homes

New homes need to be affordable for people to buy or rent

The government is aiming to build 300 000 new homes a year

In 2020–2021 only 216 490 new homes were built, mainly due to delays due to the Covid-19 pandemic

The UK's housing shortage

Many consider the process for getting planning permission to build to be slow and expensive

There are fewer smaller housebuilding companies than in the past

There is a lack of available land – some around cities is green belt land, which can't be built on

How the UK's characteristics have led to water stress

UK water supplies are facing increasing pressure

Demand for water is highest in the more densely populated South East of England, but rainfall is lowest

Mountainous areas of Scotland and Central Wales have high levels of rainfall, but the lowest population density and low levels of **water stress**

The UK's water stress

In the warm, dry summer of 2022, the shortage of water resulted in hosepipe bans in many areas of the UK

Climate change will make rainfall more unpredictable, and summers hotter and drier, increasing the risk of water stress

▲ *Figure 5* *Baitings Reservoir with very low water levels during summer 2022: one of the hottest summers on record in the UK*

Key terms | **Make sure you can write a definition for these key terms**

densely populated   population density
relief   relief rainfall   sparsely populated
temperate climate   urban   water stress

WATCH OUT

Make sure you understand the meaning of 'water stress', a term used to describe the pressure on water supplies caused by demand exceeding, or threatening to exceed, supply.

Learn the answers to the questions below, then cover the answers column with a piece of paper and write down as many answers as you can. Check and repeat.

Questions · Answers

	Questions		Answers
1	What is the UK's population?		nearly 68 million
2	What percentage of people in the UK live in urban areas?	Put paper here	84%
3	Why does the UK have a housing shortage?		there is a growing population; not enough homes are being built; and there are not enough affordable homes
4	Why are housebuilding rates slower than needed in the UK?	Put paper here	the planning permission process can be slow and expensive; fewer smaller housebuilding companies; and lack of available land
5	What type of climate does the UK have?		temperate
6	Where in the UK is rainfall highest?	Put paper here	mountainous areas of North England, Scotland and Wales
7	Where in the UK is rainfall lowest?		South East England
8	What is water stress?	Put paper here	the pressure on water supplies caused by demand for water exceeding, or threatening to exceed, supply
9	What is a water deficit area?		when the area has a low water supply (rainfall) and a high population density
10	What is a water surplus area?	Put paper here	when the area has a high water supply (rainfall) and low population density

Previous questions · Answers

	Previous questions		Answers
1	What are the advantages of aid?		it can help to address global inequalities; ACs can help LIDCs; emergency aid saves lives during crises
2	What are the disadvantages of aid?	Put paper here	countries may become dependent on aid; aid may have conditions attached which benefit the donor; corrupt governments may not spend the aid money in the right way; giving money doesn't necessarily help countries to develop their own sources of income
3	What is life expectancy?		the average age to which people can expect to live
4	What are the main causes of death in LIDCs?		infectious diseases (e.g. HIV/AIDS, diarrhoea, tuberculosis)

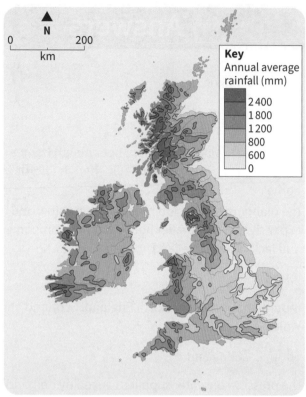

▲ *Fig. 1 – Rainfall map of the UK*

1   Study **Fig. 1**, which shows average rainfall in the UK.

  (a)   Identify **one** area of the UK with high average rainfall.   [1]

  (b)   Identify **one** area of the UK with low average rainfall.   [1]

EXAM TIP

Identify requires you to name an example, sometimes from a map, photo, or graph.

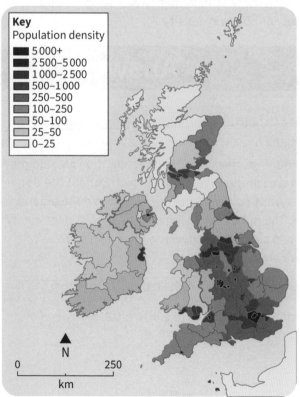

▲ *Fig. 2 – Population density in the UK*

2   Study **Fig. 2**, which shows population density in the UK.

    (a)   Identify **one** area of the UK which is densely populated.   **[1]**

    (b)   Identify **one** area of the UK which is sparsely populated.   **[1]**

3   **(a)**   **(i)**   What is the definition for an area in a 'water deficit'?

           A   Where rainfall is high and population density is high

           B   Where rainfall is high and population density is low

           C   Where rainfall is low and population density is low

           D   Where rainfall is low and population density is high

         Write the correct letter in the box. ☐   **[1]**

        (ii)   State one area of the UK which is in a water deficit.   **[1]**

    (b)   Using evidence from **Fig. 1** and **Fig. 2**, explain why some areas of the UK face water stress.   **[4]**

    (c)   Suggest one reason why water stress in the UK may get worse in the future.   **[3]**

4   **(a)**   Explain why rainfall varies around the UK.   **[3]**

    (b)   Explain how relief rainfall occurs.   **[4]**

> **EXAM TIP**
>
> **Explain** requires you to give reasons why something happens. The high number of marks available tells you that you need to include detail and supporting factual evidence.

5   **(a)**   What is the UK's population?

        A   6.8 thousand

        B   6.8 million

        C   68 million

        D   6.8 billion

      Write the correct letter in the box. ☐   **[1]**

    (b)   Which statement about the human characteristics of the UK is correct?

        A   Most people live in rural areas.

        B   The UK's population is shrinking.

        C   The most densely populated area is Scotland.

        D   London has the highest number of people per square kilometre.

      Write the correct letter in the box. ☐   **[1]**

    (c)   State the most common land use in the UK.   **[1]**

    (d)   Describe what green belt land is.   **[2]**

    (e)   Explain why there is a housing shortage in the UK.   **[6]**

Questions referring to previous content

6   **(a)**   State the main overriding aim of the UN's Millennium Goals.   **[1]**

    (b)   State any **three** of the eight Millennium Goals.   **[3]**

Knowledge

23 How is the UK's population changing?

21st century population growth trends

Since 2001, the UK's population has grown to nearly 68 million (2022). Trends in population change over time are known as **demographic transition**.

But what explains the UK's continuing population growth is not simply natural increase (births minus deaths). For example:

- most 21st century growth is due to **net migration** (the difference between immigration and emigration), particularly from Eastern Europe and Asia
- most immigrants are young, which in part accounts for rises in birth rates
- the UK has an increasingly ageing population, as people live longer.

No population trends (or future predictions) can be understood without consideration of **population structure** (the number of people in different age groups). For example, one challenge caused by the UK's ageing population is the extra strain on health and **social care** services.

The Demographic Transition Model

As a country develops, its population characteristics change. The Demographic Transition Model (DTM) uses birth and death rates to track how population changes over time (**Figure 1**). The DTM does not consider the impact of migration, which can cause a population to increase or decrease. For example, in 2021 there were 9.6 million people in the UK who were born abroad.

The UK is in Stage 4 of the DTM – only net migration stops it entering Stage 5.

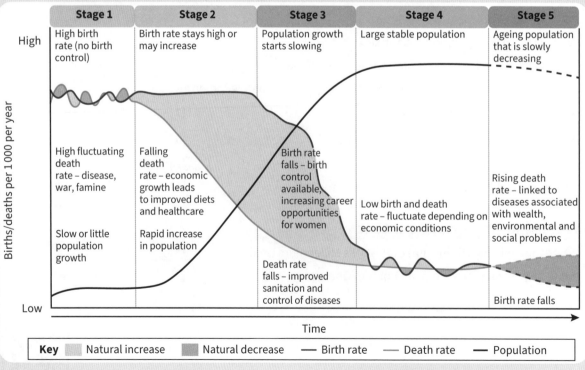

▲ **Figure 1** The Demographic Transition Model

Population structure

Countries at different stages of the DTM have different population structures – shown by **population pyramids** showing age and gender changes. The UK's population structure is shown in **Figure 2**.

Data on population structure is also used to calculate the **dependency ratio**. People aged under 16 or over 65 are dependents. The dependency ratio is the proportion of dependents to people of working age. The lower the ratio, the more workers there are to support dependents. The UK has falling numbers of children, but a greater increase in the numbers of older people, so its dependency ratio is slowly increasing.

$$\text{Dependency ratio} = \frac{\text{dependent population}}{\text{working population}} \times 100$$

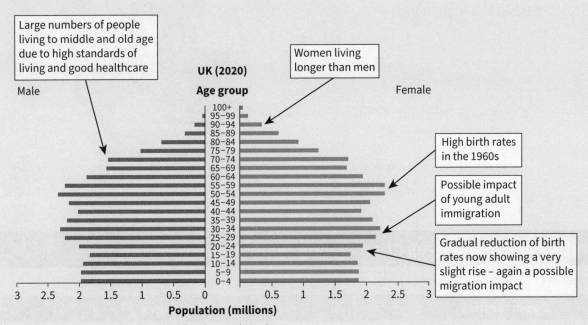

▲ **Figure 2** Population pyramid for the UK (2020)

Why is the UK's population ageing?

Life expectancy is increasing in the UK as a result of higher living standards overall.

Knowledge

23 How is the UK's population changing?

Why is the UK's population ageing?

Increased life expectancy is reflected in the UK's population distribution (**Figure 3**). Regions such as London and South East England attract many young people seeking economic, educational, and social opportunities, while other areas have a higher proportion of older age groups. Regions that tend to attract wealthier retired people tend to be more rural, with:

- warmer climates and a slower pace of life (such as South West England)
- attractive coastlines (such as North Norfolk).

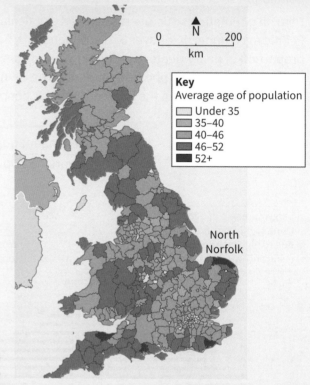

Key
Average age of population
☐ Under 35
▨ 35–40
▨ 40–46
▨ 46–52
■ 52+

North Norfolk

▶ *Figure 3 Spatial distribution of the UK population by age*

Opportunities and challenges of an ageing population

Increasing numbers of people living longer presents opportunities and challenges:

Opportunities	Challenges
• Elderly people can continue paying taxes by working part time • Elderly people can make huge contributions in voluntary work and child support • Wealthy elderly people have considerable spending power (the so-called **grey pound**) to boost local economies • Business opportunities targeting the elderly can thrive (e.g. specialist tourist travel)	• Increasing dependency ratio reflects a fall in economically active taxpayers – increasing the amount of taxes spent on pensions • Increasing demand for NHS and social care services • Increasing pressure on younger people to provide home support for elderly relatives • Economic costs of modifying infrastructure (e.g. public building and transport seating, elevated pavements, disabled access ramps, etc.)

Government responses to the UK's ageing population

- The retirement age (when people can get a state pension) is currently 66, and will increase further in future.

- Pensioners receive additional financial support (e.g. free prescriptions for ober-60s, bus passes, and winter fuel payments).
- NHS funding increases year on year.

Case study: Population change in Boston, Lincolnshire

Boston is a small market town in eastern England. In 2001, it had a population of around 56 000, of which 200 were non-UK born residents (mostly from Germany). However, since then its **ethnic diversity** has changed with the arrival of mainly young adult immigrants from the **European Union (EU)** countries of Eastern Europe coming to work in its agriculture and food processing industries. By 2011, Boston had the highest population (10%) of Eastern European residents of anywhere in the UK. As a result:

- some people perceived migrants to be 'taking' low paid jobs to the exclusion of locals
- the extra people added pressure to local services, such as healthcare and schools
- new shops, foods, and cultural traditions came into the area
- a higher birth rate helped to balance its ageing population.

Between 2011 and 2021, Boston's population increased by 9.1% to 70 500 – a rate higher than England overall (6.6%).

However, since the UK voted in 2016 to leave the EU (**Brexit**), many immigrants have returned to their home countries and the county's major farms and food processing factories have struggled to recruit workers.

▲ *Figure 4* Boston, Lincolnshire

WATCH OUT !

The UK voted to leave the EU in 2016, but it didn't actually leave until 2020, having been a member since 1973. In June 2016, 52% of UK voters voted to leave – 48% to stay a member. Boston recorded the highest leave vote (75%) in the UK.

SPECIFICATION TIP

You need a named example of a place in the UK where population structure and ethnic diversity has changed since 2001. A case study you may have studied is given here.

 Key terms Make sure you can write a definition for these key terms

Brexit   demographic transition   dependency ratio
ethnic diversity   European Union (EU)   grey pound
net migration   population pyramid   population structure
social care

Retrieval

Learn the answers to the questions below, then cover the answers column with a piece of paper and write down as many answers as you can. Check and repeat.

Questions | Answers

	Questions	Answers
1	What is demographic transition?	population change over time
2	What is population structure?	the number of males and females in a population, split into age groups – shown by population pyramids
3	What is the dependency ratio?	the proportion of people above and below normal working age
4	What are the reasons for the UK's ageing population?	improved health and social care; better diets; better living conditions; and improved lifestyles
5	What are the opportunities associated with the UK's ageing population?	elderly people can continue working part time, contribute to voluntary work and child support, and spend money in local economies and tailored business opportunities (e.g. specialist tourist travel)
6	What are the challenges associated with the UK's ageing population?	higher dependency ratios increasing the amount of taxes spent on pensions; increasing demand on health and social care services; pressure on younger people to support older relatives; and the economic costs of modifying infrastructure
7	What are the government responses to the UK's ageing population?	raising of retirement age; providing additional NHS funding and financial support (e.g. 'free' prescriptions and winter fuel payments)
8	What is meant by social care?	physical, emotional, and social support to help people live their lives
9	What is ethnic diversity?	the presence of people from a variety of cultural and ethnic backgrounds or identities

Put paper here

Previous questions | Answers

	Previous questions	Answers
1	Why are housebuilding rates slower than needed in the UK?	many consider the planning process to be slow and expensive; fewer smaller housebuilding companies; and lack of available land
2	What are the physical causes of uneven development?	extreme climatic and weather conditions; lack of clean water sources; landlocked countries cut off from sea trade; and harsh relief
3	What are the economic causes of uneven development?	poverty preventing improvements to education, infrastructure and living conditions; trade stacked in favour of richer countries

Put paper here

Exam-style questions

1 (a) (i)   In which stage or stages of the Demographic Transition Model (DTM) would you expect to find most EDCs, and why? [3]

(ii) Explain the economic impacts, and necessary responses, for a country being in Stage 5 of the DTM. [4]

(iii) Explain how a falling birth rate can reflect economic and social development. [3]

(iv) Evaluate to what extent the DTM represents a reliable indication of relative levels of economic and social development. [8]

(b) Explain how the UK's population has changed so far in the 21st century. [4]

> **EXAM TIP**
>
> **Evaluate** requires you weigh up the good and bad points to make a judgement. Likewise, **to what extent** requires you to judge the importance of something. Making judgements based on sound evidence from your understanding of the DTM is the key to successfully answering this question. Your spelling, punctuation, and grammar will also be assessed in this question.

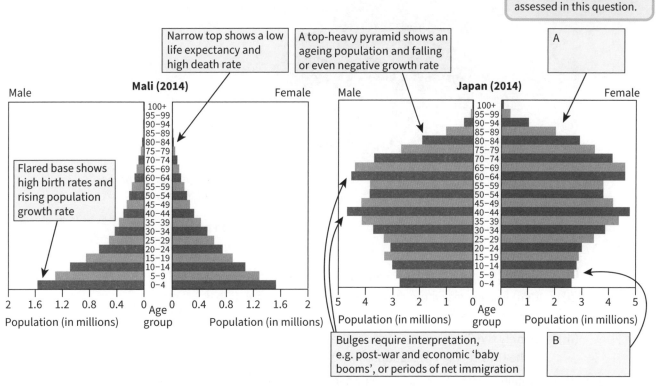

▲ *Fig. 1 – Population pyramids of Mali (left) and Japan (right)*

(c) Study **Fig.1**, which shows annotated population pyramids of countries at two different stages of development.

(i) Define the term 'population structure'. [2]

(ii) Complete the annotations for boxes A and B. [4]

> **EXAM TIP**
>
> **Labels** simply identify or name features (e.g. North Norfolk). **Annotations** include an explanation (e.g. concentration of ageing population in North Norfolk reflects people's desire to retire to the seaside). Each annotation is worth 2 marks.

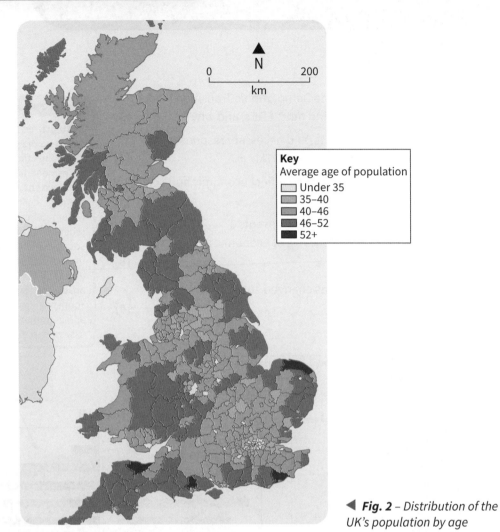

◀ **Fig. 2** – *Distribution of the UK's population by age*

2   **(a)**   Study **Fig. 2**, which shows the distribution of the UK's population by average age.

   (i)   Identify the cartographic (mapping) technique.   **[1]**

   (ii)   Identify **one** area where the average age of the population is under 40 years old.   **[1]**

   (iii)   Identify **two** key characteristics of the spatial distribution of the UK's ageing population.   **[2]**

   (b)   **(i)**   Explain how the UK's increasingly ageing population can create both opportunities and challenges.   **[6]**

   (ii)   Outline the government responses to the UK's ageing population.   **[4]**

   (c)   For a named place in the UK, explain the consequences of changing population structure and ethnic diversity and since 2001.   **[6]**

   Name of chosen place: _____

Questions referring to previous content

3   **(a)**   State **two** reasons for the shortage of housing in the UK.   **[2]**

   (b)   Outline why housebuilding rates are slower than needed in the UK.   **[3]**

24 How is the UK's economy changing?

Major economic changes in the UK since 2001

- The UK **unemployment rate** rose between 2001 and 2011 but fell to around 3.6% in July 2022.
- The highest unemployment rates are found in areas of the UK which previously relied on manufacturing, such as the north-east.
- The number of self-employed and part-time workers has increased.
- There has been an increase in people working in the **gig economy** and on **zero-hours contracts**.
- The average number of weekly hours worked has stayed the same for full-time workers and risen for part-time workers.
- The UK government's current priority is to create a more balanced economy by promoting growth in high-tech scientific and engineering manufacturing.
- They are also focusing on supporting 'green jobs' which involve sectors such as clean energy and sustainable buildings and transport.
- The closure of offices and workplaces during the Covid-19 **pandemic** of 2020–2021 meant that many people worked from home. The trend in **remote working** has continued – in 2022, more than one-third of people worked from home for at least one day a week.
- The UK government is focusing on helping the job market to recover from the Covid-19 pandemic and reduce unemployment.

> **REVISION TIP**
>
> Make sure that you are familiar with employment terms used frequently in media reporting on the UK economy – especially gig economy, zero-hours contracts, and remote working.

Core UK economic hubs

An economic hub is an area with a rapidly growing economy and many job opportunities. All this activity is associated with innovation and economic success. Examples of UK cities that are considered economic hubs include Aberdeen, Manchester, Cambridge, Oxford, London, Brighton, and Bristol. Many of these are concentrated in south-east England, so the UK government is encouraging investment outside of this region.

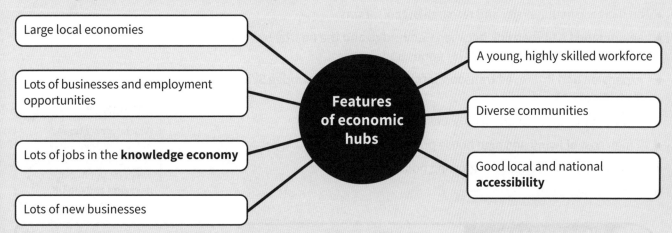

The connections between economic hubs are known as growth corridors – such as the M4 Corridor linking London to Bristol.

Knowledge

 ## Case study: Cambridge - an economic hub

Cambridge is one of the UK's economic hubs, located in eastern England. Known as 'Silicon Fen', it is Europe's largest cluster of high-tech businesses. In 'Silicon Fen', there are more than 5 000 businesses, employing 61 000 people and generating £15.5 billion a year.

SPECIFICATION TIP

You need one example of an economic hub in the UK. A case study you may have studied is given here.

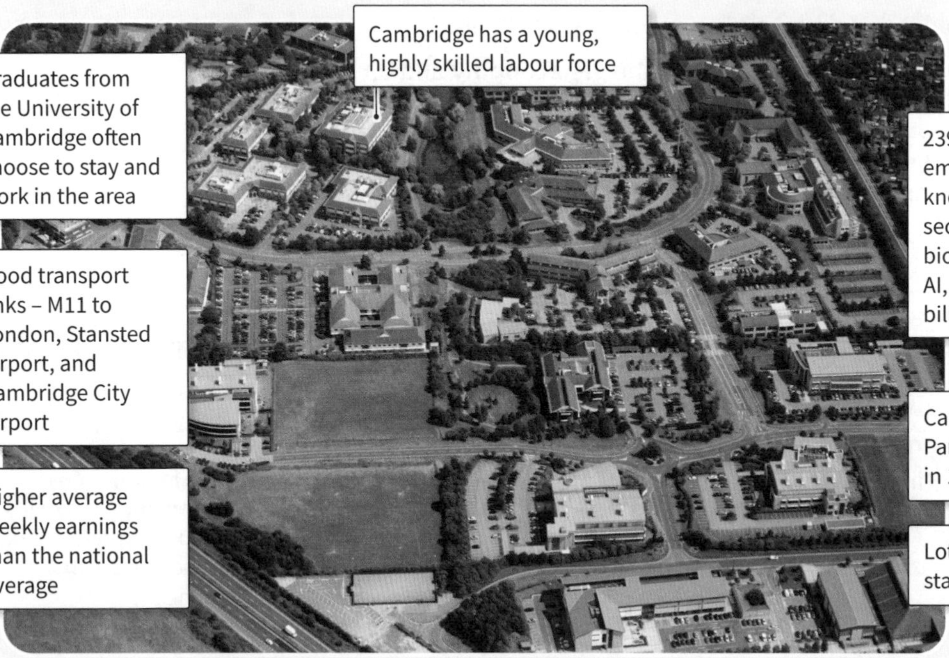

Graduates from the University of Cambridge often choose to stay and work in the area

Cambridge has a young, highly skilled labour force

239 000 people employed in 26 000 knowledge-intensive sectors – such as IT, biotechnology and AI, generating £50 billion of turnover

Good transport links – M11 to London, Stansted Airport, and Cambridge City Airport

Cambridge Science Park established in 1970

Higher average weekly earnings than the national average

Lots of new business start-ups

▲ **Figure 1** An aerial view of Cambridge Science Park

Cambridge - changes over time

Cambridge's economy grew by 7.6% in 2021. It was one of the quickest cities to recover from the Covid-19 lockdowns. Recent changes include:

- a significant increase in the number of jobs
- lots of new housing
- population growth of 6.9% between 2010 and 2020
- an increase in university and research organisations
- an upgraded A14 road link between Cambridge and the nearby town of Huntingdon to improve access for goods and people
- expansion and improved transport infrastructure for Cambridge Science Park (**Figure 1**).

However, Cambridge experiences issues with:

- a high cost of living and high house prices
- more homes needed for the growing population
- traffic congestion.

REVISION TIP

Whichever economic hub you studied, make sure you are able to write about its significance to its region and the UK.

 Key terms Make sure you can write a definition these key terms

accessibility   gig economy   knowledge economy   pandemic
remote working   unemployment rate   zero-hours contract

Learn the answers to the questions below, then cover the answers column with a piece of paper and write down as many answers as you can. Check and repeat.

Questions | Answers

#	Questions	Answers
1	What is a knowledge economy?	an economy associated with high-tech manufacturing, the service sector, and IT and communications
2	Where are the UK's highest unemployment rates found?	in areas of the UK which previously relied on manufacturing, such as the north-east
3	Since 2001, what aspects of the UK job market and working patterns have changed?	an increase in the number of people working part time; the gig economy; zero-hours contracts; remote working; self-employed people; and part-time hours
4	What is an economic hub?	an area with a rapidly growing economy, and many job opportunities – all associated with innovation and economic success
5	What are the key characteristics of the UK's economic hubs?	large local economies; lots of businesses and employment opportunities; knowledge economy focus; a young, highly skilled workforce; diverse communities; and good accessibility
6	What is Cambridge's key contribution to the national economy?	239 000 people employed; 26 000 knowledge-intensive businesses; £50 billion of turnover generated
7	How has Cambridge changed over time?	increase in the number of jobs, houses, population, university and research organisations; and improved accessibility and infrastructure
8	What issues does Cambridge face?	a high cost of living; high house prices; more homes needed for the growing population; and congestion

Put paper here

Previous questions | Answers

#	Previous questions	Answers
1	What is population structure?	the number of males and females in a population, broken down into age groups – shown by population pyramids
2	What is ethnic diversity?	the presence of people from a variety of cultural and ethnic backgrounds or identities
3	Which area of the UK is the most densely populated?	London
4	What is the majority of land used for in the UK?	farming

Put paper here

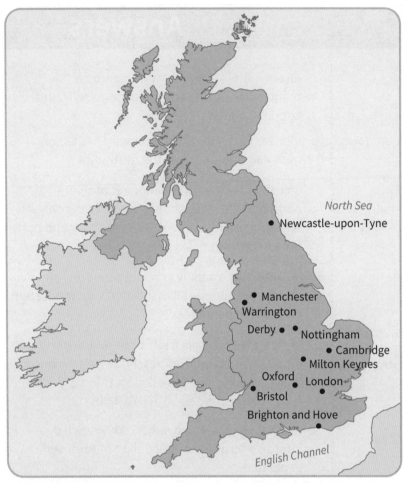

▲ **Fig. 1** – *Map showing some economic hubs in England*

1 **(a)** Study **Fig. 1**, a map showing some economic hubs in England.

  (i) What is the definition for an 'economic hub'?

  A A town or city where the economy is based on the secondary sector

  B A town or city where de-industrialisation has taken place

  C A town or city with a rapidly growing economy, and many job opportunities

  D A town or city experiencing depopulation and declining accessibility

  Write the correct letter in the box. ☐ **[1]**

  (ii) Describe the pattern of the economic hubs in England. **[3]**

  (iii) State **two** characteristics of England's economic hubs. **[2]**

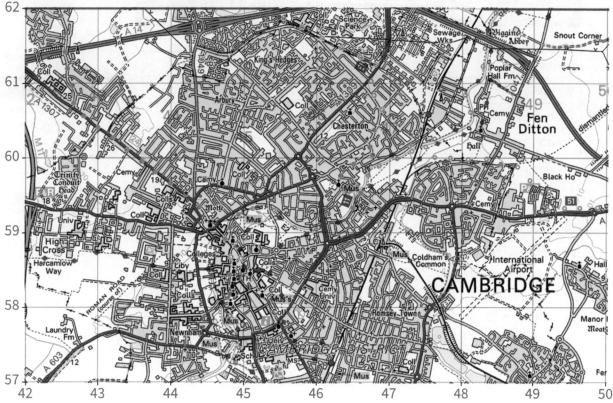

▲ **Fig. 2** – An OS map extract showing Cambridge, UK

2   Study **Fig. 2**, a 1:25 000 OS map extract which shows Cambridge, UK.

    (a)   State the four-figure grid reference for Cambridge Science Park.   **[1]**

    (b)   State the six-figure grid reference for the train station.   **[1]**

    (c)   The centre of Cambridge is in grid square 4558. In what direction
        is the international airport from Cambridge city centre?   **[1]**

    (d)   State the six-figure grid reference for the bus station in the
        centre of Cambridge.   **[1]**

    (e)   Using evidence from the map, explain why Cambridge is
        highly accessible.   **[4]**

3   **(a)**   Outline the features of **one** named UK economic hub.   **[4]**

    (b)   Examine the changes that have taken place in **one** named
        UK economic hub.   **[6]**

    (c)   Explain **two** problems faced by **one** named UK economic hub.   **[4]**

> **LINK**
>
> To understand Ordnance
> Survey maps, refer to
> page 189.

4   Study **Table 1** below, which shows economic measures for selected areas of England (2019).

Regions in England	GDP per capita (£)	Annual growth in GDP (%)
North East	24 068	0.9
North West	28 993	1.2
West Midlands	27 574	0
East of England	30 622	1.1
South East	35 631	1.6

▲ *Table 1*

LINK

To understand how to calculate the mean, refer to page 195.

(a)   Calculate the mean value for GDP per capita.   [1]

(b)   Which region has the highest GDP per capita?   [1]

(c)   Which region has the lowest annual growth in GDP?   [1]

(d)   State **one** data presentation method that could be used to show the GDP per capita data in the table above.   [1]

(e)   Using evidence from **Table 1** above and **Figure 1**, explain the variation in the UK economy.   [6]

EXAM TIP

Calculate means you need to work out the answer.

5   (a)   What is the 'tertiary sector'?

   A   Jobs in services, such as education, healthcare, and retail

   B   Jobs in research and IT

   C   Jobs in farming, mining, and fishing

   D   Jobs in manufacturing

   Write the correct letter in the box.   ☐   [1]

(b)   Define the term 'zero-hours contract'.   [2]

(c)   Explain how the UK's employment sectors have changed over time.   [4]

(d)   Explain **one** way in which the Covid-19 pandemic changed working patterns.   [2]

(e)   Examine the changes to the UK economy since 2001.   [6]

EXAM TIP

Examine requires you to investigate in detail – hence the high mark tariff. Be systematic in your answer – starting your comments about the nature of the economy in 2001 and then examining the progressive changes since.

Questions referring to previous content

6   (a)   Outline what accounts for most 21st century growth in the UK's population.   [2]

(b)   State **two** challenges resulting from your answer to (a).   [2]

25 What is the UK's political role in the world?

The UK's global significance

The UK has global significance through its membership of international organisations.

European Union (EU): The UK was a member of the EU from 1973 to 2020. In 2020, the UK and the EU signed a trade and cooperation agreement, which included a a **free trade** agreement and an agreement to cooperate on security matters. Freedom of movement between countries no longer exists. The UK is not subject to EU rules and regulations.

The Commonwealth: The UK is a key country within the 56 independent countries of the Commonwealth. The UK was one of the eight founding member countries of the Commonwealth in 1949. Members work together on issues such as democracy, trade, the environment, climate change, and gender equality.

G7 countries: The UK is one of seven members of this political group of the world's largest developed economies. The partners discuss major global issues and work closely together. The UK held the rotating presidency of the group in 2021.

The UK's links with international organisations

NATO: The UK is a founding member of the North Atlantic Treaty Organisation, an alliance of countries from Europe and North America whose 31 member countries consult and cooperate on defence and security.

United Nations (UN): The UN is the world's largest international organisation, founded in 1945 – the UK was one of the original member states. It aims to maintain international peace, protect human rights, deliver humanitarian aid, support sustainable development and climate action, and uphold international law. Today, it has 193 member states (**Figure 1**).

UN Security Council: The Security Council's primary responsibility is to maintain international peace and security. The UK is one of five permanent members of the Council, which may authorise peacekeeping missions, economic sanctions, and collective military action.

REVISION TIP

The UK left the EU in 2020, following a referendum in June 2016. It may take years for the UK to determine its new relationship with the EU, and for the consequences of Brexit to be fully established.

▲ *Figure 1 Flags of UN member states*

Case study: The conflict in Syria

Syria is a country in the Middle East, bordered by several countries including Turkey, Iraq, and Jordan, and with a coastline along the Mediterranean Sea (**Figure 2**). It was associated with the 'Arab Spring' in 2011, when mass protests against the government led to civil war. The UK originally supported the protests, but not after they were taken over by Islamist extremists wanting to establish their own state in the region. Several key dates demonstrate the complexity of the conflict since 2011:

- In 2011, the UK gave £18.4 million to Syria to supply shelter to refugees, clear mines, and provide medical care through the World Health Organisation (WHO).

- Since 2012, the UN Security Council has adopted 27 resolutions (formal statements) on Syria.

- In 2015, all members of the UN Security Council, including the UK, asked member states to take action against terrorist attacks in Syria.

- In 2018, the UK, with the US and France carried out missile strikes, which were later supported by the G7 leaders.

- Between 2012 and 2022, the UK gave £3.7 billion to 30 partners, including the UN and the Red Cross, to help the needs of people caught in the conflict.

> **SPECIFICATION TIP**
>
> You need to know the UK's political role in one global conflict through its participation in international organisations. A case study you may have studied is given here.

 Syria

▲ *Figure 2 Syria's location relative to Europe*

> **Key terms**
>
> **Make sure you can write a definition for these key terms**
>
> Commonwealth   free trade
> G7   NATO   UN
> UN Security Council   WHO

Learn the answers to the questions below, then cover the answers column with a piece of paper and write down as many answers as you can. Check and repeat.

Questions | Answers

	Question		Answer
1	What is the EU?	Put paper here	an economic and political union of 27 European countries designed to establish peace, common agreements, and laws – to promote trade, and remove economic and social barriers
2	When did the UK leave the EU?		2020
3	What is meant by the term Brexit?	Put paper here	an abbreviation of 'Britain' and 'exit' referring to the withdrawal process of the UK from the EU
4	What is the Commonwealth?	Put paper here	a group of 56 countries who work together on issues such as democracy, trade, the environment, climate change, and gender equality
5	What is G7?		a political group of seven advanced economies
6	What is NATO?	Put paper here	the North Atlantic Treaty Organisation, which focuses on defence and security
7	How many members of NATO are there?		31
8	What is the UN?	Put paper here	the United Nations, which aims to maintain international peace and cooperation
9	How many members of the UN are there?		193
10	What is the UN Security Council?	Put paper here	a body of the UN which has the authority to authorise peacekeeping missions, sanctions, and military intervention in other countries
11	What was the UK's role in Syria?		aid through the WHO; resolutions through the UN Security Council; missile strikes backed by the G7; aid through the UN and Red Cross

Previous questions | Answers

	Question		Answer
1	What is a service-based economy?	Put paper here	an economy where most people are employed in the tertiary sector
2	What are the key characteristics of the UK's economic hubs?	Put paper here	large local economies; lots of businesses and employment opportunities; knowledge economy focus; a young, highly skilled workforce; diverse communities; and good accessibility
3	What are the reasons for the UK's ageing population?		improved health and social care; better diets; better living conditions; and improved lifestyles

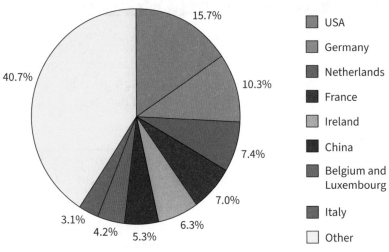

▲ **Fig. 1** – *The UK's major export destinations (2018)*

1   **(a)**   Study **Fig. 1**, the UK's major export destinations (2018).

   (i)   List the UK's top **three** export countries.   **[1]**

   (ii)   Calculate the total percentage of export trade going to the named European countries.

   A   17.7%

   B   24.7%

   C   27.8%

   D   38.3%

   Write the correct letter in the box.   ☐   **[1]**

(b)   Study the observations below, written in 2020, following Brexit.

A friendly divorce?

The UK was a member of the European Union from 1973 to 2020. Leaving the EU was a major decision taken following a referendum in June 2016. 52% of UK voters voted to leave – 48% to stay a member. While a free trade agreement has been reached with the EU, freedom of movement between countries no longer exists. Nor is the UK still subject to EU rules and regulations. However, since many working practices and standards (e.g. environmental, and health and safety) remain mutually beneficial, most are likely to continue.

> **EXAM TIP** ◎
>
> **Outline** requires you to summarise the key points, so keep your answer short and to the point.

   (i)   Outline what the EU is.   **[2]**

   (ii)   What is meant by the term 'Brexit'?   **[1]**

   (iii)   Suggest reasons why Brexit has been described as 'a friendly divorce'.   **[3]**

2   (a)   Which one of the following best describes the G7?

   A   The founding members of the Commonwealth

   B   A group of seven EU countries

   C   The group of countries on the UN Security Council

   D   A political group of seven advanced economies

   Write the correct letter in the box.   ☐   [1]

   (b)   State two international organisations of which the UK is a member.   [2]

   (c)   Explain the role that the UK plays within **two** international organisations.   [4]

   (d)   Examine the role of the UK in **one** global conflict through its participation in international organisations.   [6]

Questions referring to previous content

3   (a)   State **two** significant changes to the UK economy over the period 1950–2000.   [2]

   (b)   Outline the key changes to the UK economy since 2001.   [4]

> **EXAM TIP**
>
> Examine requires you to investigate in detail. Make sure that you include key events and dates in your examination.

⚙ Knowledge

26 How is the UK's cultural influence changing?

The UK's media exports

Many films and TV programmes that are created in the UK are watched globally.

- At its peak, motoring show *Top Gear* was shown in 214 countries around the world and many countries have produced their own versions.

- The TV show *Downton Abbey* has been shown in over 250 countries worldwide.

- The format of the TV show *The Great British Bake Off* has been reproduced in over 20 countries.

- The children's TV show *Peppa Pig* has been shown in 180 countries and *Peppa Pig* merchandise is sold all over the world.

▲ **Figure 1** *Cinema is one of the UK's major media exports*

- 147 countries watched the UK's *The X Factor* and 51 countries have made their own versions of the show.

- In 2019, UK films earned nearly £10 billion at the global box office.

- UK directors worked on 29 of the 200 highest earning films between 2011 and 2020.

Benefits to the UK from the TV and film industry

The UK TV and film industry contributes substantially to the national economy (**Figure 2**).

- In 2019/20, the UK earned £1.48 billion from the international sale of British TV programmes.

- The USA was the largest market for UK TV exports, followed by France and Australia.

- The core UK film industry contributes around £4.6 billion to the UK's GDP and over 117 000 jobs.

- The UK can attract international investment into productions from abroad, e.g. from the US (Hollywood) and India (Bollywood).

- The UK can promote its diverse cultural life through TV and film.

- Filming locations used in TV and film generated around £600 million in tourism in 2016.

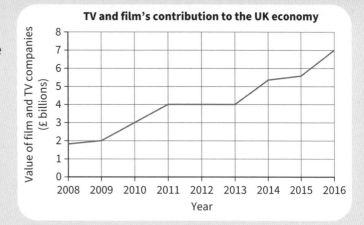

▲ **Figure 2** *Contribution the UK TV and film industry made to the national economy, 2008– 2016*

> **REVISION TIP**
>
> Make sure that you learn facts, examples, and supporting statistical data to refer to where relevant in the exam. Concentrate on two or three examples of most interest to you. Being 'invested' in any fact or example makes it far easier to remember.

Case study: Food — takeaways in the UK

One of the most obvious expressions of the UK's rich and diverse cultural heritage is its impact on what we eat. Our diets have changed markedly over the past 50 years, not least because:

- people earn more
- new delivery apps make it quicker and easier to order takeaway food
- people's lifestyles have changed and often they have less time to cook
- the media and travel have made us more aware of different cuisines
- increased **immigration** from around the world has introduced more cuisines to the UK.

SPECIFICATION TIP

You need an example of how ethnic groups contribute to the cultural life of the UK. A case study you may have studied is given here.

The takeaway industry contributed £18.9 billion to the economy in 2021

In 2022, Uber Eats was the most downloaded food delivery app in the UK

The takeaway delivery market was worth £10.5 billion to the economy in 2021

Average annual spend per person on takeaways is £641 (2021)

In 2021, the most popular takeaway cuisine was Chinese, followed by Indian

The number of takeaway restaurants has risen over the past 10 years, with only a slight decline during the Covid-19 pandemic

Indian cuisine in the UK

- Indian food was first sold at a café called Coffee House in London in 1773.
- The first Indian restaurants opened in London in the early 20th century when around 70 000 South Asians moved to the UK.
- In the 1940s and 1950s, large Indian restaurants in London employed sailors from Bangladesh.
- After the Second World War, many of these sailors bought cafés that had been abandoned during the war and began to sell curries instead of fish and chips, and pies.
- In the 1970s, more people came to the UK from India and Bangladesh and some opened catering businesses. The number of restaurants grew rapidly (**Figure 3**).

▲ **Figure 3** Indian food is a familiar takeaway in the UK

Key terms Make sure you can write a definition for these key terms: immigration   media

LINK

To understand the impact of migration on the UK's population, refer to page 136.

Retrieval

Learn the answers to the questions below, then cover the answers column with a piece of paper and write down as many answers as you can. Check and repeat.

Questions | Answers

#	Question	Answer
1	What are the UK's media exports?	TV programmes and film made in the UK that are sold and watched all around the world
2	What are some examples of UK TV programmes which have been successful abroad?	*Top Gear; Downton Abbey; The Great British Bake Off; Peppa Pig; The X Factor*
3	What is the main benefit of the TV and film industry for the UK?	it contributes substantially to the national economy
4	How much did the UK earn from the international sale of TV programmes in 2019/20?	£1.48 billion
5	How many people are employed in the core UK film industry?	over 117 000
6	Where can international investment in UK productions come from?	Hollywood, USA and Bollywood, India
7	What is the benefit of using filming locations based in the UK?	it generates money in the tourism industry
8	What are the economic and social reasons why eating habits in the UK have changed over the past 50 years?	people earn more; new delivery apps make it quicker and easier to order takeaway food; people's lifestyles have changed and often they have less time to cook
9	What are the cultural reasons why eating habits in the UK have changed over the past 50 years?	the media and travel have made us more aware of different cuisines; increased immigration from around the world has introduced more cuisines to the UK
10	What are the UK's top three most popular takeaway cuisines?	Chinese, Indian and fish and chips
11	How much does the takeaway industry contribute to the UK economy?	£18.9 billion

Put paper here

Previous questions | Answers

#	Question	Answer
1	What is the UN?	the United Nations, which aims to maintain international peace and cooperation
2	What is the UN Security Council?	a body of the UN which has the authority to authorise peacekeeping missions, sanctions, and military intervention in other countries
3	What is a pandemic?	an epidemic occurring over a very wide area, crossing international boundaries and usually affecting a large number of people
4	What is a service-based economy?	an economy where most people are employed in the tertiary sector

Put paper here

Exam-style questions

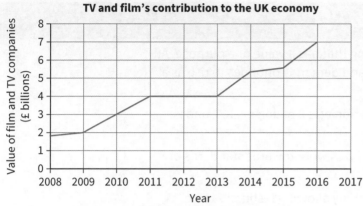

▲ *Fig. 1 – TV and film's contribution to the UK economy*

1   **(a)**   Study **Fig.1**, which shows how the contribution of the TV and film industry to the UK economy has changed over time.

   (i)   The industry contributed £8 billion to the UK economy in 2017. Complete the graph to show the data for 2017.   **[1]**

   (ii)   Calculate the percentage increase in the amount of money contributed to the UK economy between 2011 and 2016. Show your working.   **[2]**

   (iii)   Describe the trend in the amount of money that TV and film contributes to the UK economy.   **[3]**

> **LINK**
>
> To understand how to calculate a percentage increase, refer to page 195.

2   **(a)**   Which one of the following best describes the term 'immigration'?

   A   The act of coming to live permanently in a foreign country

   B   Leaving your own country to settle permanently in another

   C   The difference between people arriving and people leaving a country

   D   Moving from a rural area to an urban area

   Write the correct letter in the box.   ☐   **[1]**

   (b)   State **two** reasons for the increase in popularity of takeaway food in the UK.   **[2]**

   (c)   Explain **two** ways in which takeaway food is important to the UK economy.   **[4]**

   (d)   Explain the contribution of ethnic groups to the cultural life of the UK through food.   **[6]**

3   **(a)**   Explain the global influence of the UK's media exports.   **[6]**

   (b)   Examine the benefits of the UK media industry for the UK.   **[6]**

> **EXAM TIP**
>
> **Examine** requires you to investigate in detail. Make sure that you include named examples and supporting statistics in your answer.

Questions referring to previous content

4   **(a)**   Define the term 'service-based economy'.   **[1]**

   (b)   Outline the difference between a service-based economy and a knowledge economy.   **[2]**

Knowledge

27 Will the world run out of natural resources?

The world's key resources

A **resource** is a stock or supply of something that has a value or a purpose. All natural resources are currently overused, and demand continues to rise as a result of:

- population growth – the world's population was 8 billion in 2022 and is expected to rise to 9.3 billion by 2050
- economic development – as LIDCs and EDCs work towards standards of living enjoyed in ACs
- finite supply – despite improved technology allowing resources to be exploited in challenging environments (e.g. oil in Alaska, USA).

Globally, the three most important resources are food, water, and energy (**Figure 1**). But these are distributed unevenly across the world:

- Most ACs have plentiful supplies – and use far more than poorer countries.
- Many LIDCs lack supplies – and struggle to meet their peoples' food, water, and energy needs.

 REVISION TIP

Think about food, water, and energy resources in terms of the relationships between demand and supply.

Resource	Global importance	Global inequalities
Food	Daily calorie intake for growth, health, and productivity: 2000 calories for women, 2500 for men	<ul><li>Over a billion people are undernourished (below the recommended level)</li><li>A further two billion are **malnourished** (suffering undernutrition or overnutrition)</li><li>Obesity (overnutrition) is an increasing problem in ACs</li></ul>
Water	Vital for drinking, and producing crops and energy	<ul><li>Climate and rainfall variations affect water supply</li><li>Rainwater capture, storage (e.g. **reservoirs**), and extraction (e.g. pumping underground aquifers) is expensive – so more likely in ACs</li><li>Many of the world's poorest LIDCs suffer **water scarcity**</li></ul>
Energy	<ul><li>Energy is required for economic development</li><li>Energy powers factories and machinery, and provides fuel for transport</li><li>Energy is traded worldwide</li></ul>	<ul><li>The world's richest countries use far more energy than poorer countries (e.g. the wealthiest 10% of the world's population consumes 20 times more energy than the poorest 10%)</li><li>As EDCs become more industrialised, the demand for energy will increase</li></ul>

▲ **Figure 1** Global inequalities in availability of food, water, and energy

How environments and ecosystems are affected by demand for resources

Mechanisation of farming

To meet the demands for food for a growing world population, farming has changed from subsistence (where farmers grow crops and livestock to feed their families) to mechanised (where machinery replaces human labour, leading to large-scale commercial farming). This is particularly true in ACs.

Impacts of mechanisation of farming

While mechanised farming is more efficient, it has negative impacts on ecosystems and the environment (**Figure 2**).

Use of chemical fertilisers, pesticides and herbicides (agrochemicals) to increase food production pollute water sources (e.g. rivers, ponds, and lakes) disrupting ecosystems.

Reduced biodiversity:
- Hedgerow destruction (to make fields big enough for large machines) disrupts ecosystems and destroys wildlife habitats and their movement corridors.
- Crop monoculture (where only one crop is grown at one time in a field) leads to less diversity of plants, insects, and animals nearby.

Soil problems:
- Larger fields result in increased exposure to wind and rain causing soil erosion and leaching.
- Heavy machinery (tractors, combine harvesters, etc.) compact field entrances and plough lines leading to waterlogging.

Increased irrigation:
- Generates huge demands on freshwater supplies, with more irrigation required during periods of drought, leading to water stress.
- Needs careful management to reduce risk of waterlogging.

▲ *Figure 2 The impacts of mechanisation on environments and ecosystems*

Mechanisation of commercial fishing

Fish consumption has increased markedly since the 1950s. Global production of fish and seafood has quadrupled over the last 50 years, with about 200 million tonnes produced each year.

Millions of people depend on fish as a major source of nutritious food. Commercial fishing involves:

- fish farming in indoor pools and (mostly) sea cages
- large trawlers with huge nets sweeping through the sea or across the seabed (**Figure 3**).

Impacts of mechanisation on fishing

Commercial fishing seriously impacts marine environments and ecosystems.

- Farmed fish are prone to disease which can spread to surrounding ecosystems.
- Large trawler nets catch everything in their path, leading to unwanted species (e.g. dolphins and turtles) getting caught as **by-catch** which are then thrown back into the sea alive or dead.
- Fine-mesh nets catching smaller fish (of little commercial value) reduce fish stocks because they do not grow to maturity.
- Overfishing – over one-third of fish stocks annually are fished beyond their capacity for replacement through natural reproduction.

▲ *Figure 3 The Grateful, Fraserburgh, is a trawler that launched in 2016 with sophisticated fish-finding sonar technology, and the capacity for huge catches*

> **LINK**
>
> To understand more general sustainable management issues, such as in polar environments, refer to page 85.

Deforestation to provide energy

Deforestation – particularly in tropical rainforests, but also coniferous forest (taiga) biomes – has in part occurred due to exploitation of fossil fuels like coal, oil, and gas. The impacts of deforestation on woodland ecosystems, and the many habitats that exist on the ground and in the trees include:

> **LINK**
>
> To understand the impact of deforestation on climate change, refer to pages 33 and 81.

Reduced biodiversity: with losses of undiscovered plant species and their potential value and importance (e.g. medicinal applications)

The impacts of deforestation

Soil erosion: by wind and rain because the ground was previously shaded, and the soil bound together by the roots of trees and plants

Climate change: by reducing photosynthesis, transpiration, and the cooling effect of evaporation. Consequently, there is less moisture to condense into clouds, and higher temperatures. The 'double negative' of fewer trees (creating a carbon sink) absorbing CO_2 and burning the wood increasing emissions of CO_2, adds to the greenhouse effect

Mining to provide energy

Mining, whether for energy or minerals, is most associated with impacts on air quality (e.g. dust) and the landscape damaged (e.g. spoil heaps). But it also has huge impacts on ecosystems and the wider environment. For example:

- Open-cast mining for coal involves whole-scale stripping of vegetation and topsoil – destroying animal habitats and disrupting ecosystems (**Figure 4**). Pollution of groundwater aquifers (from chemicals used in mining operations) can also occur.

- **Fracking** for shale oil and gas has the potential to trigger small earthquakes and pollute groundwater from the toxic chemicals used in the drilling and injection process.

▲ *Figure 4 Grasberg mine, an open-cast mine in Indonesia*

Providing enough water

Global water consumption is expected to increase 20–30% by 2050 due to:

- population growth
- economic development
- increased demands for food
- increased urbanisation (increasing demand for drinking water, sanitation, and industry).

So, water supply will need to be increased. Two options are dams and reservoirs and **water transfer schemes**. However, while they bring more water, they interfere with the balance of river systems (**Figure 5**).

> **REVISION TIP**
>
> If you are asked to discuss how water supply can be increased, strengthen your points by making references to located examples whenever relevant.

Scheme	What it does	Impact
Dams and reservoirs	Dams control river water flow by creating reservoirs. Multi-purpose schemes (e.g. the Three Gorges Dam in China) provide water (e.g. irrigation, industrial and domestic), HEP, and flood control – but are expensive to build, displace many people, and lose capacity through evaporation and silting.	• Flood existing vegetation, soils, and so animal habitats • Block fish migration routes • Prevent natural flooding downstream, changing floodplain ecosystems
Water transfer	Redistributes water from areas of surplus to areas of deficit using pipelines and canals (e.g. pipelines from Wales to the English midlands).	• Can transfer invasive species of plants and animals – threatening and unbalancing existing ecosystems • Can cause nutrient imbalances – for example excess nutrients promoting excessive algae growth

▲ *Figure 5 Water schemes – and their impact on the ecosystem and wider environment*

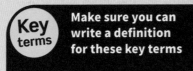

Key terms — Make sure you can write a definition for these key terms

by-catch   fracking   malnourished   reservoir
resource   water scarcity   water transfer scheme

Retrieval

Learn the answers to the questions below, then cover the answers column with a piece of paper and write down as many answers as you can. Check and repeat.

Questions | Answers

	Questions	Answers
1	What is a resource?	a stock or supply of something that has a value or a purpose
2	What are the world's three most important resources?	food, water, and energy
3	What is malnutrition?	an inadequately balanced diet whether through undernutrition or overnutrition
4	What is water scarcity?	severe water stress – when water supplies fall below 1000 m³ per person
5	What is overfishing?	when more fish of a particular species are caught than can be replaced through natural reproduction
6	What are fossil fuels?	a natural fuel such as coal, oil, or gas, formed in the geological past from the remains of living organisms
7	What is meant by pollution?	the introduction of harmful materials into the environment
8	What is fracking?	'hydraulic fracturing' of oil- and gas-bearing shale by drilling, then high-pressure injection of water, sand, and toxic chemicals
9	What is a reservoir?	an artificial lake where water is stored – mostly formed by constructing dams across rivers
10	What is meant by a water transfer scheme?	an infrastructure project for moving water from areas of surplus to areas of shortage

Put paper here

Previous questions | Answers

	Previous questions	Answers
1	What are the UK's media exports?	TV programmes and films made in the UK that are sold and watched all around the world
2	What are the cultural reasons why eating habits in the UK have changed over the past 50 years?	the media and travel have made us more aware of different cuisines; increased immigration from around the world has introduced more cuisines to the UK
3	What has happened to the amount of people employed in the primary sector in the UK since 1800?	it has fallen
4	What has happened to the amount of people employed in the secondary sector in the UK since 1800?	it rose to a peak during the Industrial Revolution, but has since fallen

Put paper here

Exam-style questions

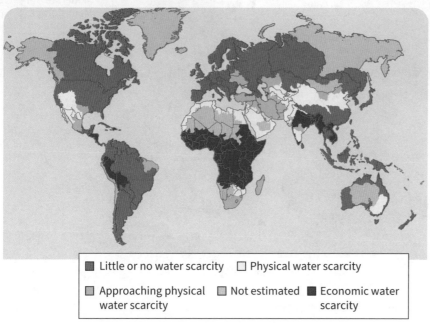

Little or no water scarcity ☐ Physical water scarcity

☐ Approaching physical ☐ Not estimated ☐ Economic water
   water scarcity   scarcity

▲ **Fig. 1** – *Projected areas of water scarcity by 2025*

1 (a) Study **Fig. 1**, which shows projected areas of water scarcity by 2025.

   (i)   What is meant by the term 'water scarcity'?   [2]

   (ii) Describe the distribution of the areas experiencing
         physical water scarcity.   [2]

   (b) Outline global inequalities in the availability of food and water. [6]

   (c) (i)   Which one of the energy sources below would best be described
             as a fossil fuel?

             A biomass

             B solar

             C natural gas

             D nuclear

             Write the correct letter in the box. ☐   [1]

        (ii) 'Fracking is now the most important source of oil and
              gas in the USA but banned in the UK'.
              Outline why fracking is so controversial.   [4]

        (iii) Describe global inequality in the use and availability
              of energy.   [4]

        (iv) Evaluate the environmental impacts of deforestation
              and mining to produce energy.   [8]

   (d) Describe the impacts of mechanised commercial farming on
        environments and ecosystems.   [6]

   (e) Explain the impacts of mechanised commercial fishing on ocean
        ecosystems.   [6]

> **EXAM TIP**
>
> **Describe** requires
> you to give the main
> characteristics of
> something. (No
> explanation is needed.)

> **EXAM TIP**
>
> **Evaluate** normally requires
> you to weigh up the good
> and bad points to make a
> judgement. Given the high
> mark tariff, the discussion
> should be comprehensive,
> include detail, and
> justify your opinions. Be
> organised in structuring
> your answer – deal with
> deforestation and mining
> separately.

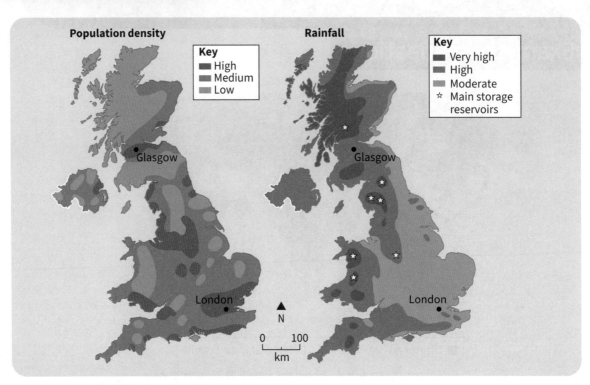

▲ *Fig. 2* UK population density and water supply

2   (a)   Study **Fig. 2** which shows UK population density and water supply.

     (i)   State whether Glasgow is likely to have a water
surplus or deficit.   [1]

     (ii)   State whether London is likely to have a water
surplus or deficit.   [1]

     (iii)   Explain the need for water transfers in the UK.   [2]

Water use	2030 (% change)	2050 (% change)
Agricultural	–3.6	–6.9
Industrial	+53.3	+119.8
Domestic	+36.5	+65.1

▲ Table 1

LINK

To understand how to calculate the range of data, refer to page 195.

(b) Study **Table 1**, which shows predicted trends in water use to 2030 and 2050.

   (i) Calculate the range in percentage change for 2030.   **[1]**

   (ii) Use the data in **Table 1** to complete the bar graph showing the

EXAM TIP

Calculate means work out.

LINK

To understand bar graphs, refer to page 189.

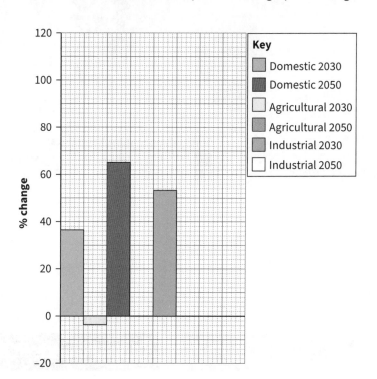

positive and negative trends.   **[2]**

   (iii) Suggest reasons why water use is expected to increase at a high rate in the industrial and domestic sectors.   **[4]**

   (iv) Outline **two** measures to increase water supply.   **[4]**

Questions referring to previous content

3 **(a)** The UK is a leading member of the Commonwealth. Outline the origins **and** functions of this international organisation.   **[3]**

   (b) Identify **and** outline the functions of **two** other international organisations the UK is an important member of.   **[4]**

EXAM TIP

Identify requires you to name an example, sometimes from a map, photo, or graph.

Knowledge

28 Will we be able to feed everyone by 2050?

What is food security?

Food security means having access to enough safe, affordable, and nutritious food to maintain a healthy and active life. Some countries have a food surplus. Most, however, do not produce enough to feed their people, and rely on imported food (a food deficit). Some of these countries also experience food insecurity as illustrated by the Global Hunger Index (**Figure 1**). This index ranges from 0 (no hunger) to 100 (the most hunger) using a range of indicators including:

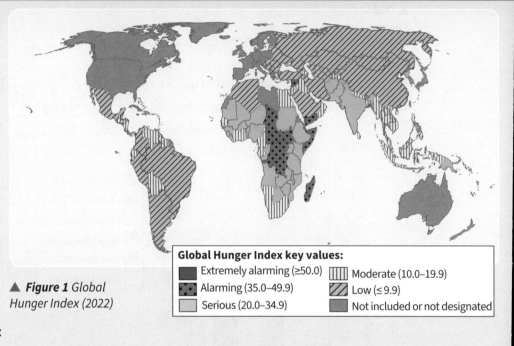

▲ *Figure 1* *Global Hunger Index (2022)*

Global Hunger Index key values:

- ■ Extremely alarming (≥50.0)
- ▨ Alarming (35.0–49.9)
- ▨ Serious (20.0–34.9)
- ▥ Moderate (10.0–19.9)
- ▨ Low (≤9.9)
- ■ Not included or not designated

- undernourishment
- the proportion of underweight and short children
- child mortality (deaths under five years old).

Human and physical

Factors affecting food security	
Human	**Physical**
• Poverty – the world's poorest people cannot afford technology, irrigation, or agrochemicals.	• Climate – regions experiencing extreme temperatures and rainfall struggle to produce food.
• Conflict – can lead to the destruction of crops and livestock.	• Pests and diseases – spread north and south from the Tropics.
• Dietary changes – especially increasing demand for meat and proteins.	• Water stress – lack of water affects many areas that suffer food scarcity.
• Population growth – by 2050 global population is expected to reach 9.3 billion.	• Soil – the type of crops that can be grown depends on the quality of the soil.
• Technology – especially in ACs, mechanisation of farming allows high levels of productivity.	

Global trends in food supply

- We currently produce enough food to supply everyone on the planet – but it is not distributed evenly.
- Many people in ACs exceed their daily food needs (calorie intake) – and obesity (overnutrition) is an increasing problem.
- Average food consumption in poorer areas (such as sub-Saharan Africa) does not reach the recommended daily intake of 2 000–2 500 calories.
- Cereals (e.g. rice and wheat) form a **staple crop** for most of the world's population, with climatic conditions influencing which crops grow best.
- Global food demand is expected to increase by over 60% by 2050.

The relationship between population and food supply

Will the world have enough food in future to cope with the rising demands of more people?

This is a question going back to the late 18th century – and revisited many times since. In 1798, the Reverend Thomas Malthus gloomily suggested that as population grows geometrically (2, 4, 8, 16, 32, …) – doubling every 25 years – food supply growing arithmetically (2, 4, 6, 8, 10, …) would not keep up. Eventually, there would be too many people to feed and population numbers would crash through:

- 'positive' checks, such as **famine**, war, and disease

- preventative checks, such as people marrying later and having fewer children.

A think tank called the Club of Rome re-introduced this neo-Malthusian view in the 1970s, widening the perspective to resources in general. Even today, some scientists fear 'a perfect storm' of resources running out by 2030.

Counter-arguments are more optimistic, and were first proposed by Ester Boserup in the 1960s. They are based on the argument that 'necessity is the mother of invention' and so agricultural innovations will ensure that no matter how many people there are, we will find ways to meet their needs.

Look at **Figure 2**. Whether neo-Malthusians or Boserupians are right is the big question. And in future – who knows? But advances in agricultural innovation are extraordinary and include:

- **biotechnology** – the controversial modification of products or processes including the development of genetically modified (GM) crops

- aeroponics and hydroponics using modern scientific techniques to grow crops without soil in artificially lit and heated greenhouses – the former using nutrient-rich water sprays, and the latter using mineral-rich-rich water in gravel.

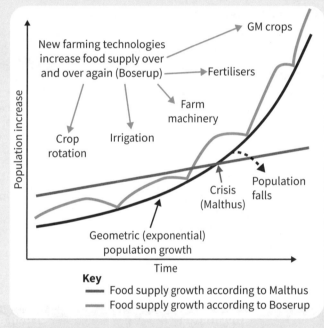

▲ *Figure 2* *Neo-Malthusian and Boserupian theories compared*

> **REVISION TIP**
>
> Remember, both neo-Malthusian and Boserupian theories could be right. So be prepared to discuss both perspectives in your answers.

Famine

Famine is the most severe impact of food insecurity – causing malnutrition, undernutrition, weakened immune systems, starvation, and death.

Famine in Somalia (2010–2012): 258 000 people died following two successive seasons of low rainfall, poor harvests, and livestock deaths. In southern and central regions, the crisis was made worse by the al-Shabab militant group blocking aid from humanitarian agencies (**Figure 3**).

▶ *Figure 3* *Somalian refugees line up to receive aid*

 Knowledge

28 Will we be able to feed everyone by 2050?

Case study: Food security in the UK

Despite most people in the UK enjoying food security, average calorie intake has decreased by around 20% since the 1980s – and yet obesity levels have risen! This is because people generally lead more sedentary lifestyles (sitting more in work and social activities) and many do insufficient exercise. Our food consumption has changed significantly in recent years as people seek:

- greater variety (e.g. exotic high-value foods from abroad)
- year-round availability (out-of-season produce)
- healthier options (e.g. **organic produce**).

Around half of the UK's food is produced in Britain, and the rest is imported. But importing food has environmental costs in terms of the distances covered ('**food miles**', **Figure 4**) and its **carbon footprint**. Two contrasting trends result from this:

- modern, mechanised, intensive, commercial agribusinesses maximise production
- locally sourced food goes directly to the public through farm shops, farmers' markets, and 'pick your own' – reducing food miles and carbon footprints.

SPECIFICATION TIP

You need a named example of attempts to achieve food security in one country. A case study you may have studied is given here.

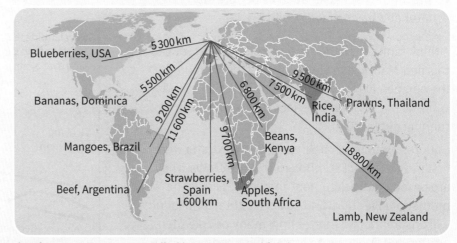

▲ **Figure 4** Distances travelled by UK imported food

Local strategies for achieving food security in the UK

Allotments	Urban gardens	Food banks

• Allotments for non-commercial crop production in urban areas have been features of UK towns and cities for over 200 years.
• Protected from development, allotments are hugely popular among all age groups wanting affordable, fresh, home-grown produce.
• The average wait for an allotment is at least 18 months.
	• This is the cultivation, processing, and distribution of food in and around settlements. Benefits include:
	  o job creation
	  o improved urban environments
	  o wildlife attraction
	  o communities coming together.
	• An inspiring example is the Incredible Edible Todmorden initiative in West Yorkshire.
		• Food banks are run by charities to give 3-days' worth of food for people and families struggling with the cost of living.
		• Social workers, health visitors and doctors issue food bank vouchers for those most in need.
		• Since 2014, food bank usage has doubled – to 2.2 million in 2022.

Key terms Make sure you can write a definition for these key terms

allotment biotechnology carbon footprint famine food bank food miles food security organic produce staple crop urban garden

Learn the answers to the questions below, then cover the answers column with a piece of paper and write down as many answers as you can. Check and repeat.

Questions | Answers

	Questions	Answers
1	What is food security?	having access to enough safe, affordable, and nutritious food to maintain a healthy and active life
2	What is food insecurity?	when a country can't supply enough food (home grown and imported) to feed its population
3	What is water stress?	where demand for water exceeds supply in a certain period or when poor quality restricts its use
4	What is a staple crop?	the major part of a diet – supplying the main proportion of energy and nutrient needs
5	Why is global food demand expected to increase by over 60% by 2050?	population growth; economic development and higher standards of living; greater availability of food; and dietary changes
6	What factors negatively affect food security?	extreme climates; lack of technology; pests and diseases; poor soils; poverty (restricting use of irrigation or agrochemicals); water stress; and conflict
7	What is biotechnology?	the modification of products or processes including the development of genetically modified (GM) crops
8	What are food miles?	the distances covered supplying food to consumers (e.g. foods imported into the UK)
9	What is the carbon footprint?	measurement of the greenhouse gases individuals produce through burning fossil fuels (e.g. cultivating and transporting food)
10	What are urban gardens?	the practice of cultivating, processing, and distributing food in or around urban areas – also called urban farming

Put paper here

Previous questions | Answers

	Previous questions	Answers
1	What is malnutrition?	an inadequately balanced diet whether through undernutrition or overnutrition
2	What is overnutrition?	when people eat too much – globally a more serious health risk than eating poorly
3	Where are the UK's highest unemployment rates found?	in areas of the UK which previously relied on manufacturing, such as the north-east
4	Since 2001, what aspects of the UK job market and working patterns have changed?	an increase in the number of people working part-time; the gig economy; zero-hours contracts; remote working; self-employed people; and part-time hours

Put paper here

Practice

Exam-style questions

▲ **Fig. 1** – Global food consumption (in calories)

1 **(a)** Study **Fig. 1**, global food consumption (in calories).

    (i) Which **one** of statements below is correct?

        A Daily calorie intake is lower in North America than in South America.

        B Daily calorie intake in Australia is 2 850–3 269 calories.

        C Daily calorie intake in sub-Saharan Africa averages 2 850–3 269 calories.

        D Daily calorie intake is higher in Asia than in Europe.

        Write the correct letter in the box. ☐ [1]

    (ii) Describe the global pattern of food consumption (in calories). [3]

> **EXAM TIP**
>
> **Describe** requires you to give the main characteristics of something. (No explanation is needed.)

(b) What is meant by the term 'food security'? [2]

(c) Describe **three** physical factors affecting food security. [6]

(d) Outline the benefits of urban garden initiatives. [4]

> **EXAM TIP**
>
> **Outline** requires you to summarise the key points. However, given the number of marks available, a located example could be included.

(e) **CASE STUDY – attempts to achieve food security in one country.**

Name of chosen country: _____

Describe a strategy or strategies adopted to achieve food security at a local scale. [6]

Study **Table 1**, changes in the Global Food Security Index (GFSI) 2019–2020 for selected countries.

Country	Change 2019–2020 (%)
Haiti	+4.7
Ukraine	+2.7
Romania	+2.6
Guinea	-3.1
Egypt	-4.3

▲ Table 1

Of the 113 countries assessed, Finland records the highest GFSI score (85.3) and Yemen the lowest (35.7).

2 (a) Calculate the range between the highest GFSI score (Finland) and the lowest (Yemen). [1]

(b) Define the term 'food insecurity'. [2]

(c) Describe **two** human factors affecting food security. [4]

(d) Outline how aeroponics and hydroponics can be used to increase food supply. [4]

(e) Explain the theories of neo-Malthusians about the relationship between population and food resources. [4]

(f) Explain how Boserupians view the relationship between global population and food resources. [4]

LINK
To understand how to calculate the range of data, refer to page 195.

EXAM TIP
Explain requires you to give reasons why something happens. The high number of marks available tells you that you need to include detail and supporting factual evidence.

Questions referring to previous content

Type of energy	%
Oil	30
Natural gas	24
Coal	26
Biomass	10
Other renewables and nuclear	10

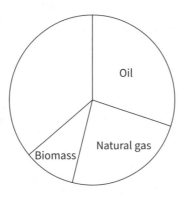

▲ **Table 2** – Global use of energy

3 (a) Study **Table 2**.

(i) Complete the pie chart to compare the data in **Table 2**. [1]

(ii) Describe the global use of energy. [2]

(b) Outline the factors responsible for increasing global energy consumption. [3]

LINK
To understand pie charts, refer to page 190.

Knowledge

29 Strategies to achieve food security

Case study: Past and present attempts to achieve food security

A past attempt: the Green Revolution

The **Green Revolution** refers to the range of agricultural innovations that began in the 1960s aiming to increase food production in LIDCs. For example:

- the development of hybrid, high-yielding varieties (HYVs) of crops (e.g. rice and wheat)
- cross-breeding of animals to improve their tolerance to difficult environmental conditions such as drought
- mechanisation and increased use of agrochemicals (**Figure 1**)
- increasing water control and irrigation schemes.

◀ *Figure 1* Crop spraying in Punjab, India, has helped double farm yields

But the Green Revolution introduced economic and social problems.

- Poorer farmers took out loans to buy HYVs and agrochemicals, but could not pay back these debts, sometimes forcing them to sell their land.
- Demand for agrochemicals created industrial jobs, but their use could be dangerous.
- Education was needed to ensure productive cultivation of HYVs, given their special agrochemical and irrigation requirements.
- Only richer farmers could afford mechanisation, which in turn increased unemployment and rural depopulation.

A present attempt: the Gene Revolution

Biotechnology – the adoption of controversial **genetic modification (GM)** – has been rapid worldwide, especially in the USA, Argentina, and Brazil. It involves transferring genetic DNA between plant species to improve resistance to drought, specified pests, or diseases.

However, concerns about the possible, largely unknown, implications for human health and the environment are widespread. GM crops are still banned in nearly 40 countries. In the UK, foods must be clearly labelled if they contain GM ingredients.

Sustainable strategies to achieve food security

Ethical consumerism

Ethical consumerism involves:

- buying particular food products (e.g. organic) known to support local businesses
- reducing 'food miles'
- promoting animal welfare.

An example of ethical consumerism is **Fairtrade** (**Figure 2**). This international movement sets standards for trade and environmentally friendly production. It helps to invest in local development projects and encourages participation in community cooperatives to ensure that farmers in LIDCs get a fair price for their produce.

▲ *Figure 2* The FAIRTRADE logo

> **WATCH OUT** (!)
>
> Take care not to confuse *fair trade* (as in making trade fairer) with the Fairtrade movement, which helps producers in LIDCs and EDCs achieve sustainable and equitable trade relationships.

Technological developments

Intensive farming (maximising crop yields using mechanisation and agrochemicals), GM crops, aeroponics, and hydroponics are all examples of technological developments making use of scientific research to ensure food security.

> **WATCH OUT** (!)
>
> Make sure when you use the term 'agrochemicals' you state which you are referring to – fertilisers, pesticides, and/or herbicides (weedkillers).

Sustainable food production

Food supplies need to be socially, economically, and environmentally **sustainable** to ensure long-term food security, and that fertile soil, water, and environmental resources are available for future generations.

Organic farming: growing crops or rearing livestock without the use of agrochemicals. Organic produce is more expensive because both production and labour costs are higher.

Sustainable fishing: setting catch limits (quotas) – and monitoring fish breeding and fishing practices to avoid over-exploitation.

Sustainable meat production: small-scale, 'high-welfare' livestock farms – using free-range or organic methods.

Seasonal food consumption: a return to local food sourcing reducing both 'food miles', and our carbon footprint.

Reducing food waste and loss: currently one-third of all food produced globally is wasted or lost! This can be addressed by:

- refrigerated food storage and distribution
- clear and sensible 'use by' food labelling
- using sealed plastic bags for fresh produce.

▲ *Figure 3* Aspects of sustainable food production

29 Strategies to achieve food security

Small-scale approaches

Small-scale approaches to ensuring food security include the 'bottom-up' approaches of **permaculture** and urban gardens.

Permaculture follows the patterns and features of natural ecosystems involving:

- harvesting rainwater
- organic gardening
- crop rotation
- managing woodland.

Urban gardens involve the cultivation, processing, and distribution of food in and around settlements. Benefits include:

- job creation
- improved urban environments
- wildlife attraction
- communities coming together.

> **REVISION TIP**
>
> You may come across exam questions directly referring to **bottom-up** and **top-down** approaches to new initiatives. A bottom-up approach refers to grassroots initiatives inspired by individuals or community groups. Top-down approaches come from governments or TNCs.

Summarising attempts to ensure food security

There are numerous, wide-ranging approaches to ensuring global food security, with considerable emphasis on scientific endeavour and innovation. But many would argue that concentrating on **appropriate technology** and a 'new' Green Revolution in LIDCs is the way forward, hence their inclusion in this summary:

How can food security be increased?

Irrigation: watering land using water extracted from rivers and aquifers. Large-scale irrigation projects involve the construction of expensive dams and reservoirs (e.g. the Indus Basin Irrigation System in Pakistan)

The Green Revolution: modern farming techniques – adopting mechanisation, irrigation, agrochemicals, and new strains of crops – introduced into poorer countries in the 1960s

Appropriate technology: often set-up by NGOs and charities – these are small-scale, low-tech projects using local skills and materials to maximum effect (e.g. water harvesting, irrigation, or crop processing, such as de-husking coffee beans using bicycle power)

A 'new' Green Revolution involves a more sustainable and environmentally-friendly approach – adopting water harvesting (collecting and storing water), soil conservation, and selectively bred seeds and livestock

Biotechnology: controversial modification of products or processes including the development of genetically modified (GM) crops

Aeroponics and hydroponics: use modern scientific techniques to grow crops without soil in artificially lit and heated greenhouses

> **REVISION TIP**
>
> If you are asked to discuss how food security can be increased, strengthen your points by making references to examples whenever relevant, including from your case study if applicable.

> **Key terms** Make sure you can write a definition for these key terms
>
> appropriate technology   bottom-up
> ethical consumerism   Fairtrade   GM
> Green Revolution   permaculture
> sustainable   top-down

Learn the answers to the questions below, then cover the answers column with a piece of paper and write down as many answers as you can. Check and repeat.

Questions

Answers

1	What is genetic modification (GM)?	when genetic material (DNA) is altered in a laboratory rather than through selective breeding
2	What is the Green Revolution?	a period in the 1960s, when scientists aiming to increase food yields in LIDCs introduced cross-bred animals and high-yielding varieties (HYVs) of rice and wheat
3	What is appropriate technology?	technology suited to the needs, skills, knowledge, and wealth of local communities and their environment
4	What are sustainable food supplies?	food production that avoids damaging natural resources, providing good quality produce, and social and economic benefits to local communities
5	What is meant by ethical consumerism?	buying particular food products (e.g. organic) known to support local businesses, reduce 'food miles' and/or promote animal welfare
6	What is Fairtrade?	an international movement setting standards for trade and environmentally friendly production
7	What does the Fairtrade movement do?	invests in local development projects, and encourages participation in community cooperatives so farmers in LIDCs get a fair product price
8	What is meant by permaculture?	a way of food production following the patterns and features of natural ecosystems involving harvesting rainwater, organic gardening, crop rotation, and managing woodland
9	What is a bottom-up approach to any initiative?	a grassroots initiative inspired by individuals or community groups
10	What is a top-down approach to any initiative?	an initiative coming from governments or transnational companies

Put paper here

Previous questions

Answers

1	What is biotechnology?	the modification of products or processes including the development of genetically modified (GM) crops
2	What is organic produce?	food produced without the use of agrochemicals such as fertilisers and pesticides

Put paper here

Practice

1   **(a)**   **(i)**   What is meant by a sustainable food supply?   **[2]**

         (ii)   Which of the following is a sustainable strategy to achieve food security?

            A   organic farming

            B   permaculture

            C   urban gardens

            D   all of the above

            Write the correct letter in the box. ☐   **[1]**

         (iii)   State **two** characteristics of organic farming.   **[2]**

         (iv)   Outline how reducing food waste and losses can increase sustainable food supplies.   **[4]**

   (b)   **(i)**   What is the Green Revolution?   **[2]**

         (ii)   Identify **two** successes of the Green Revolution.   **[2]**

         (iii)   Identify **two** failings of the Green Revolution.   **[2]**

   (c)   Evaluate the success of **one** past attempt to increase food security at a national scale.   **[6]**

   (d)   Describe the significance of biotechnology to increasing food supply.   **[4]**

   (e)   Describe how 'new' Green Revolution technology can be used to increase food supply.   **[4]**

> **EXAM TIP**
>
> **State** requires you to give a simple word or statement. So, each response is, in effect, a 1-mark answer.

> **EXAM TIP**
>
> **Evaluate** requires you weigh up the good and bad points to make a judgement. Given the high mark tariff, the discussion should be comprehensive, include detail, and justify the points you make.

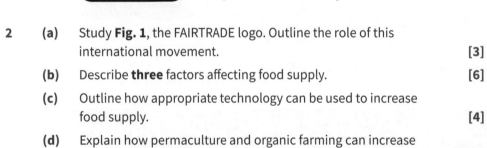

◀ **Fig. 1** The FAIRTRADE logo

2   **(a)**   Study **Fig. 1**, the FAIRTRADE logo. Outline the role of this international movement.   **[3]**

   (b)   Describe **three** factors affecting food supply.   **[6]**

   (c)   Outline how appropriate technology can be used to increase food supply.   **[4]**

   (d)   Explain how permaculture and organic farming can increase sustainable food supplies.   **[6]**

   (e)   Evaluate various methods of sustainable food production.   **[8]**

Questions referring to previous content

Country	Change in carbon content of electricity 2008–2017 (g/kWh)
Japan	+55
Norway	+3
Canada	–50
China	–125
UK	–260

▲ *Table 1*

3 (a) Study **Table 1**, which shows the change in carbon content of electricity for selected countries 2008–2017 (g/kWh).

LINK

To understand how to calculate the range of data, refer to page 195.

   (i) Calculate the range in the changing carbon content of electricity (2008–2017) between Japan and the UK. **[1]**

EXAM TIP

Calculate means you need to work out the answer.

   (ii) Use the data in **Table 1** to complete the bar graph showing positive and negative trends in the changing carbon content of electricity (2008–2017). **[2]**

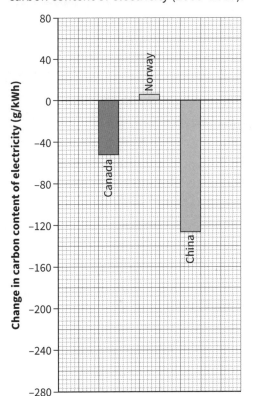

LINK

To understand constructing and reading bar graphs, refer to page 189.

   (iii) Suggest reasons why the UK recorded the highest decrease in the carbon content of electricity. **[3]**

EXAM TIP

Suggest requires you to give an explanation for something when you can't be sure. A good starting point is to think about how the forms of electricity generation in the UK have changed over recent decades.

Knowledge

30 Geographical fieldwork

Your fieldwork enquiries

You will have completed two geographical enquiries – one physical and one human. Both enquiries will have involved the collection of **primary data** on field trips (**Figure 1**) and the use of **secondary data** in support. One of your enquiries will have involved both physical and human geography and their interactions – make sure you know which!

- Physical Geography fieldwork questions will appear in Paper 1, Section B.

- Human Geography fieldwork questions will appear in Paper 2, Section B.

Exam questions will be set on your enquiries – often focusing on justifying what you did and why. They will also cover generic fieldwork issues based on fieldwork data from an unfamiliar context – for you to apply your fieldwork skills to, interpret, evaluate, or criticise.

▲ *Figure 1* Primary (fieldwork) data collection

How to be successful in the exam

Remember, in both your physical and human geographical fieldwork questions:

- you need to apply, use, adapt, and justify a variety of skills and techniques relating to your fieldwork experiences and the geographical enquiries of (unfamiliar) others

- you need to apply knowledge and understanding to interpret, **analyse**, **justify**, **evaluate**, and reach conclusions about your fieldwork experiences and the geographical enquiries of others

- the short-answer early exam questions will either be based on your own investigation or use fieldwork data from an unfamiliar context – they may use skills, including statistics

- the final question will either be based on your own investigation or use fieldwork data from an unfamiliar context – an 8-mark question using a high-level command such as 'to what extent', and also assessing SPaG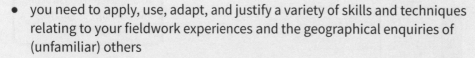

- summarising and revising your fieldwork enquiries will help you ensure a confident and anxiety-free exam.

> **REVISION TIP**
>
> Your physical and human fieldwork enquiry topics and locations could cover any topic or location accessible to you. Popular physical topics involve coasts and rivers, and common human topics involve urban and rural investigations. Practice questions have been set on all four.

> **EXAM TIP**
>
> In the exam, SPaG (spelling, punctuation, grammar, and use of specialist terminology) awards up to three additional marks for the accuracy of your writing, control of meaning, and use of specialist vocabulary.

Revision:
Summarise each enquiry into factual notes – focusing on why you did things, not what you did – including:
- an assessment of the appropriateness of your data collection and **sampling methods**
- an assessment of the appropriateness of your presentation methods
- an evaluation of the accuracy and reliability of your results and conclusion.

Then revise them.

Titles:
Learn the titles of your two fieldwork enquiries – you will be required to write them in the exam.

Aims and objectives:
Make sure that you understand the reasons behind each enquiry:
- what you were seeking to investigate and the choice of location(s)
- the potential risks in the fieldwork, and how they were minimised (**Figure 2**)
- justifying *why* you did things – your data collection/sampling methods, presentation techniques, and how you avoided **bias**.

Preparing for geographical fieldwork questions

Command words:
Make sure you understand the likely command words – calculate, explain, suggest, annotate, 'to what extent', etc.

Enquiry stages:
Make sure you understand the different stages of each enquiry – and how they fit together (**Figure 3**).

Timing:
- you have about 15 minutes for each question
- be concise (to the point) in your writing – you don't have time to waffle
- allow time to check your answers.

Managing risks in fieldwork involves assessing the potential risks (from low (1), to very high (5)) before the fieldtrip – and working out precautions.

Fall from cliff top (**1**)

Rockfall impact from cliff face (**2**)

Exposure to sunburn (**3**)

Unexpected tide coming in (**1**)

Exposure to rain or cold (**2**)

Injury through slipping, climbing, or jumping (**2**)

Breakage, loss, or failure of equipment (**2**)

▲ *Figure 2 Would you agree with these risk assessments – and if not, why?*

Knowledge

30 Geographical fieldwork

Stage

You will have followed these stages when completing your two fieldwork investigations. The exam will test your understanding of how the stages fit together.

1 The question

Deciding on a suitable question for investigation, or hypothesis to test.

2 Data collection

Selecting, measuring, and recording **quantitative** (measurable) and **qualitative** (descriptive) primary data and researching secondary data appropriate to the enquiry.

6 Evaluation

Evaluating the enquiry: reflecting critically on what you have done. For example:

- What went well?
- What didn't go well?
- To what extent are your conclusions reliable?
- How might the **limitations** be addressed, and the enquiry improved?

3 Processing and presentation of the data

Selecting appropriate ways of processing and presenting the data collected (e.g. diagrams, maps, and graphs).

5 Conclusions

Reaching evidenced conclusions supported by the data (referring to the original aims of the enquiry).

4 Description, analysis, and explanation of the data

Describing, analysing, and explaining the results (including use of statistical methods).

▲ *Figure 3 The six stages of geographical enquiry*

EXAM TIP

In the exam, as you are very likely to be asked to make a calculation or draw a sketch map or diagram, remember to include a calculator with your exam stationery.

 Key terms | **Make sure you can write a definition for these key terms** | analyse   bias   evaluate   justify   limitation   primary data   qualitative data   quantitative data   sampling method   secondary data

Learn the answers to the questions below, then cover the answers column with a piece of paper and write down as many answers as you can. Check and repeat.

Questions | Answers

#	Questions	Answers
1	What is primary data?	collected first-hand – real-time data specific to the needs of the enquiry
2	What is secondary data?	collected by others – to support the primary data, or to allow studies of changes through time (e.g. census data)
3	What is meant by generic?	not specific
4	What is quantitative data?	measurable – numerical and so verifiable and transformable into useful statistics
5	What is qualitative data?	descriptive – exploratory in nature, involving research and analysis (e.g. interviews)
6	What is bias in geography?	how findings could be influenced by opinions, e.g. bias for or against an issue
7	What is random sampling?	every item, person, or place has an equal chance of being selected
8	What is stratified sampling?	a proportionate number of observations is taken from each part of the 'population' (e.g. rock types in geology)
9	What is systematic sampling?	a sample taken at regular intervals (e.g. every 25 m along a transect, or interviewing every 20th person in the street)
10	What are limitations in geographical fieldwork?	'forced' errors or weaknesses in data collection preventing the production of fair and reliable data (e.g. insufficient time to interview sufficient pedestrians)
11	What is meant by the command word 'annotate'?	add notes to a sketch map or diagram giving explanation or comment
12	What is meant by the command word 'calculate'?	work out
13	What is meant by the command word 'explain'?	give reasons why something happens
14	What is meant by the command word 'suggest'?	give a well-reasoned guess to explain something where you can't be sure
15	What is meant by the command word 'analyse'?	to examine something methodically and in detail – to explain and interpret it
16	What is meant by the command word 'evaluate'?	weigh up the good and bad points to make a judgement
17	What is meant by the command word 'justify'?	to give evidence to support your ideas

Put paper here

Practice

Exam-style questions

Coastal fieldwork

Your fieldwork

1   **(a)**   Explain **one** way in which you attempted to make your data collection reliable.   **[2]**

      (b)   Explain how you analysed your primary data.   **[4]**

      (c)   Using an annotated diagram, explain how you used a graph (or graphs) to present primary or secondary data.   **[4]**

      (d)   To what extent did your results allow you to reach a valid conclusion to your original question or hypothesis?   **[8]**

              Spelling, punctuation and grammar and the use of specialist terminology   **[3]**

Unfamiliar fieldwork

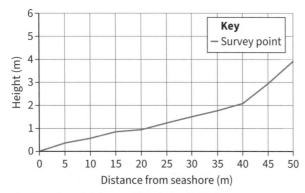

▲ *Fig. 1 – A beach profile of slope angle*

      (e)   Study **Fig. 1**, which shows a beach profile of slope angle up a beach. Explain **one** advantage of using a line graph to show a beach gradient cross-section.   **[2]**

      (f)   Outline **one** potential risk of collecting data in a coastal environment.   **[2]**

> **LINK**
>
> To understand line graphs, refer to page 192.

> **EXAM TIP**
>
> **Outline** requires you to summarise the key points.

River fieldwork

Your fieldwork

2   **(a)**   Explain how the data presentation techniques you used helped you reach conclusions.   **[2]**

      (b)   Explain your choices of the sites selected for your primary data collection.   **[4]**

      (c)   Explain the limitations of your primary data collection technique(s).   **[4]**

      (d)   Evaluate the appropriateness of the sites selected for your primary data collection.   **[8]**

              Spelling, punctuation and grammar and the use of specialist terminology   **[3]**

Unfamiliar fieldwork

(e)   (i)   A student collected river velocity data (using timed floats over a 10 m distance) at three sites along a river to test the hypothesis: 'The velocity (speed) of a river increases downstream'.

	Time taken (seconds)		
Number of observations: 5	**Site 1** (upstream)	**Site 2** (midstream)	**Site 3** (downstream)
1	15	15	19
2	14	16	18
3	18	17	21
4	16	19	23
5	16	16	19
Total	79	83	
Average velocity (m/s)	1.58	1.66	

Calculate the average velocity (m/s) for Site 3

using the formula: $\dfrac{\text{time taken}}{\text{total distance}}$ **[2]**

(ii)   Was the hypothesis proved or disproved?   **[1]**

Urban fieldwork

Your fieldwork

3   (a)   State **one** way in which you used secondary data to support your investigation.   **[2]**

(b)   Using an annotated diagram, explain the data presentation technique(s) you used.   **[4]**

(c)   Evaluate the effectiveness of **one** technique you used to analyse your fieldwork data.   **[4]**

(d)   Evaluate the reliability of your fieldwork conclusions.   **[8]**

Spelling, punctuation and grammar and the use of specialist terminology   **[3]**

> **EXAM TIP**
>
> **State** requires you to give a simple word or statement answer.

Unfamiliar fieldwork

(e)   Study **Fig. 2**, which shows an inner city area in Lincoln. Suggest an enquiry question or hypothesis that could form the basis of a geographical enquiry in the environment shown.   **[2]**

(f)   Suggest how fieldwork risks might be reduced in urban environments.   **[4]**

▲ *Fig. 2 – an inner city area in Lincoln*

Rural fieldwork

Your fieldwork

4   **(a)**   State **one** limitation of a data collection technique used in
your enquiry.   **[2]**

      (b)   Explain the ways that you collected your primary fieldwork data.   **[4]**

      (c)   Explain **one** way in which you attempted to make your data
collection reliable.   **[2]**

      (d)   To what extent did the accuracy of your data collection affect
the validity of your conclusion?   **[8]**

              **Spelling, punctuation and grammar and the use of specialist
terminology**   **[3]**

Unfamiliar fieldwork

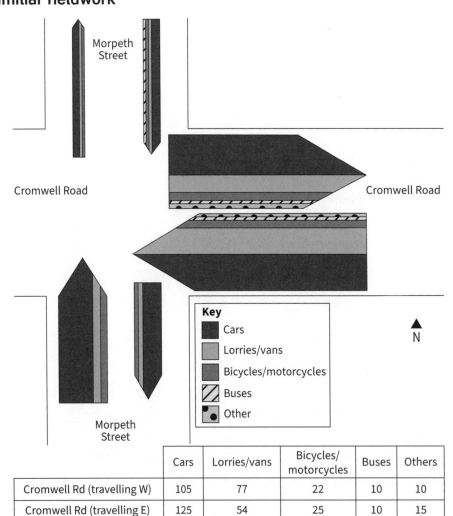

Fig. 3 – Vehicles recorded at a village road intersection

	Cars	Lorries/vans	Bicycles/ motorcycles	Buses	Others
Cromwell Rd (travelling W)	105	77	22	10	10
Cromwell Rd (travelling E)	125	54	25	10	15

   (e)   Study **Fig. 3**, which shows types of vehicles recorded at a village road
intersection.

        (i)   Identify the presentation method used in **Fig. 3**.   **[1]**

        (ii)   Suggest **one** way in which the data presentation in **Fig. 3**
could be adapted.   **[1]**

Additional unfamiliar fieldwork – using questionnaires

Date _____   Time _____

Could you help us? We are GCSE Geography students conducting a survey into aspects of tourism in the village and wondered if you would mind answering a few questions. We won't take up much of your time.

1 Do you visit Castleton

   A more than once a month? ☐

   B once a month? ☐

   C 2 or 3 times a year? ☐

   D less than once a year? ☐

2 Are you

   A staying in Castleton? ☐

   B staying within 1 mile of Castleton? ☐

   C staying between 1 and 5 miles of Castleton? ☐

   D staying between 5 and 15 miles of Castleton? ☐

   E staying more than 15 miles away from Castleton? ☐

3 Could you tell us what kind of work you do? _____

4 Are you visiting Castleton now to

   A shop for groceries? ☐

   B shop for gifts or souvenirs? ☐

   C visit a café? ☐

   D look round the village? ☐

   E visit a friend? ☐

   F for other reasons? ☐

5 Do you find this village

   A very attractive? ☐

   B quite attractive? ☐

   C average? ☐

   D unattractive? ☐

   E very unattractive? ☐

6 Put the following features of Castleton in order of attractiveness (1=most attractive).

   A the buildings ☐

   B the surroundings ☐

   C the shops ☐

   D the peace and quiet ☐

   E the amenities provided ☐

   F others ☐

That was the last question. Thank you for your help. Is there anything you would like to ask us before we go?

Fig. 4 – A questionnaire page from a village tourism fieldwork study

5 **(a)** Study **Fig. 4**, which shows a questionnaire page for a village tourism study in Castleton (a village in the Peak District).

   (i) What is the data collection method used in **Fig. 4**? **[1]**

   (ii) Question 1 could present a problem in that locals trying to be helpful might engage in the survey without the interviewer realising it until later questions are asked. Suggest and explain a better opening question to the survey. **[2]**

   (iii) Explain why the students have used mostly closed questions. **[2]**

   (iv) Explain why sample size is an important consideration in studies like this. **[2]**

   (v) Outline the relevance of Question 3. **[2]**

   (vi) The students' teacher insisted on 'interviewing in a pair, but not in a group'. Explain why they did this. **[2]**

   (vii) Explain how bias might be introduced into studies like this. **[3]**

Knowledge

31 Component 3: Geographical exploration

The Paper 3 examination

Paper 3 is where your whole GCSE Geography course comes together. It is **synoptic** in that the links, connections, and ideas within the topics covered in Papers 1 and 2 are brought together. You will be:

- applying your knowledge, understanding, and skills
- questioning and developing arguments
- making and justifying a geographical decision, or decisions.

The exam will be about a specific country, or a place within the UK, and will focus on at least two topics from Papers 1 and 2. Alongside your exam paper you will be given a Resource Booklet of information linked to a particular theme, on which the questions will be set. This information will take the form of:

- maps
- diagrams
- graphs
- photographs
- tables of data (e.g. statistics)
- short passages of text
- **stakeholder** views and opinions.

The exam format

Following careful examination of the Resource Booklet, you will answer questions on different elements of the topic and eventually an extended piece of writing requiring you to make an **evaluative judgement**.

- Early questions will require interpretation and **analysis** of the information provided.
- A synoptic 12-mark question will require you to apply your knowledge and understanding of topics covered in Papers 1 and 2.
- The final 12-mark question will require you to apply your knowledge and understanding of the information in the Resource Booklet. You will have to make a decision and **justify** it using the evidence available (**Figure 1**). There are an additional 3 marks awarded for SPaG in this question.

There is no right or wrong answer to the final decision-making question. You earn marks by how well you justify your decision.

> **EXAM TIP**
>
> SPaG is an abbreviation for spelling, punctuation and grammar. The most credit is given to clear and accurate answers which use a wide range of specialist terms

1 Read the question carefully – make sure you fully understand the issue →

2 Study *all* the evidence, considering *all* points of view – then make your final decision →

3 Always quote evidence from the resources to support and justify your decision

6 Ideally write a conclusion – referring back to the original question and the main justification for your decision ←

5 Evaluate throughout your answer ←

4 Read through and check that you have backed up your decision with relevant facts

▲ *Figure 1 How to approach the final exploration question*

How to be successful in the exam

Remember:

- do not ignore any of the resources – they were included for a reason
- you will need to interpret, assess, and analyse the resources
- you will be asked to make your decisions and judgements based on the Resource Booklet – so you must focus on the evidence to support your reasoning
- the practice you did in class and this guidance should help you have a confident and anxiety-free exam (**Figure 2**).

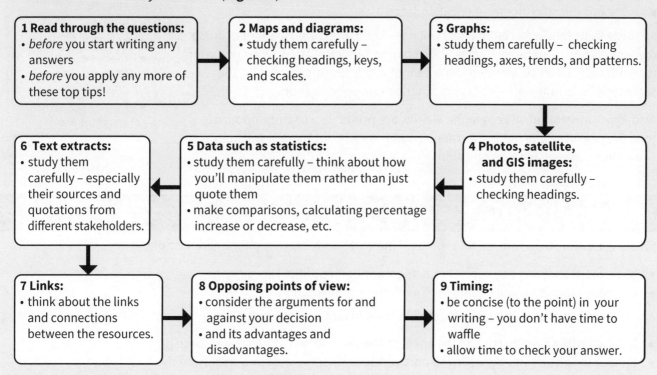

1 Read through the questions:
- *before* you start writing any answers
- *before* you apply any more of these top tips!

2 Maps and diagrams:
- study them carefully – checking headings, keys, and scales.

3 Graphs:
- study them carefully – checking headings, axes, trends, and patterns.

6 Text extracts:
- study them carefully – especially their sources and quotations from different stakeholders.

5 Data such as statistics:
- study them carefully – think about how you'll manipulate them rather than just quote them
- make comparisons, calculating percentage increase or decrease, etc.

4 Photos, satellite, and GIS images:
- study them carefully – checking headings.

7 Links:
- think about the links and connections between the resources.

8 Opposing points of view:
- consider the arguments for and against your decision
- and its advantages and disadvantages.

9 Timing:
- be concise (to the point) in your writing – you don't have time to waffle
- allow time to check your answer.

▲ **Figure 2** Top tips for a successful Paper 3 examination

Make sure you understand these key terms

analysis	identifying patterns and trends, describing them, making links, identifying anomalies, and explaining reasons
evaluative judgement	an assessment to form an idea of the quality, importance, or value of something
justify	to give evidence to support your ideas
stakeholder	an individual or group that has an interest in any issue, activity, or decision
synoptic	demonstrating understanding of the whole picture, drawing connections and supporting evidence from anywhere in the GCSE course

Knowledge

32 Geographical skills

Introduction

GCSE Geography requires you to demonstrate good literacy skills in communicating information, but also a variety of geographical skills, most of which fall into three broad categories:

- maps at different scales (cartographic)
- graphs, specialist maps, and diagrams (graphical)
- numbers and statistics (numerical and statistical).

All these skills (and associated ones) will have been integrated into your course content, although some might have been taught separately (e.g. when preparing for fieldwork). Don't be alarmed if you cannot recall specific lessons on the seemingly wide range of skills covered in the exam specification.

Also, don't forget that all geographical skills are primarily a useful, supportive tool. So, revisiting and practising them (as you would your theory) will help you when they come up in exam questions.

Atlas maps

Small-scale atlas maps are useful sources of information for geographers. For example:

- basic maps showing physical relief, settlements, and political boundaries
- thematic maps showing factors such as climate or vegetation.

Any place on an atlas map can be located by lines of latitude and longitude:

- lines of **latitude** run parallel to the equator, reaching 90° at the north and south poles
- lines of **longitude** run between the north and south poles, east and west from the Prime Meridian, 0° longitude, running through Greenwich in London (**Figure 1**).

Lines of latitude and longitude are measured in degrees (using the symbol °). Each degree is subdivided into 60 minutes (using the symbol ').

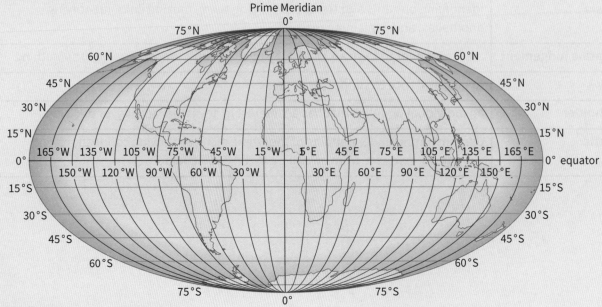

▲ **Figure 1** Latitude and longitude

OS maps

We use larger-scale Ordnance Survey (OS) maps to locate places; determine area, distance, and direction; and both visualise and understand land use, **communications**, relief, and drainage. Each map extract is a section of a national grid covering the whole of Great Britain. Scales of 1:25 000 and 1:50 000 are most common. A scale of 1:50 000 means that 1 unit on the map (e.g. 1 cm) represents 50 000 units on the ground (e.g. 50 000 cm or 500 m).

Four- and six-figure grid references

OS maps use a numbered grid made up of *eastings* (identifying longitude) and *northings* (identifying latitude). They form the basis of the four- and six-figure references used to locate features on the map. Four-figure references identify the whole square and six-figure references locate specific points (by estimating tenths of the whole square – **Figure 2**).

Calculating distance and area

Straight-line distances can be marked on the edge of scrap paper and read directly from the map's 'linear' scale line. Curving distances, such as along a road, river or coastline are measured by dividing the route into straight sections (**Figure 3**).

Calculating areas requires judgement of the proportion of a grid square (or squares) an area feature occcupies. On 1:25 000 and 1:50 000 maps, 1 square on the map represents 1 km² in real life.

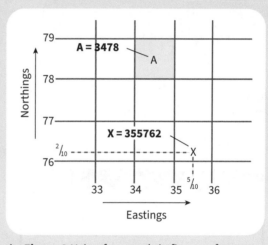

▲ *Figure 2* Using four- and six-figure references

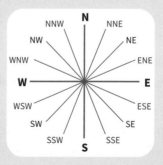

1 Place the straight edge of a piece of paper along the route to be measured. Mark the start with the letter S. Look along the paper and mark off the point where the route moves away from the straight edge.

2 Pivot the paper and mark off the next straight section. Repeat this until you reach the end of the route. Mark this finishing point with the letter F. Convert the total length to kilometres using the map scale.

▲ *Figure 3* Measuring distance along a curved line

The 16-point compass

Look at **Figure 4**. In an eight-point compass, the four main *cardinal points* (north, east, south, and west) are divided by *intercardinal points* (NE, SE, SW, and NW). A sixteen-point compass divides the cardinal and intercardinal points (e.g. ENE between E and NE).

▲ *Figure 4* The 16 points of a compass

Knowledge

OS maps

Identifying and describing landscape features

Contour patterns can be used to identify basic physical features (**Figure 5**). Remember:

- relief refers to the height and shape of the land
- drainage refers to how water is drained from the land.

▶ **Figure 5** *Contour patterns of selected landscape features*

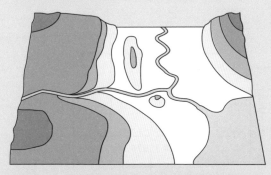

Plateau: an area of fairly level high ground

Ridge: long, steep-sided stretch of narrow upland

Floodplain: stretching from the banks of the river to the valley sides

Steep slope: contours close together

Steep river valley: contours point towards the higher land

Gentle slope: contours wide apart

Knoll: small, round, isolated hill

Estuary: where a river meets the sea

> **WATCH OUT** ⓘ
>
> The height of the land is usually indicated by *contours* (brown/orange lines of equal height, plotted at regular intervals). But watch out for spot *heights* too (usually black dots with the height above sea level written alongside).

Drawing cross-sections

A cross-section is an imaginary 'slice' through a landscape, to help you visualise what it looks like. Drawing a cross-section is not unlike drawing a line graph, although the x-axis intervals (determined by the contour spacing) are irregular (**Figure 6**).

Settlements, communications, and land use

Settlement patterns are *linear* (along a road or river), *nucleated* (focused on a central point) or *dispersed* (spread out at low density).

Function refers to main characteristics such as 'market town', or 'heavy industrial centre'.

Communications refers to transport networks, such as roads and railways. Description and explanation must be supported by specific, located evidence from the map.

Land use includes human modification or management. Reference to location is crucial, including the size and shape of the area.

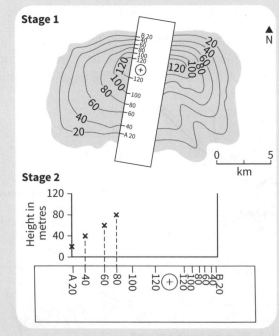

▲ **Figure 6** *Drawing a map cross-section with only a strip of paper and a sharp pencil*

> **WATCH OUT** ⓘ
>
> Beware the common mix-up of *situation* and site. The former refers to the settlement's location relative to other places. The latter describes the actual land it occupies (think of a building site and you won't go wrong).

Using photos

You are likely to come across aerial photos (taken from aeroplanes), satellite photos, and ground photos (**Figure 7**). When describing them, use directional language (e.g. 'foreground', 'backgound', 'right, 'left').

Background: concrete sea wall deflects waves

Middle right: wooden groynes maintain the beach by preventing longshore drift

Foreground: rip-rap (rock armour) dissipates wave energy before it can hit the sea wall

▲ *Figure 7 Describing sea defences at Hornsea, East Yorkshire*

GIS

A **Geographical Information System (GIS)** is a computer database system capable of capturing, storing, analysing, and displaying geographical data from a vast variety of sources (**Figure 8**). All data is identified according to location – hence a GIS is most often associated with maps and layered digital information such as satellite images, aerial photographs, statistical data, and written text.

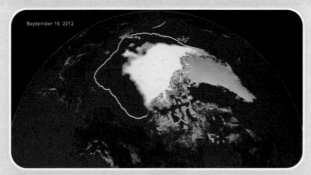

September 16, 2012

▲ *Figure 8 GIS enhanced satellite image showing the extent of the retreat of Arctic sea ice since 1979. Further GIS layering could be added to include further dates, and a scale to measure the exact rate of retreat.*

Bar graphs

A bar graph is a way of comparing quantities or frequencies in different categories (**Figure 9**). The bars are often different colours, with gaps between them because they are unconnected.

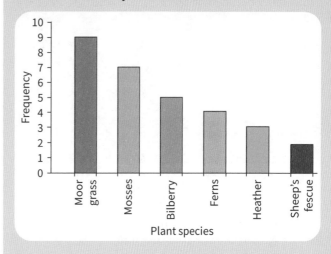

▲ *Figure 9 A bar graph showing different types of vegetation at a fieldwork location*

Histograms

A histogram also uses bars, but with no gaps because the data is continuous, or from a single sample (**Figure 10**).

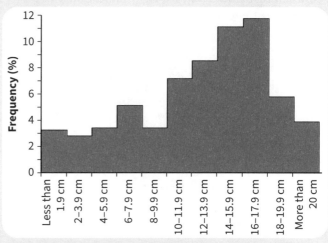

▲ *Figure 10 A histogram showing daily rainfall values over a one-month period*

Divided bar graphs

Divided bar graphs show multiple data by subdividing the individual bars. They are particularly useful when comparisons are required in place and/or time (**Figure 11**).

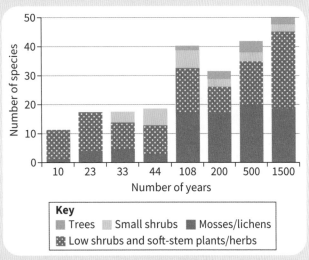

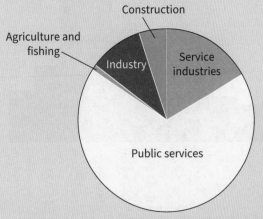

▲ **Figure 11** *A divided bar graph showing the number of species exposed by a retreating glacier*

Pie charts

Pie charts show proportions of a total as segments of a circle. They work best when kept simple – between four and six segments – and using solid, contrasting colours (**Figure 12**). Annotation using raw percentage figures can help interpretation.

▲ **Figure 12** *Types of employment in Rio de Janeiro, Brazil*

EXAM TIP ◎

Percentages are converted into degrees for the pie chart by multiplying the value by 3.6.

Line graphs

Line graphs show continuous change over time. When time is shown on the horizontal x-axis, it must have equal spacing (so dates are equally spaced). The area below a line graph can be sub-divided to show different proportions of the total. This creates a compound line graph (**Figure 13**).

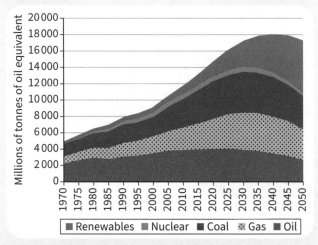

▲ **Figure 13** *Long-term global energy demand predictions*

EXAM TIP ◎

When describing graphs, use TEAM:
- **T**rends – use adjectives like rising, falling, steady, etc.
- **E**xamples – to show trends or specific values.
- **A**nomalies – data that stands out as different, such as a radical change in gradient.
- **M**anipulation – making comparisons, calculating percentage increase or decrease, etc.

Pictograms

A pictogram uses a pictorial symbol or icon instead of a bar – but the resulting half icons can prove imprecise (**Figure 14**).

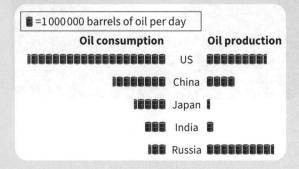

▲ **Figure 14** *Oil consumption and production in the top five oil-consuming countries*

Rose charts

Rose charts (like radial charts) are useful to display data showing orientation or direction (e.g. winds in weather studies like **Figure 15**).

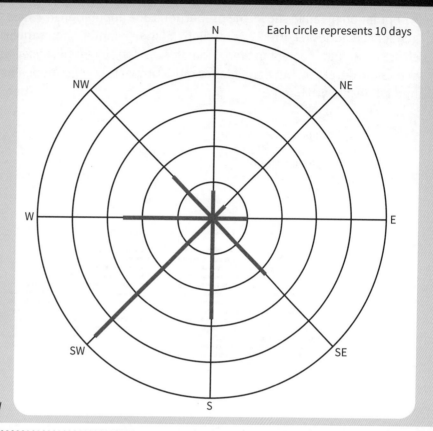

Each circle represents 10 days

▶ **Figure 15** *Measurable wind directions over a six-month period*

Scattergraphs

If two sets of data (variables) are thought to be related, they can be plotted on a scattergraph. Once plotted, the 'scattered' points may allow you to visualise a trend (correlation) or pattern.

Whether smooth curves or straight lines, trend lines should be drawn through the middle of the points, with roughly the same number of points on either side. Your trend line effectively becomes the line of best-fit.

Types of correlation

A relationship between two variables is called a **correlation** (**Figure 16**). Correlations can be shown on scattergraphs and/or tested statistically to see if the relationship is real or accidental. Occasionally a point may lie a long way from the line of best-fit. These points are called **anomalies** (outliers or residuals) and must be explained separately.

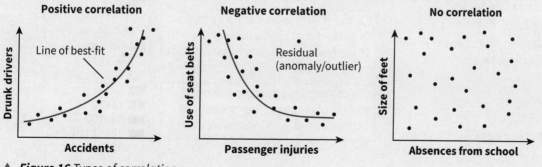

▲ **Figure 16** *Types of correlation*

Knowledge

Population pyramids

A population pyramid shows the proportions of a population in different age and gender categories (**Figure 17**). The shape of the 'pyramid' shows the population structure at that moment in time. From this we can suggest likely levels of economic development, dependency ratios, impacts of migration, and probable immediate growth trends.

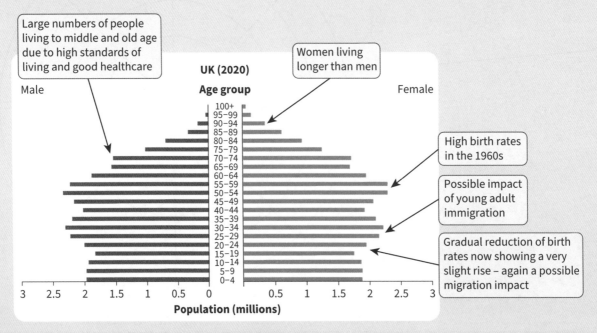

Large numbers of people living to middle and old age due to high standards of living and good healthcare

Women living longer than men

High birth rates in the 1960s

Possible impact of young adult immigration

Gradual reduction of birth rates now showing a very slight rise – again a possible migration impact

▲ *Figure 17* Population pyramid for the UK (2020)

Choropleth maps

A choropleth map uses different colours and/or density shadings to show the distribution of data categories (**Figure 18**). Ideally, there should be between four and six categories, with eight as an absolute maximum. Category values should not overlap and should preferably be equal (or if not, be in a logical geometric sequence). A drawback, however, is that they imply uniformity – by averaging values across a wide area (e.g. county or country) – and therefore hide local variations. Furthermore, the sudden changes at boundaries are unlikely in reality.

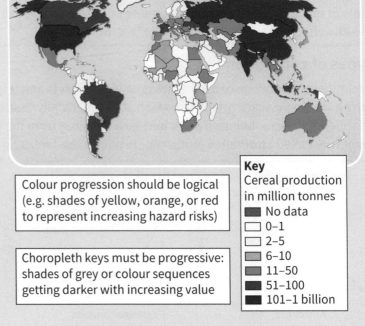

Colour progression should be logical (e.g. shades of yellow, orange, or red to represent increasing hazard risks)

Choropleth keys must be progressive: shades of grey or colour sequences getting darker with increasing value

Key
Cereal production in million tonnes
- No data
- 0–1
- 2–5
- 6–10
- 11–50
- 51–100
- 101–1 billion

▶ *Figure 18* Global pattern of cereal production, 2018

Proportional symbols

Proportional circles (and to a lesser degree proportional squares) are very useful for comparing located data (e.g. city populations). The size of each circle is proportional to the value it represents. Given thoughtful consideration of scale, and good design, proportional circle maps can be very informative (**Figure 19**).

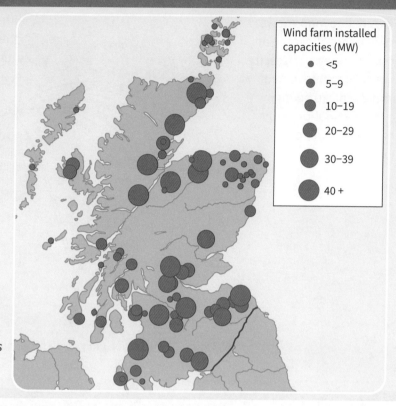

▶ **Figure 19** *Proportional circles map showing Scottish onshore wind farm capacities*

Isoline maps

Isoline maps use lines of equal value to show patterns ('iso' means equal). For example, isolines of equal precipitation plotted on weather and climate maps (**Figure 20**).

WATCH OUT ❗

Isolines should always flow in natural curves and never cross.

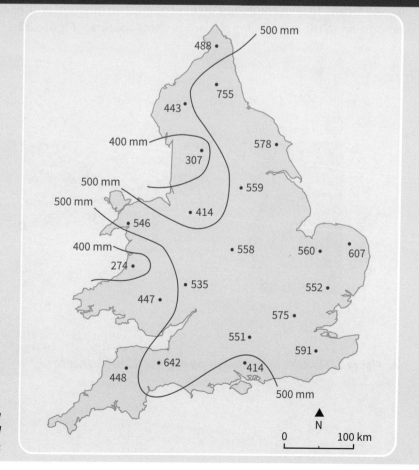

▶ **Figure 20** *Isoline map showing precipitation (mm) for England and Wales*

⚙ Knowledge

Desire line maps

A desire line map shows movements of people or goods between places. It shows direct movement from the place of origin to the destination, rather than the actual route (**Figure 21**).

▲ **Figure 21** Desire line map of international flights from Heathrow, London

Flow line maps

A flow line map shows movements between places, often along a specific route. It uses arrows to show direction of movement, and different widths (drawn in proportion to the value being shown) to show volumes (**Figure 22**).

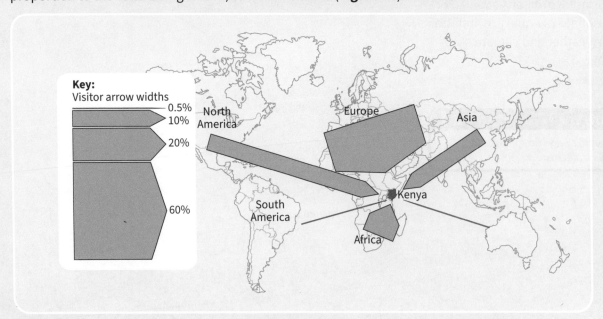

▲ **Figure 22** Flow line map showing the origin of tourists to Kenya

Using numbers and statistics in geography

Geographers frequently use numbers and statistics, which help interpret patterns and trends.

Percentage calculations, including increase and decrease

The most common calculation is working out what percentage a number is of a total:

$$\text{Percentage} = \frac{\text{number you want to find the percentage for}}{\text{total number}} \times 100$$

To calculate a percentage increase, find the actual increase by calculating the difference between the original number and the new (bigger) number. Then use the formula:

$$\text{Percentage increase} = \frac{\text{increase}}{\text{original number}} \times 100$$

To calculate a percentage decrease, find the actual decrease by calculating the difference between the original number and the new (smaller) number. Then use the formula:

$$\text{Percentage decrease} = \frac{\text{decrease}}{\text{original number}} \times 100$$

Measures of central tendency – mean, median, and mode

- Mean: the 'average', calculated by adding up the individual values for a set of data and dividing by the number of values. But this gives no indication of how data within a set are spread around the average.

- Median: the central or mid-point value in a ranked data set. Half of the data set lies above the median and half below.

- Mode: the most common value in a data set. However, as a measure of central tendency, it is only really valid when there is a substantial data set.

Dispersion and range

- **Dispersion:** refers to how data is distributed within the **range**.

- Range: the span of data across a set, calculated by subtracting the lowest from the highest value. The range therefore describes the spread of the data.

- Inter-quartile range: a statistical value to show where the middle 50% of the data lie within any set. It is based around the median and takes all data into account (so is not affected by anomalies). The inter-quartile range can be used to compare dispersions between two or more sets of data.

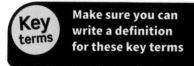
Key terms Make sure you can write a definition for these key terms

anomaly   communications   correlation   dispersion
function   GIS   latitude   longitude   range

Retrieval

Learn the answers to the questions below, then cover the answers column with a piece of paper and write down as many answers as you can. Check and repeat.

	Questions		Answers
1	What is latitude?	Put paper here	how far north or south a place is from the equator, measured in degrees and minutes
2	What is longitude?		how far east or west a place is from the Prime Meridian, measured in degrees and minutes
3	What is meant by relief?		the height and shape of the land
4	What is meant by drainage?	Put paper here	how water is drained from the land
5	What are contours?		lines of equal height, plotted at regular intervals on a map
6	What are spot heights?	Put paper here	indications of exact height above sea level on a map; on OS maps they are black dots with the height above sea level written alongside
7	What is a linear settlement pattern?		a built-up area extending along a road or river
8	What is a nucleated settlement pattern?		a built-up area that is dense and focused on a central point
9	What is a dispersed settlement pattern?	Put paper here	a built-up area that is spread out at low density
11	What is meant by a settlement's function?		the settlement's main purpose, such as 'market town', or 'heavy industrial centre'
12	What is meant by settlement situation?		the settlement's location relative to other places
13	What is meant by settlement site?	Put paper here	the actual land the settlement occupies
14	What is meant by communications on a map?		transport networks – such as roads and railways
15	What is a geographical information system (GIS)?	Put paper here	a database of located geographical information usually based on maps, satellite images, and aerial photographs layered with digital information, statistical data, and written text
16	What is a correlation?	Put paper here	a relationship between two variables – shown on a scattergraph and/or tested statistically to see if the relationship is real or accidental
17	What is an anomaly?	Put paper here	a point far from the line of best fit on a scattergraph – also called outliers or residuals
18	What is meant by dispersion of data?		how data is distributed within a range
19	What is meant by the range of data?	Put paper here here	the difference between the lowest and highest values in a data set

OS map symbols

Symbols on Ordnance Survey maps (1:50 000 and 1:25 000)

ROADS AND PATHS

M I or A 6(M)	Motorway
A 35	Dual carriageway
A 31(T) or A 35	Trunk or main road
B 3074	Secondary road
	Narrow road with passing places
	Road under construction
	Road generally more than 4 m wide
	Road generally less than 4 m wide
	Other road, drive or track, fenced and unfenced
>> >	Gradient: steeper than 1 in 5; 1 in 7 to 1 in 5
Ferry	Ferry: Ferry P – passenger only
	Path

PUBLIC RIGHTS OF WAY

(Not applicable to Scotland)

1:25 000	1:50 000	
		Footpath
		Road used as a public footpath
+++++		Bridleway
		Byway open to all traffic

RAILWAYS

	Multiple track
	Single track
+++++	Narrow gauge/Light rapid transit system
	Road over; road under; level crossing
	Cutting; tunnel; embankment
	Station, open to passengers; siding

BOUNDARIES

+ — + — +	National
+ + + + +	District
—·—·—·—	County, Unitary Authority, Metropolitan District or London Borough
	National Park

HEIGHTS/ROCK FEATURES

══50══	Contour lines
·144	Spot height to the nearest metre above sea level

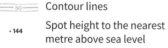

ABBREVIATIONS

P	Post office	PC	Public convenience (rural areas)
PH	Public house	TH	Town Hall, Guildhall or equivalent
MS	Milestone	Sch	School
MP	Milepost	Coll	College
CH	Clubhouse	Mus	Museum
CG	Coastguard	Cemy	Cemetery
Fm	Farm		

ANTIQUITIES

VILLA	Roman	⚔	Battlefield (with date)
Castle	Non-Roman	☆	Tumulus/tumuli (mound over burial place)

LAND FEATURES

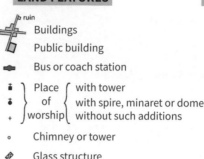

⅓ ruin	Buildings
	Public building
	Bus or coach station
⚑ Place of worship	with tower
	with spire, minaret or dome
	without such additions
○	Chimney or tower
⬦	Glass structure
Ⓗ	Heliport
△	Triangulation pillar
Ⅰ	Mast
Ⅰ Ⅰ	Wind pump; wind generator
Ⅹ	Windmill
+	Graticule intersection

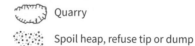

	Cutting; embankment
	Quarry
	Spoil heap, refuse tip or dump
	Coniferous wood
	Non-coniferous wood
	Mixed wood
	Orchard
	Park or ornamental ground

	Forestry Commission access land
	National Trust – always open
	National Trust, limited access, observe local signs
	National Trust for Scotland

TOURIST INFORMATION

P	Parking
P&R	Park & Ride
V	Visitor centre
i i	Information centre
✆	Telephone
⚊	Camp site/Caravan site
⚑	Golf course or links
☀	Viewpoint
PC	Public convenience
✕	Picnic site
⬗	Pub/s
🏛	Museum
	Castle/fort
	Building of historic interest
	Steam railway
	English Heritage
	Garden
	Nature reserve
	Water activities
	Fishing
☆	Other tourist feature
	Moorings (free)
	Electric boat charging point
Ⓧ	Recreation/Leisure Sports centre

WATER FEATURES

OXFORD
UNIVERSITY PRESS

Great Clarendon Street, Oxford, OX2 6DP, United Kingdom

Oxford University Press is a department of the University of Oxford. It furthers the University's objective of excellence in research, scholarship, and education by publishing worldwide. Oxford is a registered trade mark of Oxford University Press in the UK and in certain other countries.

Written by Tim Bayliss and Rebecca Priest

Series Editor: Tim Bayliss

© Oxford University Press 2023

British Library Cataloguing in Publication Data
Data available

978-138-203989-5

10 9 8 7 6 5 4 3 2

The manufacturing process conforms to the environmental regulations of the country of origin.

Printed in the UK by Bell and Bain Ltd, Glasgow

Acknowledgements
The publisher would like to thank the following for permissions to use copyright material:

Artworks: QBS Learning, Aptara, Kamae Design, Lovell Johns, Mike Parsons, Giorgio Bacchin, Ian West, Ian Foulis

Photos: p6: EUMETSAT; **p14:** imagegallery2/Alamy Stock Photo; **p18:** US Air Force Photo/Alamy Stock Photo; **p26:** Associated Press/Alamy Stock Photo; **p29(L):** think4photop/Shutterstock; **p29(R):** Caribbean Helicopters; **p30:** Sean Pavone/Alamy Stock Photo; **p32, p37:** NASA Image Collection/Alamy Stock Photo; **p45:** Tim Bayliss; **p48:** Tim Bayliss; **p49:** Tim Bayliss; **p51:** Gary Clarke/Alamy Stock Photo; **p54:** Bob Digby; **p55:** Crown Copyright; **p58(R):** Tim Bayliss; **p58(L):** Tim Bayliss; **p61(T):** Ordnance Survey; **p61(B):** Tim Bayliss; **p62:** Tim Bayliss; **p65:** Tim Bayliss; **p67:** Crown Copyright; **p68:** Matt Cardy/Getty Images; **p69:** Airfotos/Northumbrian Water; **p74, p78:** Colin Marshall/Alamy Stock Photo; **p80:** NASA Image Collection/Alamy Stock Photo; **p82:** iacomino FRiMAGES / Shutterstock; **p85:** Vladislav Gurfinkel/Shutterstock; **p87:** ASK Images/Alamy Stock Photo; **p88:** Tyler Olson/Shutterstock; **p90:** Dmitry Chulov/Shutterstock; **p86:** evgenii mitroshin/Shutterstock; **p93:** Soltan Frédéric/Getty Images; **p97:** Aurora Photos/Alamy Stock Photo; **p100:** Tim Bayliss; **p101:** Martin Fowler/Shutterstock; **p104:** Crown Copyright; **p105(L):** Bristol Live/BPM MEDIA; **p105(R):** Eric James/Alamy Stock Photo; **p108:** Elena Mirage/Shutterstock; **p111:** Michal Staniewski/Shutterstock; **p113:** REUTERS/Alamy Stock Photo; **p120:** Thiago Trevisan/Alamy Stock Photo; **p124:** Alex Saurel/Getty images; **p132:** Aerial Media Hub/Shutterstock; **p139:** Caron Badkin/Shutterstock; **p144:** Cambridge Aerial Photography/Alamy Stock Photo; **p147:** Crown Copyright;

p149: Andrew F. Kazmierski / Shutterstock; **piv, p154:** Mr.Music / Shutterstock; **pv, p155:** MBI / Alamy Stock Photo; **p159:** Sobrevolando Patagonia / Shutterstock; **p160:** Tim Bayliss; **p161:** akhid7790 / Shutterstock; **p167:** journalturk / Getty Images; **p172:** P.S.Virk / Shutterstock; **p173(T), p176:** PSL Images / Alamy Stock Photo; **p173(B):** Nick Turner / Alamy Stock Photo; **p178:** Tim Bayliss; **p179:** Tim Bayliss; **p183:** Tim Bayliss; **p190 (T):** Tim Bayliss; **p190(B):** NASA;

The publisher would also like to thank Adam Robbins, Arissa Buckley, and staff and students at Heathfield Knoll School and King Charles I School in Kidderminster for sharing their expertise and feedback in the development of this resource.

MIX
Paper | Supporting responsible forestry
FSC® C007785